I0605646

Praise for
Be Good Bankers

"To plumb the depths of the Holy Scriptures—and, in a preeminent manner, the Gospels—is to deepen our knowledge and love of God, who has most perfectly revealed himself to us by the redemptive Incarnation of God the Son. By pondering the Gospel according to Saint Matthew deeply, while translating it anew from the original text, Professor Michael Pakaluk helps us to receive the Word of God through the lens of the good banker—the good householder who dedicates himself to safeguarding and fostering our greatest treasure, our life in Christ in his holy Church. The fruit of his study is a most worthy instrument for our daily conversion to Christ and our growth in him along the way of our earthly pilgrimage to our lasting home—eternal life with him."

—**Raymond Leo Cardinal Burke**

"Few things are more opposed in the popular mind than commerce and Christianity. Investment, gain, loss, debt, payment, receipts, ledgers—what have these to do with salvation? Quite a lot, it turns out. In *Be Good Bankers*, Michael Pakaluk shows how Matthew the tax collector reveals the economy of salvation by way of what is most immediately familiar to most of us—the material economy. Pakaluk thus deepens our understanding of and gratitude for redemption. And along the way, he brings a new appreciation for the goodness of the economy that points to it."

—**The Reverend Paul D. Scalia**, Episcopal Vicar for Clergy at the Diocese of Arlington and Pastor at Saint James Catholic Church

"*Be Good Bankers* is one of those books that will challenge everything you thought you knew about the Gospel of Matthew. Thanks to

Michael Pakaluk's deep knowledge of Scripture, ancient languages, and the economic way of thinking, you will see Christ through the eyes of Saint Matthew himself. *Tolle lege*!"

—**Samuel Gregg**, Friedrich Hayek Chair in Economics and Economic History at the American Institute for Economic Research

"If a conservationist, an engineer, a physician, and an abstract artist were all asked to write the same story, while the substance may be the same, the narrative would differ markedly in approach, style, emphasis, and the use of metaphor. In what may be his most creative work yet, Michael Pakaluk convincingly demonstrates that the erstwhile tax collector's commercial background profoundly influenced the manner in which he narrates his Gospel, thus opening for the earnest reader a new and profitable dimension of an ancient story, especially with this wonderful new translation of the Gospel."

—**Henry T. Edmondson III**, Carl Vinson Professor of Political Science and Public Administration (Emeritus) at Georgia College and State University

"The Keynesian obsession with 'econometricizing' every aspect of the economy takes human action out of our understanding of economic life and opens the door to central planning as the dominant force in the exchange of goods and services. Likewise, the modern obsession with sentimentalizing the Christian life renders a cogent understanding of our spiritual walk and journey impossible and closes the door on vital theological and practical truths. Dr. Pakaluk's work in Matthew doesn't just rediscover missing economic messages in the Bible; it illuminates missing instructions for the properly ordered Christian life."

—**David L. Bahnsen**, Founder and Managing Partner at the Bahnsen Group

"This is a bold and insightful analysis of the Gospel according to Matthew. Michael Pakaluk demonstrates that commercial and banking practices help understand why Matthew, a former tax collector, organized his account of Christ's public ministry the way he did. The worldly and divine economies come to life in this important contribution to New Testament studies."

—**Alexander William Salter,** Georgie G. Snyder Associate Professor of Economics at Rawls College of Business at Texas Tech University and Comparative Economics Research Fellow at the Free Market Institute

"This book will surprise you. With his typically direct and inquisitive style, Michael Pakaluk once again takes us deep into the heart of Matthew's Gospel by 'an economic way of thinking' which is as illuminative as it is unexpected. His economic interpretation is neither reductively materialist, nor trapped by historicism, but rather his interpretive path penetrates to the core of what it means to become wise to discern what is right and just amidst all the exigencies of our everyday trade. Exemplary!"

—**C.C. Pecknold**, Associate Professor of Systematic Theology at The Catholic University

BE GOOD BANKERS

BE GOOD BANKERS

The Economic Interpretation of Matthew's Gospel

with a Fresh Translation

MICHAEL PAKALUK

REGNERY GATEWAY

Gateway Editions and Regnery books may be purchased in bulk at special discounts for sales promotion, corporate gifts, fund-raising, or educational purposes. Special editions can also be created to specifications. For details, contact the Special Sales Department, Gateway Editions, 307 West 36th Street, 11th Floor, New York, NY 10018 or info@skyhorsepublishing.com.

Gateway Editions™ is an imprint of Skyhorse Publishing, Inc.®, a Delaware corporation.

Visit our website at www.regnery.com.

Please follow our publisher Tony Lyons on Instagram @tonylyonsisuncertain.

10 9 8 7 6 5 4 3 2 1

Library of Congress Cataloging-in-Publication Data is available on file.

Cover design by David Ter-Avanesyan
Cover photograph by Angela Castaño

Print ISBN: 978-1-5107-8234-1
eBook ISBN: 978-1-5107-8235-8

Printed in the United States of America

To Catherine Ruth

Contents

Preface xiii
Introduction xxv

Part One: The Deposit (Matthew 1:1–16:12) **1**
First Part of the First Part: Recognition of the Deposit (Matthew 1:1–9:8) 3
(i) Confirmation and Credentialing by Third Parties (Chapters 1–4:16) 3
(ii) Attestation from Jesus's Own Words and Deeds (Chapters 4:17–9) 31
Second Part of the First Part: Crediting of the Deposit to an Account (Matthew 9:18–16:13) 73

The Dividing Point: Announcement of the Passion (Matthew 16:13–28) 128

Part Two: The Payment (Matthew 17:1–27:66) **133**
First Part of the Second Part: Payments Looked for in the Followers of Jesus (Matthew 17:1–20:19) 137
Second Part of the Second Part: The Payment of the Redeemer (Matthew 20:19–27:66) 162

The Recapitalization of the Household of God (Matthew 28:1–19) 229

Conclusion 235
Postscript: Matthew's Authorship and "Marcan Priority" 239
Acknowledgments 253
Select Bibliography 255

Preface

"Be good bankers"—this book had its origin when I first encountered that phrase. I remember the occasion with crystal clarity. I was a graduate student in philosophy at Harvard University, sitting at the check-out desk of the philosophy department's Robbins Library, where I worked as the head librarian. I was reading *Introduction to the Devout Life* by Saint Francis de Sales to review what the saint had written about friendship, the topic of the dissertation I was writing under the political philosopher John Rawls.

A recurring theme in classical writing on friendship is that we should deliberately select our close friends, not leaving something so important to chance. After all, friends tend to become like their friends. Therefore, if we take seriously that we should become virtuous, we should deliberately choose friends who are virtuous.

However, de Sales was a Christian who believed in Original Sin. Therefore, he took a stricter approach. All friends will have their flaws. These flaws can lead us astray. Indeed, the flaws of good friends are potentially more insidious than the influence of bad friends, because we tend to ignore or downplay them. Therefore, de Sales advises, in his characteristically amiable style, rich in classical allusions:

> Friendship requires great communication between friends. Otherwise, it can neither be born nor exist. Because of this it often happens that with this communication of friendship many other communications insensibly pass and glide from one heart to another by a mutual infusion and reciprocal intercourse of affections, inclinations, and impressions. This happens especially when we have a high esteem for the one we love. Then we open our heart in such manner to his friendship that with it his inclinations and impressions, whether good or bad, enter rapidly and completely. Certainly, the bees that gather the honey of Heraclea seek nothing but honey, yet with the honey they insensibly suck the poisonous qualities of the aconite from which they gather it. Therefore, Philothea, on these occasions we must carefully practice what the Savior of our souls was accustomed to say, as the ancients have informed us, "Be ye good bankers," or changers of money; that is to say, receive not bad money with the good, nor base gold with the fine. "Separate the precious from the vile." Yes, for there is scarcely any person that has not some imperfections. Why should we receive promiscuously a friend's tares and imperfections together with his friendship? We must love him indeed, notwithstanding his imperfections. But we must neither love nor receive his imperfections, for friendship requires a communication of good, not evil. Wherefore, just as they that draw gravel out of the river Tagus pick out the gold they find, in order to carry it away, and leave the sand on the banks; so they who have

> communication of some good friendship ought to separate the sand of its imperfections and not suffer them to enter into their souls.[1]

When I read the line "Be good bankers," I was astonished. De Sales described it as something Jesus "was accustomed to say," suggesting a repeated and characteristic teaching. But how so exactly? The maxim is not in the New Testament. I had studied the main works of the Church Fathers, yet I had never come across it. Where could it be found, exactly? What did it mean?

The book's translator gave only this footnote:

> These words are not found in Holy Scripture but are reported by Origen, Clement of Alexandria, St. Ambrose, St. Jerome, and other fathers. Cf. Alardus Gazeus' commentaries on the *Collationes Patrum* (Bk. I, chap XX) of John Cassian.

Aha! Good enough. But I did not know this work by Cassian. And I had no idea who Alardus Gazeus was. His edition of Cassian's book would certainly be somewhere in Harvard's vast library system. But to hunt it down would require descents into the bowels of various library stacks. Busily writing my dissertation as I was, I could not afford the luxury of such a foray. However, I did make a mental note to return to this saying later. It seemed too important and too fascinating to ignore.

My questions remained on the back burner when, as a young scholar, I went on to publish books and papers mainly on classical

1 Saint Francis de Sales, *Introduction to the Devout Life*, trans. John K. Ryan (Garden City, New York: Doubleday & Company, 1955), pt. 3, chap. 22, 177–78.

philosophy. I got my chance to look into them much later, when I began writing a series of books on the four Gospels, of which this current book is the third.

My approach in this series has been to view each Gospel in relation to a key person who helped form it. Why? Because the Gospels were written by those reputed to be eyewitnesses, or by persons who interviewed reputed eyewitnesses within one generation of the events they report. The relevant persons were still alive, and they had big personalities. Consider the famous "fragment of Quadratus of Athens," from about 126 AD:

> Our Saviour's works, moreover, were always present: for they were real, *consisting of* those who had been healed of their diseases, those who had been raised from the dead; who were not only seen while they were being healed and raised up, but were *afterwards* constantly present. Nor did they remain only during the sojourn of the Saviour *on earth*, but also a considerable time after His departure; and, indeed, some of them have survived even down to our own times.[2]

It would be like someone today taking oral histories about what it was like to live through the September 11, 2001 attacks. The distance in time is the same, about twenty-five years. (Or provide your own example relative to the time when you are reading this.) The disciples of Jesus were mainly manual laborers who lacked formal training. They were not like scholars in the age of print books who can sit in

---

2 Alexander Roberts, James Donaldson, and A. Cleveland Coxe, eds., *Ante Nicene Fathers,* vol. 8, trans. B. P. Pratten (Buffalo, New York: Christian Literature Publishing, 1886), 749.

a library with multiple texts before them, citing them as they see fit to compose their own versions. Their main sources would be persons, not texts.

In my first book on the Gospel of Mark, *The Memoirs of St. Peter: A New Translation of the Gospel According to Mark*, I found ample evidence that Mark had written down what he heard Peter preach when he accompanied Peter in Rome. Even Mark's language when most faithfully rendered had a spoken quality to it. Mark's Gospel was indeed "the memoirs of Peter," as Justin Martyr had said around 150 AD, and as the early Church believed.

Next, when I turned to the Gospel of John in *Mary's Voice in the Gospel According to John: A New Translation with Commentary*, I asked whether there aren't signs of the influence of Mary, since according to solid tradition they lived together for many years in Jerusalem and Ephesus. I found many such signs indeed. My investigation yielded what Newman called an "accumulation of probabilities," amounting to a kind of proof. It was possible to discern "Mary's voice in the Gospel of John," as I put it.

Therefore, when I decided to write a successor book in this series, on Matthew—the book you are reading now—I wondered how I might adopt once more this method of looking for "the person behind the Gospel."

Perhaps it was Jesus? I don't mean simply that the Gospel was about Jesus, or that Matthew's Gospel was influenced by Jesus—obviously so. I mean, rather, suppose that Matthew's Gospel was written in accordance with express directions given by Jesus. How might one confirm or support such a hypothesis?

The hypothesis is not improbable. Why do we suppose that Jesus acted only spontaneously, without any planning for the future? What founder would do so? Why wouldn't Jesus have understood that he needed someone to make a record? After all, his disciples saw the need—that is why they later wrote such records. You and I see the need now, after the fact. And yet *Jesus* couldn't have seen the need? And why mightn't he have chosen a tax collector as an apostle specifically for this purpose? After all, tax collectors did their daily work by making records. Might Jesus have suggested a basic outline, at least, to get Matthew started? Might he have helped Matthew select and arrange material?

Questions like these are fascinating. But I decided to adopt a different approach. Something else grabbed my imagination. I kept thinking about the famous painting by Caravaggio, *The Calling of Matthew*, where Caravaggio represents the common idea that, when Jesus called Matthew, he asked him to leave behind the world of money. And yet what if Matthew didn't leave it behind? I know certain adult converts to Christianity who are experts in banking or finance and who became highly admirable Christians precisely because they applied to Christianity what they had learned in the world of business. Suppose then that "the person behind the Gospel of Matthew" was . . . Matthew, the tax collector. Suppose that, as an Apostle, he remained a man savvy about balances, income and expenses, Roman law and administration, and market transactions in general. Suppose he did not leave all of that behind, but Jesus selected him in part because of that background. Maybe his background enabled him to see more clearly some important dimensions of Jesus's teaching. What if, somehow, "banking" themes were salient in his Gospel?

Obviously, I would need to return to "Be good bankers." Many years later, here was my chance. Was there a match between Jesus's teaching as expressed in that maxim and the Gospel of Matthew, as written by a tax collector? Wouldn't the maxim be a pledge of the fruitfulness of the interpretation I was considering?

How times have changed! Earlier I would have needed hours or days to find John Cassian's *Collationes*. Now it takes only a few minutes to find the volume and call it up online.

John Cassian, a monk, lived in Southern France in the late fourth and early fifth centuries. He wrote one important treatise on the exterior life of monks ("Institutes") and another on a monk's interior life (the *Collationes* or "Conferences"). In one chapter of the latter, he urges monks to be on guard against misguided teachings that come from the devil or from mere human beings, rather than from God. To do so, he says, "We should prove ourselves to be good bankers [Latin, *probabiles trapezitae*] in accordance with the command of the Lord."[3]

Bankers, he explains, are skilled at detecting three types of counterfeits:

1. Coinage that is *debased* through the intermixture of base metals
2. Coinage that *has a false veneer*, appearing only superficially to be a precious metal
3. Coinage that is *not the proper weight*

Likewise, he says, monks must be skilled at discerning the following:

1. Teachings that contain traces of superstition or empty philosophy
2. Teachings that look like good interpretations of Scripture but are actually deceptions

3 John Cassian and Michael Petschenig, *Iohannis Cassiani Conlationes XXIIII* (Vindobonae: apvd C. Geroldi filivm, 1886), 29.

3. Teachings that are innocent in themselves but have a tendency to lead someone into sin

In this last analogy, Cassian construes a thing's tendency as a kind of weight: the teaching is wrongful because it "pulls" us in the wrong way.

I was not surprised that a monk would interpret "Be good bankers" solely in relation to money-changing. Monks lived apart from the world, not immersed in commerce. A monk would naturally think of a banker in relation to original task of banking, which was money-changing. But did other authorities and the Fathers of the Church deal with the maxim similarly?

My next step, then, would be to find Gazeus's commentary on this passage and track down the sources for the maxim in early Christian authorities. "Gazeus," I discovered, is a Latinization of Alard Gazet (1565–1626), a Benedictine from the Habsburg Netherlands famous as the editor of the complete works of Johannes Cassian printed in 1616. The book is quite rare. In my graduate school days, I would have had a hard time consulting it. But again, in about one minute, I was able call up online a scan of the first edition held by the Katholieke Universiteit Leuven.

I saw that Gazet in his commentary first quotes a passage in Saint Jerome:

> You know how I have gladly listened to that word of the Apostle: "Test everything; hold fast to what is better" [1 Thess 5:21]. Also the words of Our Savior, when he said: "Be reliable money changers" [Latin: *Estote probabiles nummularii*]: And so, if a coin is debased, or it does not bear the image of Caesar, or it lacks the impress of public money, then it should be rejected; but if it shows the face

> of Christ with a clear light, store it away in a purse close to your hearts.[4]

Then he quotes Origen:

> Jesus said to those careful to keep his commandments, "Be upright bankers" [Latin: *Estote probi trapezitae*], which is the teaching of Paul, too, when he says "Test everything; hold fast to what is better."[5]

Then he quotes Saint Clement of Alexandria:

> Understandably Scripture, wanting us thus to become that sort of dialectician, exhorts: "Be skillful bankers" [Greek: *ginesthe dokimoi trapezitai*], rejecting everything while holding fast to that part which is good.[6]

This last passage was most interesting to me, for two reasons. First, Saint Clement regarded the maxim as undoubtedly from Jesus, even calling it "Scripture." Second, he interpreted it philosophically. "Bankers" for Clement were savvy Christian philosophers who know how to draw the right distinctions in any domain—which is clearly a very different ability from that of Cassian's spiritual money-changers.

Gazet next lists various other places where the maxim is cited: Saint Jerome's *Commentary on Ephesians* (no longer extant); the opening of Saint Ambrose's *Commentary on Luke*; Saint Basil the

---

4 This letter is referred to as number 119, to Nimerius (Minervus) and Alexandrus.
5 Book 19 of his *Commentary on John*, no longer extant.
6 Quoted from *Stromata*, 1.

Great's *Commentary on the Prophet Isaiah* (1:47 ad loc); and the *Apostolic Constitutions* (Ii, 21,5), which Gazet ascribes to Saint Clement of Rome.[7]

After giving these quotations and references, Gazet asks why "Be good bankers" was regarded as "Scripture" by early Christians. He goes through a catalogue of purported scriptures, which have since been lost. Perhaps, he suggests, it was contained in the lost document that Saint Jerome refers to as the "gospel according to the Hebrews." Or perhaps it was in the lost translation of the Gospel of John into Hebrew that Eusebius mentions. Or perhaps it was in the original Hebrew version of the Gospel of Matthew, if that is different from the "gospel according to the Hebrews." Or maybe, he says at last, it was simply passed down in tradition as a commandment of the Lord, even if it is not found expressly in any putative Gospel.

So, at last I had found where the earliest Christian teachers had cited the maxim.[8] I confirmed that the maxim was accepted as coming from Jesus. And I had found that, although generally they interpreted it to mean "distinguish good from bad; keep the good, reject the bad," (often citing 1 Thessalonians 5:21 as a complementary text), they could be quite creative in how they interpreted it.

Once I could consult Gazet, I could also see how the maxim was expressed in Greek and Latin. I saw in particular that the Latin uses a future imperative, which is employed for a command that is to be fulfilled in the future. When such a command is general (as is "Be good bankers"), then the sense of the future is that the command will need to be fulfilled in diverse circumstances, through personal

7 Clement of Rome was the fourth bishop of Rome in 80 to 99 AD, following Peter, Linus, and Cletus. Scholars today regard the *Apostolic Constitutions* as considerably later, from the fourth century AD.

8 Many more sources can be found in Alfred Resch, *Agrapha: Aussercanonishe Schriftfragmente* (Leipzig: J.C. Hinrich'sche Buchhandlung, 1906).

initiative, and in such a way as to exhibit growth and development. "Be good bankers" would need to be interpreted in that spirit.

Another thing I saw is that the word for "banker" in Greek really does mean a banker. In the New Testament, every time a mere money-changer is mentioned, the word is *kollubistēs*, which means literally "a small-change man" (from the word for small change, *kollubos*). However, in the maxim "Be good bankers," the word is different: it is *trapizetēs*, which comes from the word for table (*trapezos*) and means "a man who does his work at a table." The word *kollubistēs* takes its meaning from what the men dealt with; *trapizetēs* from where they worked. The former is the more specific term; the latter is the more general term. This more general word, *trapizetēs*, is used only once in the New Testament, in the parable of the talents: "Then you ought to have invested my money with the bankers, and at my coming I should have received what was my own with interest" (Matthew 25:27). In the parable, it refers to bankers who pay interest on deposits.

The one time that Jesus uses it, it does not refer to mere money-changers!

So I had the "divine warrant" I was looking for to underwrite my approach. The maxim "Be good bankers" really could be traced back to Jesus, and he apparently meant by it something much broader than "be a good money-changer."[9] My project was on its way.

9 As James Hardy Ropes points out, there are five independent streams of tradition that witness to "be good bankers." James Hardy Ropes, "The So-Called Agrapha," *American Journal of Theology*, 1:3 (July, 1897): 758–76.

Introduction

1. My Worldview

For my economic interpretation of Matthew's Gospel, I presuppose a worldview that will be familiar at least to some economists, but it is unusual for a book on the Gospels. It consists of three main ideas:

> First, we are "designed" to do business to earn a living.
> Second, the Creator knows this fact about us and uses it to teach us about himself.
> Third, that is why there are deep analogies between the spiritual realm and the world of business.

Let me explain each of these briefly.

First, we are "designed" to do business to earn a living. It is built into human nature that we engage in business activity. By "business activity" I mean *working together with others to provide a good or service on the market that is of value to others, such that to obtain this good or service, others are willing to provide to us, in exchange, with some good or service of their own.*

Defined in this way:

- Business activity must start from thinking about others—about what is good or of value *to them.*
- Business activity is not selfish but *collaborative*. Even if someone is a sole proprietor, he still must work on good terms with suppliers and assistants.
- Business activity is not "greedy," as people say, but rather it depends on a strong sense of what *the other person* would count as a fair exchange for the good or service that you are providing.
- Business activity results in a sort of friendship, since it implies long-term relationships that the participants regard as fair. Businesses survive over time only through cultivating loyal customers—which is not possible if they come to believe that you are not dealing with them fairly.
- Profit is a natural reward for cooperating with others in a win-win relationship. Profit is like the fruitfulness we see elsewhere in nature where natural systems are working as they should.

I say it is "built into human nature" that we engage in business activity because all of us need to keep body and soul together. We all want to live in relative comfort if possible. We all want to enjoy some free time from hard labor. Yet no one attains any of these things by living and working on his own. As Milton Friedman once famously pointed out, none of us can make on his own even something as simple as a pencil.[1]

1 Milton Friedman and Rose Friedman, *Free to Choose* (New York: Harcourt Brace Jovanovich, 1980), 11–13. Friedman draws upon an essay by Leonhard E. Read, "My Family Tree as Told to Leonard E. Read," *The Freeman*, December 1958, 32–37. Read's essay is typically referred to as "I, Pencil."

Saint Thomas Aquinas taught that this "inclination" to keep ourselves in existence is one of three fundamental motivations in human nature.[2] Adam Smith is famous for saying that by nature we have a propensity to "truck, barter, and exchange."[3] Aristotle in his *Politics* says that this propensity has a natural term of growth, which he called "the city" (*polis*). People, he said, continue to provide additional goods and services to one another and exchange them until just about everything they need is attainable on a common market. When a community has grown to such an extent, it can be called a "complete community" or a "political community."

This fact, that we are designed to do business together so that each of us may earn a living, is often obscure to scholars, because they work in a community of ideas rather than a market. The universities in which they work have largely been sheltered (rightly so) from so-called market forces.

Second, the Creator knows that he designed us for business activity and uses this fact about us to teach us about himself. We understate the case if we say merely that we have a "propensity" toward business activity. The truth is, most of us are compelled to work long days. Nothing else has the same persistent urgency as needing to work in order to meet one's commitments. We live "from hand to mouth." Anxiety over paying our bills can keep us up at night. We wonder how we will afford a child or the next child. We look everywhere for ways of making more money. We are keenly aware of what we owe, say, in a mortgage or on our credit card balances.

2 That is along with the *inclinatio* to form a family and pass down our ideals through our children, and the *inclinatio* to worship God and serve some higher cause. *Summa Theologiae*, I–II, 94, 2.

3 Adam Smith, *An Inquiry into the Nature and Causes of the Wealth of Nations*, vol. 1, Cannan ed. (London: Methuen, 1776), I, i, 2.

I assume in this book that God exists and that God made us. It follows that our propensity and need to engage in business activity is by his design. If he designed us in this way, then there is a reason. One reason, surely, is that we become better human beings by engaging well in business activity. The commitment, sacrifice, service, and risk-taking required by business are good for us.

But another reason is that the world of business creates a concrete "language" for God to speak to us about himself. God is a spirit and invisible: divine realities are also invisible. The invisible can be revealed to us only through the visible. Ponder the images Jesus uses in his teaching: kneading dough, pastoring sheep, tending a vineyard, cultivating a tree, sweeping the floor. They refer to the world of work. Likewise, much of the imagery of Saint Paul's letters is "economic."

Third, there are deep analogies between the spiritual realm and the world of business. But it is not simply that in business activity God created a "language" for communicating truths about himself. There are also deep analogies between the logic of business activity and the logic of the spiritual realm, which should not be surprising, if they both come from the same source.

For example, spiritual wealth is analogous to material wealth. If not, Jesus could never have taught, "Lay up for yourselves treasure in heaven" (Matthew 6). Likewise, spiritual debt is analogous to monetary debt. And spiritual payment is analogous to monetary payment. The one sort is far more important than the other and more lasting, but they are analogous.

If, just now, you wondered about my use of the phrase "spiritual payment"—think carefully about the main doctrines of Christianity. Christianity's most fundamental claim is that Jesus is the Redeemer. To redeem is literally to make a payment; it is to buy someone back—from debt and consequent enslavement. Jesus's favored image for the plight of a sinner in need of salvation is a debtor under a load of crushing debt.[4]

On this worldview that I have sketched, it becomes plausible that God would choose as one of his Apostles, and maybe even as one of his Evangelists, someone who was positioned to attain a good grasp of these key ideas. Who would such a person be, then, except Matthew? Matthew was a tax collector. In his work, he had to examine and assess businesses.

So then, let's begin to think of what I call the "economic interpretation of the gospel" and connect it to "Be good bankers" by turning to what it meant to be a banker at the time of Jesus.

2. We Are All Bankers Now

Banking originated with men sitting at tables changing coins. The word "banker"'just meant a man who sat at a table (*banc* in Old French). Our word "bench" is the closest equivalent. Even today we speak of judges as on a bench. A banker is a bench-er.

By working at tables, bankers were unusual. Most men worked in the field, as farmers or in husbandry. Others worked on boats as fishermen. Or they made things in shops. Perhaps they worked on the road, like merchants or soldiers. But bankers sat there all day, working at a table. Bankers had the original desk job; they were the first sedentary profession.

---

4 Scripture scholars have observed how sin in the Jewish tradition changes from being conceptualized as a heavy burden to a debt. After this book was written, my colleague Reinhard Hütter recommended in this regard Nathan Eubank, *Wages of Cross-Bearing and Debt of Sin: The Economy of Heaven in Matthew's Gospel* (Berlin: De Gruyter, 2013), https://doi.org/10.1515/9783110304077. My approach is different from but consistent with Eubank's.

Although banking originated in money-changing, these "table men" soon took on the other tasks we associate with banking today, through a series of natural developments.

A money-changer in the ancient Mediterranean world needed to accept coins from many cities and provinces in exchange for the local currency and for the currency of the empire. Therefore, he needed a large stock or "capital" of these "currencies of account." Therefore, he needed a secure storage box or "safe" for holding these coins.

Right from the start it was recognized that a banker, if he was to keep money safe, needed not simply this physical instrument but also a spotless reputation for honesty. Otherwise, who would trust him with the handling of their wealth? In addition, he needed good habits of keeping records. Every banker had to be a bookkeeper and accountant. That is to say, besides handling material capital, a banker needed recognizably to possess this "human capital," these virtues, as well.

Once a banker had a safe and he was trusted, people generally might leave their large sums of money with him for safekeeping. Thus, he would acquire "depositors."

A depositor might instruct the bank to pay from his own deposits certain sums to others, upon their presenting the right documentation. This would be a rudimentary form of what we call "checking" today. Or a depositor at one bank, after bringing his goods to market in another city, might deposit the proceeds from his sales in a bank in that other city, which would then guarantee the funds for withdrawal from the bank in the merchant's home city. This would be a rudimentary "interbank transfer."

Because bankers dealt with the relatively rapid flow of relatively large sums of money, even if their margins on transactions were small, they could acquire significant wealth of their own. They could then put this money to work with loans and investments. Thus, bankers were the first venture capitalists. For instance, they might underwrite a trading voyage, fronting the capital for the purchase of the cargo and the hiring of the crew. They might invite depositors to share in a loan or investment for a proportionate share in the profits. These would be the first securities.

The banker's original task of money-changing was not without its challenges. Currencies have always been at risk of debasement by governments, counterfeit by fraudsters, and devaluation through the accidental nicking or deliberate removing of small bits of coins. Bankers had to be able to spot these alterations and assess the precise loss of value. If they got it wrong by excess, their rates would not remain competitive. If they got it wrong by deficiency, they would operate at a loss. This accurate assessment of value required considerable experience and skill.

Because bankers were trusted in handling large sums of money, they became trusted agents and intermediaries in general. They could be called upon for assistance in any serious transaction. They often played a role like that of the closing attorney in a real estate transaction today. Their attestation of an event was regarded as reliable for purposes of law.

Roman bankers had acquired all of the roles I have mentioned by the time of the Roman occupation of Palestine beginning in 63 BC. Roman banking set the standard in the ancient Mediterranean, and anyone who wanted to refer to best practices in banking would refer to Roman banking. If Jesus referred to a banker, this is the kind of person he would mean.[5]

---

5 Jean Andreau, *Banking and Business in the Roman World* (Cambridge: Cambridge University Press, 1999); William Linn Westermann, "Warehousing and Trapezite Banking in Antiquity," *Journal of Economic and Business History* 3 (November 1930): 30–54; and George M. Calhoun, *The Business Life of Ancient Athens* (Chicago: University of Chicago Press, 1926).

In sum, a banker's profession required the following:

- Acquiring value
- Conserving value
- Growing value
- Assessing value
- Trading for value
- Assessing risk
- Taking risks for value

It also required these attributes:

- Trustworthy good judgment and integrity
- Good record-keeping and accounting

Note that value in the ancient world was conceived of not abstractly but rather as concretized in the specie money of gold and silver. Money has traditionally been regarded not simply as a medium of exchange and a unit of account but also as a store of value. We live today in a regime of fiat currency, in which our money is not backed by any commodity. We think of money abstractly, as a claim on the goods and services of others (or even more abstractly as a government's ability to back a sovereign note with taxation). But in the ancient world, money was a commodity. To hold gold or silver in one's hands was to hold value. Gold especially was valued for its fascination and beauty, apart from its value in exchange. Since it was also rare, it was used to signal prestige, exclusivity, attainment, and status.

Once we describe a banker in these general terms, we can see that all of us are bankers, first, in the mundane sense that, in running our households and managing material wealth, all of us must carry out tasks similar to a banker's. A banker simply carries out publicly, visibly, at arm's length, with greater sums of wealth, and with a public trust what all of us must do privately and on a smaller scale.

However, there is a deeper kind of wealth rooted in persons, which we also need to conserve, apprise, trade for, and so on. Call this not material wealth but "wealth of persons." We have already mentioned "human capital," such as a skill. A skill is a kind of wealth of persons, which we need to deal with in the manner of bankers—we need to *acquire* such wealth by education, *conserve* it by continuing education, *assess* its value rightly by making education a priority over activities, and *trade for it* by giving up other things to get it.

But relationships and persons themselves also seem to belong to this deeper kind of wealth. If someone says, "I suffered a loss when my friend betrayed me, but I gained him back when he begged forgiveness, and I forgave him," he is talking about a loss incurred of such deeper wealth, and a gain realized. He is saying in effect that, by trading away his right to hold a grudge and exact punishment in retaliation for the harm that had been done against himself, he gained back a friend. He is looking back on that exchange and assessing that, rather than enduring a loss to himself as it may have seemed when he wrote off his claim, he actually came out better off. Again, if someone cites the proverb "Make new friends, but keep the old, one is silver and the other gold," he is saying that we should be good bankers regarding this deeper wealth of persons—in particular, we should not acquire new friends at the cost of old friends.

Our very selves constitute such wealth. What if, by trading oneself away, sometimes one gets oneself back, but at a greater value?[6] Then too, if God exists and he is a person and he is all-powerful, God himself and our relationship to him would also count as wealth. Someone with a philosophical sensibility might even find it easy to believe that God

6 See Catherine Ruth Pakaluk, "The Lord Repays: Self and Sacrifice," chap. 19 in *Hannah's Children: Stories of Women Quietly Defying the Birth of Dearth* (Washington, D.C.: Regnery Gateway, 2024).

was his sole wealth. Thus, Newman wrote, "My God I believe and know and adore Thee as infinite in the multiplicity and depth of Thy attributes. I adore Thee as containing in Thee an abundance of all that can delight and satisfy the soul. I know, on the contrary, and from sad experience I am too sure, that whatever is created, whatever is earthly, pleases but for the time, and then palls and is a weariness." Newman continues, "My God, I take Thee for my portion. From mere prudence I turn from the world to Thee; I give up the world for Thee."[7] The key phrase here is "mere prudence." Newman is saying that the mere prudence of a good banker would suffice for assessing properly the value that is to be found in the world, and, for seeing that, to trade all for God—if he exists—would be a sensible trade to one's own benefit.

So then, we are all bankers now, in our personal finances and in the goods that belong to us specifically as persons. Therefore, the maxim "Be good bankers" speaks directly to all of us.

3. A Glimpse of the Divine Economy

There can be no bankers where there is not an economy. The good bankers that Jesus spoke of must be located, then, in some kind of economy. Let us give it the name "the divine economy." But what is this? We can get a glimpse of it, I suggest, through drawing a contrast with an idealized merely "human economy."

By an "economy" I shall understand *any system by which persons, through each pursuing what he understands to be his genuine good, cooperate with one another through mainly spontaneous reciprocal exchanges, with the result that they increase and share among*

7 John Henry Cardinal Newman, "XXXIII, God the Sole Stay for Eternity," in *Meditations and Devotions*, ed. William P. Neville (London: Longmans, Green, and Company, 1907), 433–34.

themselves some kind of wealth. By this definition, there are various "economies" besides what we usually mean in speaking of "the economy." The economy in that usual sense turns out to be an abstraction of activities embedded within other economies that are inherently more important.

We said there are different kinds of wealth. Let us look at this idea with more attention. Wealth consists of goods. But a good is always a good *of* someone and therefore good relative to some aspect of a person. If, therefore, there are different, ranked aspects of a human person, then the goods of a human person will also be different and ranked in the same way. There will be different and ranked kinds of wealth.

But there *are* different and ranked aspects of a human being. The classical philosophers such as Plato and Aristotle recognized that this was so, and on this basis, they offered lists like the following:

Aspect of a Human Being	Type of Good	Examples
external to him but belonging to him	external goods	clothing, shelter, money, tools
his body	bodily goods	strength, vitality, health, comfort
his soul	character goods	the virtues, knowledge, skills, culture, friendship, family relations, admirable achievements, rational liberty, tranquility, self-possession

These goods have contrary evils. For external goods, the evils would be various kinds of material poverty. For bodily goods, they would be sickness, disability, weakness, and physical discomfort or pain. For character goods, these would be vice, ignorance, lack of culture, friendlessness, lack of a family and home, befuddlement of the will, domination by emotion, addictions, and purposelessness.

These goods also have fraudulent, deceptive goods that mimic them but have no real value (as Plato pointed out in the *Gorgias* 464a–e). For example, debased currency mimics genuine currency. Cosmetics and plastic surgery produce an artificial beauty, which mimics the vitality that naturally flows from youthfulness and health. Hypocrisy and moral posturing mimic virtue. Flattery mimics friendship. Fame mimics achievement.

In an economy, or system by which persons cooperate so as to increase and share among themselves any kind of wealth, generally one person or group possesses one specialized good within that kind, and others possess others, and then each shares from what they have, with reciprocity, so that all benefit from and have their "poverty" alleviated by the wealth of others.

The clearest case of such an economy is a rudimentary barter economy involving the most basic material goods. We are born into this world unprotected from the elements—we need clothing. We lack instincts for finding nourishment, and we have no natural or dedicated sources of food—we need to "make" our own food. We lack hooves or tough pads on our feet for walking on rocky ground—we need shoes. We are not provided with any natural lair—we need to build a shelter. Each family could make all of these things for itself; in that case, such a family would constitute a small economy. However, such a self-subsistent family would need to work very hard, almost constantly, to meet its material needs, and it could hardly make anything particularly well. On the other hand, if families cooperate, then, by each family's specializing in just one good, and subsequently trading with other families for all the rest, corporately they will make all of these things more easily, more plentifully, and to a higher standard. Hence we arrive at the ideal of a simple material economy, roughly that of a village. Such an economy has the possibility of developing over time into the even more efficient and more complete material economy of a city. A city also opens up the possibility of reliable protection against aggressors, significant leisure, and through the use of this leisure a common devotion to higher goods. The city represents a kind of endpoint that transcends the mere meeting of natural needs, which is why Aristotle said famously in his work *Politics* that "man is by nature an animal fit for a city" (1253a1). (The Greek word *politikon*, often translated as "political," means more exactly "city-dwelling" or "living best in a city.")

But let us go up the hierarchy of goods. There can be an economy too of bodily goods. We would call it a "culture" or "community" centered around wellness, healthiness, fitness, and beauty of physical form. But the basic principle is the same. In such a community, people tend to specialize; they focus on some approach to eating well or some kind of training or a particular sport. Each specialization is its own contribution to a general culture of fitness. They share with one another the goods of health and fitness that they enjoy. They do not do so by buying and selling—at least not mainly so but through other types of reciprocity: by mutual encouragement, by teaching and the sharing of expertise, and through common athletic activities, especially competitions. Such a culture is indeed "a system by which persons cooperate with one another so as to increase and share among themselves any kind of wealth." It meets our definition of an economy. Such a culture of fitness typically develops spontaneously. It consists of many interwoven networks and initiatives, quite illustrative of what Friedrich Hayek called "spontaneous order."[8]

An economy of health and fitness is higher than the economy of material goods, as shown by such things as that we work *in order to*

8 See among many sources F. A. Hayek, "The Principles of a Liberal Social Order," *Il Politico* 31, no. 4 (December 1966): 601–18, http://www.jstor.org/stable/43206528.

play sports, and we can hardly use material goods if we are seriously ill. Yet we use analogies drawn from the material economy to talk about this economy of goods of the body. We say, "No pain, no gain," which suggests one must "spend" pain in order to "gain" fitness; or, "The best investment you make is in your own health;" or, "Repetitions in weight training are valuable only at the margin;" and so on. The reason we do so, as has been said, is that the material economy is the clearest even if it is the lowest economy.

There are economies of goods of the soul also. There might for instance be (as one would say) "a strong music community" in a certain area, by which we would mean that there are many people who specialize in different areas of music and in different instruments or types of performance—for instance, Nova Scotia historically has had a strong community of Celtic music. These people freely exchange what they know and love. They share their favorite music with one another. They often get together in groups of various sizes to play music together. The same can hold true of a strong "intellectual" or "literary" or "academic" or "art loving" or "chess" community.

What is especially interesting about this third-level economy is that traditionally we have founded institutions that, as it were, aim to concretize such an economy as some kind of unified whole. Right from the start, in the economy of knowledge, Plato founded his Academy and Aristotle his Lyceum. The modern university aims to bring together into one place every specialization in knowledge, ostensibly for common benefit and effect. A conservatory likewise with its own virtuosi and ensembles aims to locate an economy of music within a single building, to attain the highest standards and to convey all of the wealth acquired and shared within that economy to a new generation.

For these economies involving goods of the soul, too, we use analogies drawn from the market economy: "That tedious exercise on your musical instrument will *pay dividends* in the long run;" "It is always *a savvy investment* for a medievalist to learn Arabic;" "The research *output* of that scientist is outstanding;" and so on. Again, we make such comparisons because the market economy is for us the clearest example of an economy: its goods are clear, the specializations are clear, the reciprocal exchanges are clear, and the effects of wealth are clear. And yet the economy of goods of the soul is higher, as shown by how we regard it as sensible to earn money *in order to* free up time for music and study.

In each of these three economies, the wealth that we create, share, and develop is the result of our ingenuity and industriousness and our canniness in collaborating with others. Each type of wealth depends upon many natural gifts and on an assumption of that continued, generally beneficent order in the world, which traditionally is called "providence." Assuming we have a modicum of virtue, stay at peace, and cooperate on friendly terms with one another freely, then the nature of these economies rightly ordered is that, if we work at it consistently, over time we tend corporately to become wealthier with all three kinds of wealth: external goods, goods of the body, and goods of the soul.

The ideal of this hierarchy of three economies, as rightly ordered in the lives of individuals and in a polity, can be entrancing, like a pretty toy. At least, many thinkers have found it entrancing—I can report that in my own studies of Plato and Aristotle, I have found it so. Presumably, it was even more entrancing when the Aristotelian conception of the cosmos, as concentric spheres of quintessence rotating around the air and the sea and earth, was still accepted. Within such a classical worldview, if we do not think too hard, it might be easy to accept a naturalistic view of nature as self-sufficient and complete. What need, then, of God, religion, or salvation? It is a very pretty toy, indeed—we simply need to discern its intended order and put that into effect. Such has been the dream of many philosophers.[9]

However, the reality that we actually see is not like this, and it cannot possibly become the way it is "supposed" to be. The reason is that there is something that, as it were, radiates down through this hierarchy of economies and threatens to make it a wreck—or has made it a wreck for almost everyone at certain times and for some almost all the time. It threatens to do so through war—which is mainly murder, theft, and rape—but also through nearly the constantly occurring thefts, lies, adulteries, betrayals, deceptions, outrages, oppressions, and enslavements of human life—not to mention jealousies, abandonments, rejections, insults, greed, vanity, rage, contentiousness, hubris, envy, self-deception, addictions, debasements, and various types of despicable weakness and simple foolishness. It threatens too through disease and various calamities and disasters, which we sense are not unconnected with disorders within us. Consider carefully your own life and the lives of those around you, and you can see that this wreck is well verified.

Even the remedies we propose, such as rules and government, themselves become part of the problem to be remedied. Rules are gamed for self-interest. Government gets corrupted for the benefit of a few. Governments indeed seem to specialize in lies. Famously, they steal; sadly, they often kidnap and murder. The actual exercise of political authority tends to corrupt those subject to it, leading many to suspect that laws are simply the means for the powerful to control others for their own advantage.

---

9 For example, Plato in his *Republic* sketches such an ideal. He is pessimistic that it can be attained, not it seems because he recognizes something irreparably flawed in our nature, but rather because he thinks the right sort of leaders would never be formed, selected, or tolerated.

We find that we cannot do what we know we should do and wish we would do. We are tormented by our lack of self-possession. We hate what we are drawn to and what we have become. We often discover, after the fact, a complete insensibility to what we ought to have kept in mind when we acted and to what we realize we should have seen—and then we feel ashamed, while aware (if we gained wisdom) that we are likely, right now, making a similar mistake in some other important matter, which we do not see. We do not know ourselves. We lack internal integrity. All of us grow old and start to break down just as it seems we have begun to learn how to live. If we do not die early and when we are elderly become satisfied that we have lived a suitably long life, it is only because we have become reconciled to not doing or achieving all that we dreamed of while we were young.

For a Christian, what I have detailed are signs of an original sin. The pretty toy was deliberately thrown to the ground by the child. The three lower hierarchies were intended in God's creation to be well ordered, and they were so, Christianity says, in a state of "original justice" under God. But somehow that justice with God was destroyed, and our bond with him was broken, with the result that everything else is at constant risk of subversion. Indeed, all goods are at risk of being lost for us if we "lose" our souls—that is, if the basis on which we enjoy any good at all is undone. It is not possible, we sense, for any good in a lower hierarchy to remedy this wreck radiating downward from the top. It is foolishness to suppose that a new idea or new system or new arrangement or structure could be the cure—many people accept this foolishness, which is further evidence of the wreck. Ideas have no power of themselves, and from experience we can judge that any new system will inevitably become just as corrupt as the system it replaced. Moreover, systems require a good will to implement them, but our will itself is corrupted.

Therefore, the intended order of things, which we may still discern if we are astute, has been wrecked. What then? For the purposes of this book, we assume that God, a personal being, exists. He is a good Creator. The order he intended became wrecked through the free choices of his rational creatures.

Suppose then that God, the Creator of the intended order, sees this wreck that I have just described. He has pity on us. He desires to remedy the disaster and save his creation, and to do so he sends the Savior. If there is a divine economy in which good bankers are situated, it would be within some kind of a new economy—an additional, fourth economy, at the top of the hierarchy of the other three, which results from this sending of a savior.

4. The Savior Founds a Divine Economy

Here we need to pause and ask just what we mean by a "savior." We use the term all the time, but what does it mean? A savior is someone who brings salvation. But what is salvation? I want to say that there is an objective meaning of the term. We are not free to invent meanings as we wish or feel. The terms "salvation" and "savior" have a standard meaning, a core meaning, which consists of four elements:[10]

- First, salvation presupposes peril. For someone to be in a position to be saved, he must be in danger of some great loss, of his life or worse. But it is not simply that danger threatens or that it is imminent; it is rather that he is captured by it. He cannot extricate himself from it. That is why, after he is saved,

10 See Michael Pakaluk, "Philosophy as a Path of Salvation in the Ancient World," in *Proceedings of the XIX Session of the Pontifical Academy of St. Thomas*, eds. Serge-Thomas Bonino and Guido Mazzotta (Vatican City: Urbaniana University Press, 2020), 11–27.

we say that he was "set free" or "liberated." In the classical world, a storm at sea was the paradigm of this kind of danger—a ship in the grips of a fierce storm that seemed bent on destroying it.

- The second element of salvation is that there must be an agent who intervenes, of a higher status than those in peril—as must be the case, if what seems impossible to those in peril is possible for this agent. Here's the classical example: in response to supplications by the crew, a god from above might intervene to rescue the ship from destruction.
- The third element is some process of translation, from peril to safety, involving some element of cooperation or consent on the part of the saved. In salvation, it is not that an evil is removed from a person, but rather that the person is removed from an evil. He is rescued from that evil and set in a safe place. That is why his consent is needed, either his explicit consent or an imputable consent. In the classical example, the boat in peril is saved by being brought safely to port. To be saved is to be brought home, where the crew wants to be.
- Fourth, the saved person incurs a debt of gratitude, which he must discharge afterward by explicit actions and signs. In the classical example, the crew, now safely home, sacrifices an animal to the god who saved them and erects a trophy.

So, salvation requires: (1) peril; (2) a higher agent, who "condescends" to save a lower being; (3) a translation from evil to safety; and (4) gratitude in reciprocation. Objectively, these are the core elements of the concept of salvation.

In the classical world, the standard example as mentioned was rescue from water. The Bible gives such examples as well: consider the parting of the Red Sea; Jonah; "fishers of men" (Matthew 4:19);

the calming of the storm (Matthew 8:23–27); and Jesus's pulling up Peter when he starts to sink into the water—Peter's very words are "Lord, save me!" (Matthew 14:22–23).

But another common image, much more common in the teachings of Jesus than rescue from the sea, is financial: a man finds himself bankrupt; he cannot extricate himself; his creditors therefore have the right to imprison him or sell him into slavery. Yet then a wealthy person, showing mercy, intervenes to pay his debt, placing him on a sound footing. The rescued man in turn is meant to show gratitude by remitting as necessary the debts of those indebted to him. It is this other image of salvation—let us call it "the financial image"—that is best for understanding the divine economy.

Let us see if this financial image can be applied in a thoroughgoing manner to the gospel, while keeping in mind that anything involving God is a mystery and goes beyond our capacity to understand completely. All images are limited; we must use discretion and not stretch them beyond their intelligent good use.

On the financial image of salvation, one likens creation in general to an investment by God. It is wealth infused by God, which continues to be possessed by God and is meant to produce even more wealth. The Psalmist says, "Know that he, the Lord, is God. He made us, we belong to him, we are his people, the sheep of his flock" (Psalm 100:3). A flock of sheep in the ancient world represented wealth (see Genesis 13:2). The "flock" for the Psalmist seems to be the entire human race. But smaller social groups such as the people of Israel and individuals are to be conceptualized similarly. Israel was likened by Jesus to a vineyard—that is to say, a productive business (Matthew 21:33). Jesus likened any individual to a tree cultivated by its owner to bear fruit (Luke 13:8–9) and also to someone who was granted a large lump sum meant to be put to productive use, certainly not to be squandered (Luke 15:12).

But now (continuing with the financial image) let us suppose that one of God's well-capitalized, created entities were to run itself into the ground, subvert its own value, and go bankrupt. The upshot in the ancient world, as we said, would be that the operators of that business, or the tenant farmers, would be sent to debtors' prison, or sold into slavery, to help pay their debts. But what does God the Creator do if he sees that his creation has gone bankrupt and "his people" are somehow liable to prison and enslavement?[11] If we continue to think in economic terms, what options would God have? Recall that in the ancient world money was a commodity and not a fiat currency. A debt could not be made simply to disappear; it could not be remitted except by someone's bearing the cost.

At first glance, there would seem to be three and only three options: closure, buyout, or bailout. First, God could shut down the business and perhaps, if he wished, start another business afresh. Second, he could enlist a third party to assume the debts of the bankrupt business. Third, he could write off the debts, which would be the same as for him to assume them himself, and then recapitalize the business, if that seemed good, which would amount to a bailout.

The first option seems untenable, since it would impugn God's dignity and wisdom. He would look like a failure at starting businesses. More important, he would make himself irrational by treating a debt as though it wasn't a debt. And if he showed himself to be irrational regarding the meaning of a debt, he certainly would not be in a position to start another business afresh.

---

11 Imprisonment *by whom*, enslavement *to whom*? The financial image strains a bit at this point, perhaps, but in the tradition, it was sometimes thought to be the devil, in accordance with retributive justice.

The second option, if carried out, would in effect make his original creation a subsidiary of some parent business. Such an arrangement, for rational creatures, would fail to represent correctly the right relationship between him and them. Rational creatures are created to be independent of any decisive, supervening authority except God's. In the business world, it would be as if an entity that was meant to operate as a partnership based on shared principles—say, a law firm or accounting firm—were purchased by a private equity interest and operated as though it were a corporation, for purposes other than those inherent in sound professional practice. The professionals would lose their freedom and independence; they would cease being members of a learned profession and would become mere employees.

The third option is untenable because it would fail to address what led to the original bankruptcy. It would create what economists call a "moral hazard," which is when bailing someone out from his imprudent actions encourages him to act with equal or worse imprudence in the future. More important, a bailout would not address the problem of the lack of sense of his rational creatures. If they were bailed out, they would not even need to acknowledge the debt or understand its seriousness. They would live in a state of fundamental falsehood, and they would lack a sound will.

So all three options fail. The first would impugn the intelligence of God, the second would place rational creatures under an authority other than God, and the third would actually fail to address any of the real problems.

And yet, there just might be a fourth option. What if the original investor were to join the business and through his own actions make it so that the business could itself repay the debt? And what if at the same time, by his example, he impressed upon others the reality of the debt and its seriousness? In that case, he could prudently save the business and infuse it with new capital, without any risk of confirming its members in their bad practices and bad conceptions.

Readers familiar with Saint Anselm's *Cur Deus Homo* (Why God Became Man) will recognize that I have just now briefly reformulated, using the financial image, his basic argument for the Incarnation. In a crucial summarizing passage, the saint writes:

> The substance of the inquiry was this, why God became man, for the purpose of saving men by his death, when he could have done it in some other way. And you . . . have shown that the restoring of mankind ought not to take place, and could not, without man paying the debt which he owed God for his sin. And this debt was so great that, while none but man must resolve the debt, none but God was able to do it; so that he who does it must be both God and man. And hence arises a necessity that God should take man into unity with his own person; so that he who in his own nature was bound to pay the debt, but could not, might be able to do it in the person of God.[12]

According to the Christian teaching of salvation—speaking within the financial image—God's plan was not simply to bail us out but rather to repay the debt on our behalf, in such a way as to teach us the seriousness of the debt and to begin to address our tendencies to fall into debt. He does so through a series of "purchases" in the following way.

---

12 St. Anselm, *Proslogium; Monologium; an Appendix in Behalf of the Fool by Gaunilon; and Cur Deus Homo*, trans. Sidney Norton Deane (Chicago: Open Court, 1926), 279 (with modifications of the author).

First, originally, he enjoys of course the wealth of divinity and all its glory in heaven. But he (or more precisely his Son) must divest himself of this wealth: "though he was in the form of God, [he] did not count equality with God a thing to be grasped, but emptied himself, taking the form of a servant, being born in the likeness of men" (Philippians 2:6–7). Theologians refer to this "emptying" by its Greek name, *kenosis*. *Kenosis* implies the hiding of his divinity by taking on a humble human nature. On the financial image, we understand it as a payment, by the Son, of the necessary price for God to become man through the Incarnation. The very fact of the Incarnation is already purchased by the Son. It comes as a free gift to us, but it comes with a cost to him, the loss of the visible expression of his divinity. There is no free lunch even in the divine economy.

Second, on the financial image, the Incarnation implies a deposit—namely, the Deposit of the divinity of the Son, and the wealth of that divinity, into human nature. We may think of the Deposit as credited to the common account of the entire human race and in principle available to each of us to draw upon.

If we put together these two ideas—divestment of divine glory and deposit into a human account—then on the financial image we may conceive of the Incarnation as a transfer of wealth from heaven to earth and placed into the account of the human race at the cost of this divestment. As Saint Thomas Aquinas says in his famous hymn "Pange Lingua" his precious body and blood have a price, or purchase value, more than the entire world.[13]

Third, this wealth deposited into the account of the human race is to be spent, in payment of our debt, in the Passion of Our Lord. Saint Paul in the passage already cited goes on to say, "And being found in human form he humbled himself and became obedient

13 *Sanguinísque pretiósi, Quem in mundi prétium.*

unto death, even death on a cross" (Philippians 2:8). That is, the Son's additional divestment now of his humanity, through death, is conceived of a second payment, made by him, but now on our behalf. "You are not your own," Saint Paul repeatedly insists, "you were bought with a price" (1 Corinthians 6:19–20 and 7:23).

The seriousness and price of sin, therefore, is clearly seen in the Passion of Christ. There can be no risk that someone who attends to his Crucifixion will think that our Redemption was accomplished without any cost. Whatever else it is, the Passion is certainly not a bailout.

The Passion rescues us, but it does so with new obligations. As Saint Paul says, "You are not your own." On the financial image, we conceive of these obligations as additionally arising from a new capitalization, a new creation. The Passion does not merely pay the price for sin on our behalf, but it also recapitalizes the human race, or at least those who draw upon this capital, principally through baptism. It proposes a new way going forward, a new kind of business, which in this book we are understanding to be the full meaning of the phrase "Be good bankers." Saint Augustine distinguishes well this second capitalization from the original one when he says, "God created us without us: but he did not will to save us without us";[14] that is, the first capitalization did not require our consent for us to enjoy its wealth, but the second does.

In sum, we see that Redemption on the financial image has all four of the objective components of salvation:

1. An evil from which we cannot extricate ourselves—namely, insolvency

---

14 *Sermo* 169,11,13: *Patrologia Latina* 38,923, as cited in the *Catechism of the Catholic Church* (New York: Doubleday, 1995), n. 1847.

2. A rescuer from a higher plane who condescends to save us out of pity, who pays the price to come down to our level—the Redeemer
3. Our necessary cooperation in being saved, as after all we must draw on the common account and make a claim on the funds—which is faith
4. A response of gratitude; that is, our willingness to participate in a new economy as recapitalized

The financial image of the atonement was used in the early Church at least as early as the second century in Saint Irenaeus. We see its influence on Saint Augustine in a famous passage: "Men were held captive under the devil and served the demons, but they were redeemed from captivity. For they could sell themselves. The Redeemer came, and gave the price; He poured forth his blood and bought the whole world. Do you ask what He bought? See what He gave, and find what He bought. The blood of Christ is the price. How much is it worth? What but the whole world? What but all nations?"[15]

As a result of this recapitalization of the creation, another kind of wealth became possible, which we would need to add now to the original hierarchy of three implicit in creation:

Aspect of a Human Being	Type of Good	Examples
His spirit in relationship to God	"Spiritual" goods and properly "divine" goods	The theological virtues (faith, hope, and charity), grace, a clear conscience, Christian liberty Being a child of God, being a friend of God

15 *Ennarationes in Psalmos* 95, n. 5, as quoted by Joseph Pohle, "Merit," in *The Catholic Encyclopedia*, vol. 10 (New York: Robert Appleton, 1911), http://www.newadvent.org/cathen/10202b.htm.

Thereafter, the hierarchy of goods we sketched previously looks like this:

A. Divine and spiritual goods
B. Character goods
C. Bodily goods
D. External goods

And we are now in a position to see clearly that on many occasions Jesus advises us to trade well in the divine economy that he has instituted. He tells us that if our eye causes us to sin, we should pluck it out (Matthew 18:9)—trade C for A. That the Kingdom of Heaven is like a pearl of great price which a merchant bought with all that he had (Matthew 13:45)—trade D for A. That anyone who would save his soul, should lose his soul (Matthew 16:25)—B for A. That we should fear the one who can cast our soul in hell, not the one who can harm the body (Matthew 10:28)—C for B. He clearly held that it made sense for some men to destroy a roof so that their friend could be healed (Matthew 9:2)—D for C.

But just as we can trade for this higher wealth, we can acquire it, conserve it, develop it, and take account of it. That is to say, we see that the Incarnation and Redemption establish a divine economy in which one can be a good banker in the sense intended by Jesus.

5. Sources of the Divine Economy

Any economy, as I have defined an economy, develops spontaneously, not through commands and external direction. Therefore, to give an economy, it is enough to stipulate its participants, their typical inherent motive, their typical mode of transaction, and the mode of diversification of the goods they swap. For example, in the basic material economy we described earlier, the participants are originally the inhabitants of a village or city, but potentially the whole human race;[16] the motive of each participant is to remedy his own material needs; the mode of transaction is a market exchange in which each in a free agreement swaps some portion of his surplus for some portion of the surplus of someone else; and the mode of diversification is the natural distribution of talents and resources, accentuated by the division of labor. Posit these, and a material economy based on them will develop spontaneously over time.[17]

For the divine economy, the participants are the entire human race together with God. Although God is divine and we are not, we form a unity with him nonetheless on the principle that a human being is created "in the image of God"; therefore, to treat the image in a certain way is as if treating God in a certain way. Human beings can act reciprocally with God and act reciprocally directly with their neighbor, but in the first case they are indirectly treating their neighbors in a certain way too, and in the second they are indirectly treating God in a certain way also.[18]

The motive for the divine economy is the need to respond with gratitude to one's having been saved. We said earlier that the fourth component in the concept of salvation is gratitude on the part of the saved person. Now it is time to get a little more precise and say that

---

16 An important insight of Adam Smith in his attack on barriers to free trade is that the material economy is "meant" to bind together the whole human race, because it originates to remedy needs faced by the whole human race. Adam Smith, *An Inquiry into the Nature and Causes of the Wealth of Nations*, Cannan ed. vol. 1 (London: Methuen, 1776), IV.3.

17 We presuppose too for any material economy that human beings are inherently fond of reciprocal transactions. We have by nature a "propensity to truck, barter, and exchange." Smith, *Inquiry into the Nature*, I.1.

18 See the wonderful discussion of how "every virtue . . . and every vice is put into action by means of your neighbors" in Saint Catherine of Siena, *Dialogue*, trans. Suzanne Noffke (New York: Paulist Press, 1980), 33ff.

this gratitude has as if three aspects and three kinds of expression, precisely on account of the three other components of an act of salvation, which it is a gratitude *for*. Because gratitude is a mode of discharging a debt, we can speak alternatively of these three motives as three debts needing to be discharged. Here is the basic mapping, which will become clear as we proceed:

Component of Salvation	Form of Gratitude
The savior's rescue	A debt of justice
The savior's mode of rescue	A debt of love
The savior's condescension	A debt of emulation or zeal

Let us consider first how the aspect of rescue gives rise to a debt in justice, as this is easiest to grasp. Perhaps it is best to articulate the point in the first person. Someone might say, "Before being saved by Christ, I was enslaved by sin. I hardly had possession of myself, I did not know or understand myself, and I was a 'wretch'—on a pathway to eternal death and loss. But when I was rescued by him, he gave me back my life, my very self, my freedom, and my future. Nothing that I now have, therefore, is of my own doing or making. In justice, then—or such is my conviction—I ought to offer to him, and to place in his service, my life, my self, my freedom, and any material goods I may happen to have command over."

As we have already seen, Saint Paul uses such logic in explaining why Christians should regard even their bodies as subject to God's laws: "Do you not know that your body is a temple of the Holy Spirit within you, which you have from God? You are not your own; you were bought with a price. So glorify God in your body" (1 Corinthians 6:19–20). Saint Alphonsus Liguori puts the point this way: "Therefore, O my Jesus, I cannot any longer, without injustice, dispose of myself, or of my own concerns, since Thou has made me Thine by purchasing me through Thy death. My body, my soul, my life are no longer mine; they are Thine, and entirely Thine."[19]

The reciprocal transactions corresponding to this debt would be, for example, when we offer up in intention all that we have to God in an act of worship, or, for instance, when we make all that we have available in principle to our neighbor in gratitude to God. Saint Paul seems to envision Christian *koinônia* in this way: "as a matter of equality your abundance at the present time should supply their want, so that their abundance may supply your want, that there may be equality" (2 Corinthians 8:13–14).

Because the Incarnation itself is regarded as a divine exchange of divinity for human nature, then, whenever one Christian takes upon himself the need of another, this transaction is conceived of as a win-win exchange on the same model. Suppose a prosperous Christian assists a starving Christian. On the financial image we conceive of it as an *exchange*, rather than as one-way altruism: namely, the prosperous Christian trades away his material goods in exchange for the opportunity of expressing gratitude to Christ and, as it were, paying down his debt, which is a win for him; while the starving Christian trades away his need, in exchange for both the alleviation of that need and giving someone the opportunity to express gratitude to Christ, which is a clear win for him as well.

So much for the debt of justice. A second debt of gratitude, the *debt of love*, arises not from a consideration of the evil from which one has been saved, but from a consideration of the motive of the superior power who saves. We take this debt to correspond to the component of translation in an act of salvation. More specifically, it involves the mode of the translation and the manner of the savior's engagement.

19 Saint Alfonso Maria de Liguori, *The Passion and Death of Jesus Christ*, trans. Eugene Grimm (New York: Benzinger Brothers, 1887), 31.

Bear with me here: the classical example of salvation from a storm at sea can easily illustrate this interesting and very important point. Suppose two scenarios: In the first scenario, a crew at sea is in danger of shipwreck in a storm, and mighty Zeus by the nod of his head calms the storm in the vicinity of the ship, protecting it so that it can get safely to the port. In the second scenario, once again, a crew is in danger of a shipwreck, but this time Zeus also sends dolphins to escort the ship to port, and, more than that, Zeus himself takes human form and rides upon one of the dolphins. Both scenarios would be acts of salvation. From the point view merely of what the crew gains—safety, rescue from shipwreck—they are exactly same. However, in the second, Zeus not only rescues the crew but also makes a point of showing to the crew his particular care for them. His evident care gives the rescued crew an *additional* reason to give thanks to their rescuer.

Something similar holds true on the Christian understanding of salvation. Sound theology holds that for Christ to save us from sin and death, it was not necessary that he undergo torture and death on a cross. The tiniest cut to his pinky finger would have sufficed. He is God after all. But Christ chose to save us in an extreme way, to express the extreme intensity of his love for us. As Saint Bernard of Clairvaux put it, "*Quod potuit gutta, voluit unda*": "What he was able to do with a tear, he wanted to do with a flood." Saint Bonaventure commented, "He chose to suffer as much pain as if he himself had committed all our sins."[20] Such intense love gives rise to a second debt, a debt of love, which is an urgent desire to repay love with love. Once again Saint Alphonsus Liguori gives an apt formulation: "If thou, my God, art thus become mad, as it were, for

20 Quoted by Liguori, *Passion and Death*, 247.

the love of me, how is it that I do not become mad for the love of God?"[21]

It is not the role of the book to trace out all of the implications in Christian culture of this felt urgency to repay in love. Christian love, so conceived, was the principal reason why marriage was transformed within Christianity, from being a mainly utilitarian relationship, marked solely by warm affection, to a romantic bond of extreme and intense reciprocal love. Again, Christians have felt compelled to found hospitals, orphanages, and schools, not solely from cold calculations about meeting the needs of others, but more so to express an extreme of love. Cathedrals arose from such love.[22] We single out Father Damien of Molokai for the intensity of his love rather than for the success of his hospital, which a government agency in theory might have operated more efficiently. That businesses get evaluated today as much on the friendliness of their service as on their competence is a development of the same originally Christian viewpoint.

So, a debt of love is a second, original motive for the divine economy.

The third kind of debt, a debt of emulation or zeal, arises from what I have been calling the condescension of the Savior, whereby he freely relinquishes a position of honor and higher standing as the price of directly assisting a humbler creature in need.[23] One might call it "magnanimity" as much as condescension. Max Scheler

21 Liguori, *Passion and Death*, 40.

22 Henry Adams, "The Dynamo and the Virgin," chap. xxv in *The Education of Henry Adams* (Boston: Houghton Mifflin, 1918; New York: Barnes & Noble, 2009), 302–10. Citations refer to the Barnes & Noble edition.

23 No Christian should scruple over this notion of condescension. One of the finest expressions of wonderment at it is the "Fifth Choir of Angelicals" from Newman's poem "The Dream of Gerontius" in *Verses on Various Occasions* (London: Longmans, Green, and Company, 1903), 363–64. These verses serve as the lyrics to the beloved hymn "Praise to the Holiest."

correctly saw that Christian culture has depended upon the emulation of this noble attitude and that Nietzsche's criticisms of Christianity flow from an obliviousness to it.[24] For a Christian, there is nothing admirable about poverty or lowliness as such, but there is something highly noble in voluntarily taking on poverty, when there was no necessity of doing so, to help someone in poverty precisely through suffering along with him.

This third motive to repay can be construed as the wish to do the same thing or something similar on a smaller scale for someone else. Here is how such a motive arises. An elementary impulse of reciprocity is to repay, in the same way, what one was paid. This is the so-called *lex talionis*, the law of "such for such."[25] If my neighbor treats me well, the most obvious friendly thing to do in return is something similar. If, for instance, he offers to help me when I am away by cutting my grass, I might offer to help him in return by cutting his grass when he is away. The reason is that we wish to affirm and repeat that which is good. But the next best way of affirming it through repeating it, besides doing the exact same thing, is to swap the agent and the patient—thus, I affirm the worth of a good service from another, when I was the recipient, by my repeating the good service toward that other, when I am able, as the doer. However, God is never in need of our good services—he suffers no evil from which he needs to be extricated; he lacks no ability to extricate. We cannot affirm the goodness of what he did for us, then, by such close reciprocation of doing good for him. On the other hand, each human being is made in the image of God, and human beings do indeed have many needs. Therefore, what we could not reciprocate toward God, we can

---

24 Max Scheler, *Ressentiment*, trans. William W. Holdheim (New York: Schocken, 1972).

25 Aristotle calls it "Rhadamanthine" justice in *Nicomachean Ethics*, vol. 5.

reciprocate in kind to God in our neighbor. I can affirm, then, the goodness of God's showing mercy to me by showing mercy to others. I can affirm the goodness of God's forgiving my debt when I could not have repaid it by remitting the debt of others to me when they cannot repay it. "Do you know what I have done to you? You call me Teacher and Lord; and you are right, for so I am. If I then, your Lord and Teacher, have washed your feet, you also ought to wash one another's feet" (John 13:12–14). This is how a felt debt to repay through emulation follows from Our Savior's "condescension."

In sum, each aspect of Christ's salvation—the rescue itself, which is a beneficence; his extreme of love; and his condescension, or mercy—becomes the basis for a need or debt to repay reciprocally, and thus for a distinct kind of reciprocity. If we are earnest and faithful in following them out, these motives give rise spontaneously to a divine economy.

6. Life in the Divine Economy

We mentioned Saint Paul's repeated insistence "you have been bought for a price." But the same image is in Saint Peter also: "You know that you were ransomed from the futile ways inherited from your fathers, not with perishable things such as silver or gold, but with the precious blood of Christ, like that of a lamb without blemish or spot" (1 Peter 1:18). Peter, too, is presuming that the salvation brought by Christ is a close analogy of the payment of a pirate's fee or a kidnapper's ransom.

We have postulated that if the value of salvation, the most fundamental good for a Christian, is itself analogized in Scripture to a commercial transaction—it is a redemption, a buying back of what is rightfully one's own, but not with silver or gold, but with something of far greater value—then we might expect that financial images would suffuse how early Christians explained their new life in Christ.

And that is exactly what we do find. These images tend to become softened over time by translators so that we can lose sight of their original commercial meaning. But the images are there all the same. Let us look at just a few of them.

We should recall once again that we employ such images to illuminate realities that in themselves, because they are divine, go beyond human understanding. The mysteries control the images, so to speak, not the images the mysteries. In particular, in no way is it the case that because commercial images can illuminate Christian mysteries, then the life of faith in Christ is "reduced to" economics, or that Christian prudence becomes one more application of cost-benefit reasoning or utility-maximization. We are exploring here analogies.

First, consider the phrase "the deposit of faith." This phrase expresses a commercial comparison: a deposit (*parathêkê*) is wealth entrusted to someone, typically a banker. In the Greek translation of the Old Testament (the "Septuagint" or LXX), the same word is used for someone who defrauds his neighbor by stealing some good that was left with him on deposit (Leviticus 6:2). So, when Saint Paul on two occasions uses this word when writing to Timothy, saying "safeguard the deposit" (1 Timothy 6:20; 2 Timothy 1:14), he is presuming that the faith is like a precious good, which belongs to God, left in Timothy's care. Timothy could indeed fail to safeguard it, either by altering the good for his own purposes or by neglecting part of it, thereby diminishing or even destroying its value. But in either case he would fail in a fiduciary duty and be committing fraud, because the deposit does not belong to him.

Or consider how naturally Saint Paul thinks of his relationship with the churches as if mediated through a system of accounting:

> And you Philippians yourselves know that in the beginning of the gospel, when I left Macedonia, no church

> entered into partnership with me in giving and receiving except you only; for even in Thessalonica you sent me help once and again. Not that I seek the gift; but I seek the fruit which increases to your credit. I have received full payment, and more; I am filled (Philippians 4:15–18).

It is a perplexing passage. One scholar has argued that since Paul is using the technical language of accounting (as he is), he must be referring to an actual written ledger for a common account. Such a ledger would record the deposits made by the Philippians, which were intended to underwrite Paul's expenses as though they were their own, and it would also record Paul's expenses, by which he drew upon their wealth as though it was his own. This scholar refers to the passage as the earliest evidence of accounting in Christian writings.[26] The more traditional interpretation is that Paul is simply using an accounting metaphor, and his meaning is that, as Saint Thomas Aquinas puts it, "No church entered into a partnership with me in giving temporal goods and receiving spiritual goods."[27] But even on this traditional interpretation, Paul is so fluent in accounting and financial concepts that he readily uses them to describe his work as a kind of joint venture.

Or consider Saint Paul's notion of "redeeming" or "buying back" time. What does this strange phrase mean? Saint Paul uses it twice. (Ephesians 5:16; Colossians 4:5). The word that Paul uses in both passages is *kairos*, which means time in the sense of opportunity. When he says that Christians should in effect pay something to attain

---

26 J. M. Ogereau, "The Earliest Piece of Evidence of Christian Accounting: The Significance of the Phrase *eis logon doseos kai lempseos* (Phil 4 :15)," *Comptabilités* 6 (2014): 1–16.

27 Thomas Aquinas, *Commentary on Saint Paul's Letter to the Philippians*, F. R. Larcher, trans. (Albany, New York: Magi Books, 1969), ad loc.

the *kairos*, he seems to be saying that they should make small sacrifices—forego some small, licit pleasures and comforts—in order to "purchase" opportunities for God's grace in their lives.[28] A *kairos* does not come along without any cost: there is no free lunch in the Christian life anymore than there is in business. The *kairos* must be purchased in the coin of the realm, which is some small suffering accepted out of love. Regardless, Paul's use of the expression "buying back time" shows, again, how easily he thought of the Christian life in commercial terms.[29]

Or consider this passage:

> Slaves, obey in everything those who are your earthly masters, not with eyeservice, as men-pleasers, but in singleness of heart, fearing the Lord. Whatever your task, work heartily, as serving the Lord and not men, knowing that from the Lord you will receive the inheritance as your reward (Colossians 3:22–24).

Slaves of course get paid nothing. This is what it means to be a slave rather than a hired hand. But Paul is teaching slaves to work with a good heart for the Lord, because the Lord will pay them, even if their earthly masters do not. In the passage, Saint Paul uses a commercial term, *apolambánô*, which originally meant to receive payment for services rendered. He is saying that slaves who work with the intention of serving the Lord will reliably receive compensation for services rendered—not earthly compensation, but something better.

---

28 This foregoing of small pleasures moment to moment in the Christian tradition is called "mortification."

29 See Michael Pakaluk, "Redeeming the Time the Christian Way," The Catholic Thing, June 8, 2022, https://www.thecatholicthing.org/2022/06/08/redeeming-the-time-the-christian-way/.

Furthermore, it is good that they work with the expectation of that other compensation, as then in their daily work they live in a relationship of reciprocity with the Lord.

Or consider this famous passage from Hebrews:

> By faith Moses, when he was grown up, refused to be called the son of Pharaoh's daughter, choosing rather to share ill-treatment with the people of God than to enjoy the fleeting pleasures of sin. He considered abuse suffered for the Christ greater wealth than the treasures of Egypt, for he looked to the reward (Hebrews 11:24–26).

The Greek word awkwardly rendered here as "the reward" is *misthapodosia*, which actually means due compensation, wages due for service. Our word "reward" may suggest, misleadingly, that Moses was looking forward to something like a bonus, a gratuitous gift that only might be given to him in the end. But the Greek term implies, rather, that he was relying on a payment that would be strictly due to him for his choice of Christ over Pharaoh's daughter.[30]

The writer of Hebrews even says this: "And without faith it is impossible to please him. For whoever would draw near to God must believe that he exists and that he rewards those who seek him" (11:6). The word rendered here as "he rewards" is related to *misthapodosia* and means someone who is reliable in giving compensation—like an employer who will not fail to pay his workers. As Saint Jerome puts

30 Theologians refer to what is strictly due as a matter of "condign merit," whereas a bonus would be "congruous merit." An employee on payroll is paid on the basis of condign merit. A child may, at his parents' good pleasure, get ice cream as an unexpected reward for cleaning his room as a matter of congruous merit.

it in the Vulgate, someone who approaches God must believe that he is a reliable *remunerator*.[31]

The usual Greek term for financial profit (*kerdainô*) is also used in the New Testament. Consider the following interesting passage:

> For though I am free from all men, I have made myself a slave to all, that I might win the more. To the Jews I became as a Jew, in order to win Jews; to those under the law I became as one under the law—though not being myself under the law—that I might win those under the law . . . To the weak I became weak, that I might win the weak. I have become all things to all men, that I might by all means save some (1 Corinthians 9:19–22).

The passage is a good example of how translators systematically soften commercial terms. The English verb "to win" means to acquire as a result of a contest. But what Paul is speaking about has nothing to do with winning in that sense. (The NAB even has "win over" instead of "win.") The term he uses means "to gain" in the manner of a successful business enterprise. It means, precisely, to gain as profit. (The Douay-Rheims and KJV both use "gain" rather than "win.") Clearly, he is relying on the logic of redemption, conceived of as a purchase. Businesses make profits by earning back through their activity more than they spend. Paul is saying that by becoming a slave and by becoming weak, which he conceives of as akin to commercial expenditures—they are like the expenditures paid by Christ in the Incarnation and in the Passion—he gains in the wealth that consists in saved souls.

31 *Sine fide autem impossibile est placere Deo. Credere enim oportet accedentem ad Deum quia est, et inquirentibus se remunerator sit.*

The word for "gain" and the word for "loss" are correlative and standardly mean commercial gain and loss, and we find them both used by Paul in the following famous passage:

> Indeed I count everything as loss because of the surpassing worth of knowing Christ Jesus my Lord. For his sake I have suffered the loss of all things, and count them as refuse, in order that I may gain Christ (Philippians 3:8).

Paul could have put this thought in other forms. He could have said that he *gave up everything* to know Christ. Or that he *jettisoned* everything or *sacrificed* everything or *abandoned* everything. But he uses commercial terms suggestive of a business accounting after the fact. He is saying that when he looks back now at the ledger, he sees, on one hand, the losses he sustained, and, on the other hand, his gains. The fact that he adds that he counts his losses "as refuse" shows that his analogy is indeed commercial, because in a commercial reckoning we would regret the losses, even if they were necessary for the gains. And yet Paul wants to make clear that in this case, in contrast, he does not recognize any value at all in what he lost!

How might we summarize what we are seeing here? We can say that the Apostles found it natural to use commercial images for the Christian life, because the Christian life, as placed within a divine economy, is marked by reciprocal exchanges by which we grow in genuine wealth, with respect to the vital interests of our eternal life, for which the material economy serves as a clear model. The debts, obligations, risk of bankruptcy, possibility of gains in value by trading, payment for services rendered, and the value to us of something earned are all very clear in the material economy. Here as elsewhere, we use that which is clear to illuminate what is less clear.

But the material economy is thus clear because it was designed to be clear. That is one of its purposes, if we look at the matter teleologically. We hunger and thirst for food and drink because our bodies need food and drink. But food and drink also represent other, higher desires, and they are designed to represent them: Jesus could not have said, "Happy are those who hunger and thirst for justice," unless hunger and thirst were like the desire for justice but clearer. The pain, immediacy, urgency, and felt need to do something, which are implicit in the body in its experience of those desires, are meant to illuminate for us what the desire for justice should look like. Likewise, the material economy has a representational purpose. Jesus could not have likened discipleship to working in a vineyard for pay, unless it was like working in a vineyard for pay. Working in a vineyard for pay therefore has a representational purpose, of standing for discipleship in the kingdom. The point can be generalized to the material economy as a whole.

It is a gross mistake to regard the material economy as sufficient on its own—to misconstrue its wealth as ultimate wealth, and trading in its goods as the sole form of personal reciprocity. People with such a narrow vision are bad judges of value and poor bankers. The best way to avoid this disastrous mistake is not to avoid the financial image altogether but rather to apply it resolutely, so that the divine economy, placed now "on the same turf" as our material concerns, can begin to assert its proper claims on us.

7. Matthew the Tax Collector

What have we established so far? We have seen that Jesus liked to teach "Be good bankers," which meant more than "Be good money-changers." It meant also: be good traders, investors, risk-takers, and assessors of value. We have seen that salvation from of old was conceived of as a buying back, paid for by the death of the Christ. We have seen that Christians naturally turned to commercial images to describe the Christian life. In short, we have located what might be called a *mode of explaining the gospel* that would most adeptly be grasped and handled by someone with some kind of financial background. Jesus himself was a carpenter and handyman. His four chief Apostles were fisherman. But he deliberately called a tax collector to be an Apostle also. A tax collector spent his time valuing transactions and entities in light of the relevant laws and making careful records of the same. Was it just an accident that Jesus called a person like that, or was it that Matthew's background matched this mode of presenting the gospel?

In what follows, I will assume that Matthew was called to be a disciple for the reasons mentioned. I will assume also that Matthew the tax collector was indeed the author of the Gospel traditionally ascribed to this Matthew. I dissent from a common view among New Testament scholars that someone else wrote the Gospel of Matthew and that this author depended on the Gospel of Mark in writing it and needed to depend on it (the thesis of "Marcan priority"). Interested readers may find a full account of my reasons in the postscript at the end of this book.

I proceed then on the assumption of Matthew's authorship and ask, What light does this shed on his Gospel?

In imperial Rome, tax collectors worked within a hierarchical structure, with some overseeing other lowlier "tax farmers." We do not know exactly how much authority Matthew the tax collector held. Apparently he wasn't at the bottom, because he had money to host his colleagues at a feast, and they came to that feast when he invited them (Matthew 9:10). Capernaum, the city where he worked, was at a crossroads; it had a moderate business importance and opened up to broader markets.[32] Besides, any tax collector in Palestine would have needed to know how to navigate among both religious and secular authorities. For all we know, Matthew as an individual had exceptional curiosity and ambition. That he was selected by Jesus would suggest that he did. Therefore, I shall assume that he was aware of Roman best practices in accounting and those provisions of Roman law that had implications for accounting. Two of these practices turn out to be highly relevant to this book.

Accounting in the Roman period consisted mainly of lists. Modern double-entry bookkeeping, which creates a record of the movement of funds, had not been invented.[33] Roman numerals did not lend themselves to being arranged in columns in order to be summed. Managers did not use accounting to make good estimates of the comparative efficiencies of different parts of their business. It was all rather primitive, compared with modern accounting. And yet, for all that, accounting was comprehensive and exact. Lists would be drawn up by managers for their work of a day, recorded in a daybook or *adversaria*. From these, summaries would be carefully made of receipts and expenditures upon various classifications—which farm, which commodity, which client, which time period, and so on.[34] And then, in the Roman world at the time of Christ, a consolidated summary would be compiled for larger

32 See for instance Sharon Lea Mattila, "Revisiting Jesus' Capernaum: A Village of Only Subsistence-Level Fishers and Farmers?," in *The Galilean Economy in the Time of Jesus*, eds. David A. Fiensy and Ralph K. Hawkins (Atlanta: Society for Biblical Literature, 2013), 75–138, https://doi.org/10.2307/j.ctt1b7x6b4.8.

33 Fra. Luca Pacioli, a Franciscan and a mathematician whose books on proportion and on chess were illustrated by Leonardo da Vinci, described the double-entry system of the Venetian merchants for the first time in his 1494 *Summa de arithmetica, geometria*.

34 See, for instance, Roger S. Bagnall, *The Kellis Agricultural Account Book*, P. Kell. IV Gr. 96 (Oxford: Oxbow Books, 1997).

households, which functioned for tax and legal purposes as the official record of the business or economy of that household. This kind of consolidated summary was called a *codex accepti et expensi*, "a book of what is taken in and what is spent." Most of what we know about the *codex accepti et expensi* comes from Cicero, who died in 43 BC—that is, just a few generations before Matthew composed his Gospel.

From Cicero's language and from a passage in Pliny the Elder's *Natural History*, scholars have long believed that a *codex accepti et expensi* was formatted with receipts in one column of a page and expenditures in a parallel column, or perhaps with the receipts on one page of a pair of facing pages and the expenses on the other.[35] The idea is that by comparing the offsetting lists, a manager or tax official could more easily figure out the profit and balances. Whether the formatting was uniformly bifurcated like that is unclear.[36] But it is certain that the codex, regardless of formatting, was conceptualized as bifurcated. Its entries were thought of, functionally, as composing two distinct and offsetting groups.[37] Here's a comparison: Suppose in your library at home you have a shelf of books about cooking and a shelf of books about music. But over time you acquired many more books about cooking than music, and you had no extra shelf space, so that you let the cooking books flow over to the music shelf. Despite the absence of strict, spatial bifurcation, you might nevertheless still

35 For the standard view, see William Smith, William Wayte, and G. E. Marindin, *A Dictionary of Greek and Roman Antiquities* (London: John Murray, 1890), 465–66.

36 See doubts raised in G.E.M. Ste. Croix, "Greek and Roman Accounting," in *Studies in the History of Accounting*, ed. A. C. Littlejohn and B. S. Yamey (London: Eastern Press, 1956), 14–74. About what strictly can be inferred from the passage in Pliny, see B. R. Rees, "N.H. ii.22," *Classical Review* 8, no. 3/4 (December 1958): 213–15.

37 For this notion of functional position, see Lance Elliot LaGroue, "Accounting and Auditing in Roman Society" (diss., University of North Carolina, Chapel Hill, 2014).

think of your books, functionally, as placed on either the cooking shelf or the music shelf.

We can say with confidence that a tax official who was accustomed to examining *codices accepti et expensi*, or who knew that best practices of certain tax officials involved the examination of this kind of record, would naturally think of the economy of a household in the same way, as ultimately divided up into a complete list of receipts on one hand and a complete list of expenditures on the other hand. I will assume that Matthew conceived of the accounting of a household economy in this way also. This is the first practice of Roman accounting that is highly relevant to this book.

As mentioned, a *codex accepti et expensi* had official standing. As Cicero informs us, people disputing a debt, for instance, might bring this codex into court and expect that its record of a transaction from even many years earlier, down to the smallest unit of currency, would be decisive for legal purposes. Obviously, therefore, if someone doctored the books, he might create an obligation that did not really exist, say, if he added a line representing an outflow to someone as a loan that, in the *codex*, was nowhere offset by any inflow from that person. Or suppose Decimus were to record in his codex, with the consent of Lucanus, that he had paid a certain sum to Lucanus, and yet Decimus and Lucanus both understood that he had not yet paid Lucanus any such sum. Such a record would create a debt, because Decimus at any time could take Lucanus to court and demand repayment of the sum which was due to him, because *there* was the decisive evidence of the loan, recorded in the codex.

This is a good way to understand how a certain mode of creating an obligation to pay arose in Roman law at the time of Christ in connection with the *codex accepti et expensi*. It was called a "literal" obligation—meaning "based on the writing," or perhaps even "based on the account books"—because the obligation arose from the mere writing of an entry into the record, not from any business reality. "The debtor must consent to the entry," one authority observes, "and no doubt he would normally make a corresponding entry in his own book." The device was used "as a sort of novation or recast of an existing transaction, or as a way of opening a credit for the debtor."[38]

For our purposes, it is important to understand that this device was also used to make a third person responsible for a debt. For example, suppose that a wealthy man, Marcus, had a very dear friend of modest means, Terence, who because of a bad gambling habit had become broke and could not meet his obligation to pay a third person, Antonius, 500 denarii for corn. By the creation of a literal obligation, Marcus could assume Terence's debt. Here's how that would be done: Marcus and Antonius would agree that Antonius should make an entry into his own codex for 500 denarii loaned to Marcus. Marcus would then become liable to Antonius for the very amount of Terence's debt. This kind of arrangement, in which one person is made to substitute as debtor for another, was called an obligation "*a persona in personam*" by the Roman jurist Gaius, who is our main source of knowledge of these literal obligations.

This method of creating a debt—by making a record of the payment in the official financial record of a household, the literal obligation—arose along with the *codex accepti et expensi* and declined along with it.[39] Both reached their zenith around the time of Christ,

---

38 W. W. Buckland, *A Text-Book of Roman Law from Augustus to Justinian* (Cambridge: Cambridge University Press, 1921), 456–57; Alan Watson, *The Law of Obligations in the Later Roman Republic* (Oxford: Oxford University Press, 1965); and Peter Birks, *The Roman Law of Obligations*, ed. Eric Descheemaeker (Oxford: Oxford University Press, 2014).

39 Ralf Michael Thilo, *Der Codex accepti et expensi im Römischen Recht: Ein Beitrag zure Lehre von den Literalobligation* (Gottingen, Germany: Muster-Schmidt, 1980).

and sometime between 200 and 500 AD they went into desuetude.

These are our two relevant items from Roman accounting practice: I am assuming that Matthew, as an ambitious tax collector familiar with the best practices of Roman accounting, first, would naturally conceive of a household's receipt of wealth and expenditure of that wealth as corresponding to entries in a *codex accepti et expensi*, and that, second, he would naturally suppose that a debt could be created by the mere recording of it in the official record of a household's economy.

Our next question then becomes, How might his embrace of these conceptions have informed his account of the economy of the household of God?

8. The General Structure of Matthew's Gospel

I will give only general remarks here: there will be many occasions in the commentary to look at details.

Everyone who examines Matthew's Gospel agrees that it is so ambitious that it must have been composed according to a definite plan. The common view is that Matthew conceived of his work as like a layering. He began with an already existing narrative of actions of Jesus, especially miracles, and probably a distinct collection of teachings of Jesus, and then he inserted the one into the other: five strata of teaching ("discourses") intermingled with this narrative—"like a layer cake," as people say. There is truth to this analysis, but even on its own terms it is flawed because there is certainly a sixth long discourse and there are many shorter discourses. A more important objection, however, is that such an analysis appeals to nothing fundamental; it identifies no compelling principle of organization besides the idea of weaving in discourses.

I approach the matter in a different way. I begin with the idea that, for someone who is not an author of long discourses by trade,[40] the most natural and most obvious way of organizing an ambitious composition, assuming the subject matter is at all suitable, will be by dichotomy. That is, you conceive of your composition as divided in half, and if you need more structure than that, you are disposed to divide again those halves into halves.

Furthermore, if you wished to be more artful, then, inspired by the human face and by beautiful works such as fine buildings, you would exploit symmetries and reflection among these parts.[41] Therefore, I expect antecedently to see in Matthew divisions into halves and perhaps the use of devices of symmetry or reflection.

And that is what I do find. I find division into halves. The public life of Christ would be naturally suited to such a division, as it had two basic parts: his ministry in Galilee and then his going up to Jerusalem to suffer and die. Note that I am not claiming that the parts must be the same in length, but only the same in weight and importance. However, in Matthew's Gospel one does find that the two parts are very close to being the same in length. The point of division, we may say, is Peter's famous "You are the Christ" (16:16), which is almost exactly halfway through the Gospel whether we count by verses (544 out of 1,071) or Greek words (9,457 out of 18,345).

And I also find reflection between the two parts, as summarized in this table:

---

40 In the ancient world, orators would be like this. They were mainly defense attorneys who wrote lengthy speeches to defend their clients.

41 See the work of my sometime colleague Roger Scruton in *The Face of God: The Gifford Lectures* (London: Bloomsbury Continuum, 2014), who developed theologically his theories in *The Aesthetics of Architecture* (Princeton, New Jersey: Princeton University Press, 2013).

First Part	**Second Part**
Coming from: genealogy	Going to: sending out of the Twelve
Womb	Tomb
Anointing to be baptized	Anointing to die
Temptation in the desert	Distress in the garden
Call of the Twelve to him	Flight of the Twelve from him
Evangelization	Martyrdom
Bread = the word	Bread = the body
Going down to Galilee	Going up to Jerusalem
Parables of sowing	Parables of harvest
Many receive, a few reject	Many reject, a few receive

And there are many more. A Christian will of course believe that such symmetries are present by God's design in the life of Christ. Presumably, they constitute one reason why that life has proved so compelling to so many. My point is that Matthew's recognition of these and other symmetries, which he does not fail to highlight, would have made organization by division look compelling as well.

But if Matthew understood Peter's profession of faith to mark the halfway point, why would he do so? Because this is the first occasion that Jesus teaches that he is going to be crucified. As Matthew puts it, "From that time Jesus began to show his disciples that he must go to Jerusalem and suffer many things from the elders and chief priests and scribes, and be killed, and on the third day be raised," (Matthew 16:21). Therefore, from that point on, the meaning and emphasis of Matthew's account must change. We can easily overlook the phrase "From that time" (*apo tote*). But the old commentators on the Greek have not overlooked it: it is "a note of time marking an important epoch" (Meyer);[42] "an important note of time"

42 Heinrich August Wilhelm Meyer, *Commentary on the New Testament*, ed. Frederick Crombie, trans. Peter Christie (Edinburgh: T. & T. Clark, 1880), 301.

(Cambridge Bible);[43] "It is clear, therefore, that He had not shown it them before. The Gospel may be divided into two parts, from which the Divine plan of Jesus shines forth. The first proposition is, *Jesus is the Christ*; the second, *Christ must suffer, die, and rise again*" (Bengel's *Gnomon*).[44]

And as if to confirm the point, the very next time the disciples show that they had forgotten that the Christ was fated to suffer, Christ reminds them, "Whoever would be first among you must be your slave; even as the Son of man came not to be served but to serve, and to give his life as a ransom for many" (Matthew 20:28). "Ransom" (Greek, *lutron*) here is "ransom money"—that is, paid for the release of a slave. The turning point of Matthew's Gospel, then, halfway through, is the revelation of the Cross, which is at the same time the revelation of the payment of a ransom.

Once we recognize that Matthew's account is divided into two basic parts, we are led to ask whether it makes sense to compare those two parts to that standard instrument of record-keeping for prominent households of the time, the *codex accepti et expensi*, which as we saw was also divided into two parts. And now, thinking back to our discussion of the principles of divine economy, we see that, of course, Matthew's account may be so compared. As we saw, on those principles, the Lord's death is understood as a purchase, which is to say an expenditure. It is an *expensum*, or rather it is *The Expensum*, which includes many smaller *expensa*: "We are going up to Jerusalem; and the Son of man will be delivered to the chief priests and scribes, and they will condemn him to death, and deliver him to the Gentiles

---

43 A. Carr, *The Gospel according to St. Matthew*, The Cambridge Bible for Schools and Colleges (Cambridge: Cambridge University Press, 1893), 212.

44 Johann Albrecht Bengel, *Gnomon of the New Testament*, vol. 1, trans. James Bandinel (Edinburgh: T. & T. Clark, 1863), 329.

to be mocked and scourged and crucified, and he will be raised on the third day" (Matthew 20:18).

But no household can spend what it does not have. We have seen that each of these expenses is as it were infinite. How did the household acquire such infinite wealth? Again, as we have seen, it did so by a Deposit—which is the Incarnation—of divine nature into the human race. Accordingly, the first half of Matthew's book begins with an announcement of the Deposit, just as the second half begins with an announcement of a Payment. The two main mysteries of the Christian faith, the Incarnation and the Passion, are the two sides of a ledger—the one a Deposit, the other a Payment.

I have been speaking of a deposit, but strictly for a household I should be speaking of a receipt, an *acceptum*, into the economy of that household. To understand the difference, think of the financial concept of a beneficiary. The beneficiary of an account is that person who has rights to the assets in that account. The beneficiary may be someone other than the account holder; it may even be someone other than the one in whose benefit the funds were originally deposited into an account. For instance, a man may deposit funds into an account for his son's college education, the son being the beneficiary, but when the son grows up and decides to learn a trade instead of going to college, the man might redesignate his wife as the beneficiary. So, when we speak of a deposit, we are not yet bringing in the notion of the beneficiary, but when we speak of the receipt or *acceptum*, we are now bringing in the notion that the household is the beneficiary.

One must draw this distinction because, as we will see below, the deposit of the Word into human nature is represented by Matthew as in its original intention "for" Israel, the people of the covenant. And yet it works out, as a result of the rejection of Christ by his own people, that that intention gets broadened, so that the Gentiles as well become designated "officially" as beneficiaries. This is the development or change that one sees in the second part of the first half of Matthew's Gospel. Matthew gives there an account of how the beneficiary of the deposit changes and therefore how there is a corresponding change in the "household" within which the deposit may be accounted (or "recognized," as an accountant would say) as a certified "receipt."

Another concern of Matthew in the first half of his book is *credentialing*. To understand why, think back to our original discussion of banking in the very opening of this introduction, where it was explained that a banker needs to be not simply reliable in fact but also reliable in appearance, so that he can be trusted as reliable. "Be good bankers" also has the sense of "Be trustworthy and reliable bankers." A similar point needs to be made here. In all financial matters, it is necessary not simply that value be present (in the account where it is supposed to be) but also that that value be in some sense certified or confirmed as present. With persons, we call this process "credentialing," from the Latin, *credentia*, which means believability. Typically, credentials involve origins. Today, minted coins and bills say where they were minted or printed. Good wines tell us where they were bottled—a savvy patron at a restaurant will not *smell* the cork pulled from a very expensive bottle but rather *inspect* it, to see whether what is printed on the cork matches what is given on the label. Smilarly, produce has its Controlled Designation of Origin, or DOC. We compose *curricula vitae* (CV) which give education and job experience; we insist on their accuracy even in small matters because a CV really is akin to a financial statement.

Strangely, but importantly, credentialing and confirmation are often accomplished just by a slip of paper that states something. Paper has power in such matters. A receipt at the store is sufficient to confirm that one made a purchase. A diploma on the wall serves to credential a physician or professor. In general, documentation serves to confirm, even if it can hardly be verified itself.

Matthew thought in this way also. As someone with the sensibility of an accountant, he sees that the genuineness of the deposit has to be confirmed, and accordingly, he conceives of the first part of his Gospel as also a matter of confirmation and credentialing—sometimes, as we shall see, simply with a paper.

But this leads to the last general observation about the Gospel of Matthew that I wish to make here. It has often been observed that Matthew takes pains to say that certain prophecies are fulfilled by events in the life of the Lord. There are about twenty such instances, more or less, depending upon how one counts, such as the following:

> All this took place to fulfill what the Lord had spoken by the prophet: "Behold, a virgin shall conceive and bear a son, and his name shall be called Emmanuel" (Matthew 1:22–23).

We may ask, Why did Matthew refer so often to the fulfillment of prophecy? And what exactly is this relationship of fulfillment, anyway?

Regarding the first question, commentators often say that Matthew refers to prophecies so frequently because he was writing for a Jewish readership that would find these prophecies authoritative. Regarding the second, commentators typically say that the fulfillment relation is the converse of the foreseeing relation—that is, if some reality is precisely what God intended in what the prophet foresaw, when the prophet foresaw and said it, then that event fulfills what the prophet said.

These common answers are plausible enough and in their way surely true. Yet the interpretation we have been developing suggests a different approach.

We have been understanding Matthew's Gospel as like the ledger of a household. But suppose we take the household he ultimately has in mind as stretching back to include the nation of Israel? Suppose, even, we understand his genealogy at the beginning of his book to be a way of asserting that continuity? In law, one finds the notion of "incorporating by reference," which is when one code of law by referring another code intends that the force of that other code be carried over and taken to apply to everything that is said in the present code. What if Matthew's giving of a genealogy stretching back to Abraham plays a role like that, as if merging two economies and two sets of records—that of Israel and that of the Kingdom of Heaven? We saw that the mere writing of an entry into a *codex accepti et expensi* was sufficient to create a literal obligation. Suppose Matthew saw the analogy, at least intuitively, and regarded a prophecy as establishing an obligation to be repaid. Then, his frequent references to these prophecies would also be a way of emphasizing the payment of a debt in the life and death of Christ, while also showing the interconnectedness of the two economies.

It turns out that the word that Matthew commonly uses for the fulfillment of prophecy (*plêroô*) was applied commonly to the fulfillment of a commercial obligation. It meant to render or to pay in full. One instance given in the standard lexicon involves, tellingly, paying back the debt owed to one's country by giving up one's life in battle: "[the warrior Magareus] either will die and *pay the earth the full price* (*plêrôsei*) of his nurture, or will capture two men and the city on the shield, and then adorn his father's house with the spoils" (*Seven against Thebes*, 477, emphasis mine).[45] Sometimes the word refers to payment in full of the interest due on a loan, and sometimes to the payment of the price for the worth of some good received. If, in a

45 Aeschylus, *Aeschylus*, trans. Herbert Weir Smyth, vol. 1, Suppliant Maidens, Persians, Prometheus, Seven against Thebes (Cambridge, Massachusetts: Harvard University Press, 1926), 361.

codex accepti et expensi, an entry had been made in order to establish a literal obligation and later on that debt was paid in full, a natural way to describe this relationship would be to say that what had earlier merely been written had now been paid in full—the promised payment had been *fulfilled*.

TABLE 1: THE STRUCTURE OF MATTHEW'S GOSPEL		
Part One: The Deposit (Matthew 1:1–16:12) First Part of the First Part: Recognition of the Deposit (Matthew 1:1–9:8) (i) Confirmation and Credentialing by Third Parties (chapters 1–4:16) • Genealogy confirms • Kings confirm • Trip to Egypt confirms • The Baptist and his baptism confirm • The temptations in the desert confirm (ii) Attestation from Jesus's Own Words and Deeds (chapters 4:17–9) • Sermon on the Mount • Miracles Second Part of the First Part: Crediting of the Deposit (Matthew 9:18–16:13) • Apostles appointed and sent out • Faith, not heredity, the principle of inclusion • Scribes and Pharisees reject him • Nazareth rejects him • Parables for pagans • Mission to pagan territory • Feeding of the four thousand in pagan territory	**The Dividing Point: Announcement of the Passion (Matthew 16:13–28)**	**Part Two: The Payment (Matthew 17:1–27:66)** First part of the Second Part: Payments Looked for in the Followers of Jesus (Matthew 17:1–20:19) • Marriage without divorce • Accepting children • Detachment from wealth • Use of time as a vocation • Authority and honors Second Part of the Second Part: The Payment of the Redeemer (Matthew 20:19–27:66) • Rejection by the elders, Scribes, and Pharisees • Betrayal • Trial, false accusations, unjust sentence • Handed over to the Romans • Unjust sentence • Scourged • Beaten • Mocked • Crucified **The Recapitalization of the Household of God (Matthew 28:1–19)**

Let these remarks suffice for how in general we intend to approach Matthew's Gospel as the work of a former tax collector. Our working hypothesis (argued for in the postscript) is that the Apostle Matthew, a tax collector, was indeed the author of the Gospel traditionally attributed to him. We discussed two relevant provisions of accounting and contract law of the time, which presumably this Matthew would have been familiar with. We have proposed that his Gospel is structured like a *codex accepti et expensi* and also shows his attention to various literal obligations. In the commentary, we will look at how his Gospel thereby teaches and explains "Be good bankers."

Table 1 above gives the basic structure of Matthew's Gospel on the interpretation I am proposing. The translation and commentary below will follow this structure, rather than the traditional division of the text into twenty-eight chapters. (Those chapter and verse numbers are not original but were added to the Bible in the sixteenth century.)

9. *Brief Notes on My Translation*

I have aimed to make this translation completely accurate. By this I mean that I aim to construe each Greek sentence as a sentence in good English that says everything the Greek sentence says and neither says nor implies anything not in the Greek sentence, while minimizing changes in sentence structure and word order.[46]

Matthew's own writing is in a plain style, which I like to call his "business Greek." Typically, in any clause he will combine just two ideas on the pattern: participle + finite verb. For example, "Walking

46 My main Greek text has been Nestle et al., *Novum testamentum Graece*, 26th ed. (Stuttgart: Deutsche Bibelstiftung, 1983).

[participle] alongside the sea of Galilee he saw [finite verb] two brothers" (4:18). I regard his simple style as expressive of his record-keeping background. An entry in a ledger involves recording the amount of a receipt or expense, together with a note explaining why. The former is as if the definite act is expressed by a finite verb, while the latter is as if a qualification is added to that definite act. For example, "buying corn, I paid one denarius." Every entry in a ledger gives a definite quantified act and a qualification of the same. Matthew writes in a similar way.

A special problem is presented by Matthew's frequent use of the Greek word *idou*, which literally means "look!" It is traditionally rendered uniformly as "behold!" But "behold" is archaic; moreover, *idou* plays many different functions for Matthew. My practice is to replace *idou* with an English expression playing the same function whenever doing so is not awkward.

A similar problem is presented by Jesus's use of "Amen, I say to you," which I always render as just that because the function of this expression seems always the same, meaning, "You can have full confidence in what I am about to say; take it seriously."

I generally omit "and" (*kai*) when it occurs at the beginning of a sentence, since I regard its function there as segregating assertions, which in English is already accomplished by a period. (Matthew's Greek text was originally without our punctuation.) A word which is always used in the same place and in the same way has lost its original meaning and retains only a parsing function, in the way that many English speakers today begin every sentence with "So." But I do render *kai* as "And" in those few cases when in my judgment it is not serving simply as a full stop.

All quotations of Scripture besides my translation are from the RSVCE.

PART ONE

The Deposit (Matthew 1:1–16:12)

The value of the economic interpretation of Matthew's Gospel will show itself right away, in the illumination it provides of the opening genealogy and the infancy narrative.

First Part of the First Part: Recognition of the Deposit (Matthew 1:1–9:8)

(i) Confirmation and Credentialing by Third Parties (Chapters 1–4:16)

Matthew's first confirmation of the Deposit, and the first credential, is his documentation of the genealogy of Jesus. Matthew uses the Greek word *biblos* ("papyrus" or "paper"), not *biblios* ("book"). The former is used for a written document—for content precisely as written down. For example, the frequently mentioned "book (*biblos*) of life" (Philippians 4:3; Revelation 3:5, 20:15) is a written record of the saved. Matthew, in the spirit of an accountant, provides a genealogical document.

I present the genealogy as a list, as Matthew gives it. For clarity, here I have removed the traditional verse numbers. But in removing these editorial additions from the sixteenth century, I also render the documentation the way Matthew intended.

This genealogy is a document precisely of origin; that is, it verifies how something properly came to be. Therefore, one must use a word like "begot," which states causation. Rendering it as "Abraham was the father of Isaac," and so forth (as nearly all translations do today), is a serious mistranslation because it improperly gives only the effect of the causation, not the relation of causation itself.[1]

1 For more on this important point, see Michael Pakaluk, "The Gospels Begin with Sex," The Catholic Thing, January 5, 2022, https://www.thecatholicthing.org/2022/01/05/the-gospels-begin-with-sex/.

Documentation (*biblos*) **of the origin of Jesus Christ, David's son, Abraham's son.**

David's son, Abraham's son—These phrases are used as patronymics and should be rendered accordingly—think of his full name as Jesus Abrahamson Davidson Christ.

Abraham begot Isaac.
Isaac begot Jacob.
Jacob begot Judah and his brothers.
Judah begot Perez and Zerah by Tamar.
Perez begot Hezron.
Hezron begot Ram.
Ram begot Amminadab.
Amminadab begot Nahshon.
Nahshon begot Salmon.
Salmon begot Boaz by Rahab.
Boaz begot Obed by Ruth.
Obed begot Jesse.
Jesse begot
David the king. David begot Solomon by the wife of Uriah.

The decisive genealogy is from Abraham to David, because he is Abrahamson Davidson. The rest of the generations are measured in terms of this span, as explained below. To get the number fourteen, one has to count the persons, not the steps.

Solomon begot Rehoboam
Rehoboam begot Abijah.
Abijah begot Asa.

Asa begot Jehoshaphat.
Jehoshaphat begot Joram.
Joram begot Uzziah.
Uzziah begot Jotham.
Jotham begot Ahaz.
Ahaz begot Hezekiah.
Hezekiah begot Manasseh.
Manasseh begot Amos.
Amos begot Josiah.
Josiah begot
Jeconiah and his brothers, at the time of the Babylonian resettlement.

To get fourteen in the next list, Jechoniah has to be counted again:

After the Babylonian resettlement,
Jeconiah begot Shealtiel.
Shealtiel begot Zerubbabel.
Zerubbabel begot Abiud.
Abiud begot Eliakim.
Eliakim begot Azor.
Azor begot Zadok.
Zadok begot Achim.
Achim begot Eliud.
Eliud begot Eleazar
Eleazar begot Matthan.
Matthan begot Jacob.
Jacob begot
Joseph the husband of Mary, of whom
Jesus was born, who is called Christ [“Anointed”].

I'll now resume using chapter and verse:

> **1:17 Therefore, the whole of the generations from Abraham until David are fourteen generations.**
> **From David until the Babylon resettlement, fourteen generations.**
> **From the Babylon resettlement until Christ, fourteen generations.**

In this commentary, I will mainly raise questions directly related to the economic interpretation advanced here, of Matthew the tax collector and the divine economy. But sometimes I raise a question simply of general interest. Often, the one kind of question dovetails into the other.

Such is the case here. For example, we want to ask simply out of general interest, "How does the genealogy give the origin of Jesus, if Joseph is not the father? Doesn't the last step make the whole preceding list pointless?" I answer (not as contributing to the economic interpretation): no, because Matthew is presuming that God is able to accomplish through a miraculous process what would have been so in a natural process. The supernatural intervention, he thinks, does not subvert or replace but brings along with it Joseph's paternity. If so, then presumably Jesus would have looked like both Joseph and Mary, not simply Mary; also, Joseph could have claimed a direct paternal authority over Jesus. Jesus was not simply an adopted child for Joseph. Nonetheless, to be sure, Matthew has drawn up the list to make patent the failure of ordinary human paternity at this point—which is how it should be, for the specific credentialing of a divine-and-human savior.

There are well-known difficulties in the list and in the numbering:

- In the second group of fourteen, Matthew omits generations. Between Joram and Uzziah, there were Ahaziah, Joash, and Amaziah.
- Also, between Josiah and Jeconiah, there was Jehoiakim, who was actually the one who had the brothers.
- In the third group, to get the number fourteen, Jeconiah after the Babylonian exile has to count as different from Jeconiah before the exile.

Of course, Matthew was aware of these things. It's foolish to say that he wasn't. Therefore, these changes were deliberate.

To understand Matthew's deliberate procedure here, one must understand what it meant to count in the ancient world. To count was to measure, using the first unit as the standard. For example, I mark a length of fabric, and then I use that length as a measure for the rest of the roll. The "unit measure," then, has a different status from the other, measured quantities. Measuring was conceived of as essentially normative. It was the imposition of the standard set by the unit measure on something originally indistinct. And if, for instance, there were irregularities or imperfections in what was measured, then it would be the unit measure *as normative*, or rather the measurer wielding that measure as normative, who would decide where to draw lines. The measurer would surely not permit his decision to be settled by the thing measured, with all its irregularities. The unit measure alone *measured*; the rest *was measured*.

Then notice that in verse 17 Matthew uses the phrase "the whole of the generations" only for the first group, from Abraham to David. Why? Because Jesus is Abraham's son and David's son. Therefore, he reasons, the whole and complete enumeration of the generations from Abraham to David must constitute the measure for the rest of the genealogy. He then applies this measure as a normative standard.

Because the standard is normative, he is free, at his discretion, to decide what to include or exclude from the measured, if there are irregularities in the measured, so that the normative measure fits as he judges it should. For example, he evidently decides not to count three kings notorious for their wickedness.[2]

He would find the number 14 confirmatory of his original inspiration to add up the generations, because this number would be the double of a perfect number, 7 + 7. He might even have conceived of Abraham as the reason for the one 7 reaching forward, just as David was the reason for a second 7 reaching back. The number 14 then would be as if Abraham and David joined together.

He is also clearly pleased that the measure in its first judicious application measures out to the resettlement (dislocation, deportation) of the Jewish people from Jerusalem to Babylon. This exile stands for our own dislocation from God because of sin. That even this disaster is measured would presumably show, for Matthew, that Abraham and David were meant together to be brought to bear against sin.

We therefore find that the tripartite division of the genealogy reflects all three figures who were characteristically anointed in the Old Covenant: first, Abraham, who is the *prophet* of the vast descendants of the nation of Israel; second, David, who stands for the figure of a *king* ruling over these descendants; and the disastrous Babylonian resettlement showing the need for reconciliation through, third, a *priest*. *Christos* in Greek simply means "anointed one." The Anointed One, the Christ, had to combine all three offices together. But there would be no other occasion for such a figure to arise except after the third group of fourteen was measured. Thus, his measuring is complete leading up to the Christ.

---

2 As Psalm 1:6 would authorize, "The way of the wicked will perish."

18 But the origin of the Christ was as follows. When his mother, Mary, was betrothed to Joseph, before they had come together, it was found that she was carrying in her womb from the Holy Spirit.

Before they had come together—that is, before, as betrothed, they stopped living separately.

it was found that she was carrying in her womb from the Holy Spirit—"Carrying in her womb" is a Greek description of pregnancy. Attend to this phrase carefully: not, "it was found she was pregnant, which later proved to be by the Holy Spirit," or "which was inferred to be by the Holy Spirit," but rather, "it was found that it was by the Holy Spirit that she was carrying in her womb." That is to say, her immediate family and Joseph found (or discovered) it to be so. But how did they discover that this was so? Presumably, they believed Mary's word—although we cannot rule out that they additionally had confirming signs, whether mystical or miraculous. Going forward, then, Matthew is taking it as a fact, in his narrative, that the offspring is of the Holy Spirit. Note that, in the ancient world, testimony by a known honest person did not have secondhand status, as compared with one's own direct observation.

19 Joseph her husband, as he was an upright man, and not wanting to expose her, intended to release her quietly.

to release her quietly—His problem is that he does not want to take her for himself because he believes that she belongs to God, and yet he does not want it to look as if he is accusing her of fornication. The word for "release" means to tell her that he does not consider her bound by her former promise to him. It is not that Joseph intends to put her away.

20 He had just been pondering these things when—this is astonishing!—an angel of the Lord appeared to him in a dream, saying, "Joseph, David's son, have no fear of taking Mary as your wife since that which is begotten in her is from the Holy Spirit. 21 She will bear a son. And you shall give him the name 'Jesus,' since he will save his people from their sins."

this is astonishing!—"Behold" (Greek *idou*). Matthew invites you to share in his wonder. It's as if his enthusiasm can't help breaking out from his accountant's professional manner.

have no fear of taking Mary—The angel knows and adverts to the reason for Joseph's holy fear, namely, that the child is begotten from the Holy Spirit. We should add no comma before "since" (punctuation is an editorial decision; there were no punctuation marks in the original text) because what follows, "that which is begotten in her . . . ," gives what the divine messenger and Joseph both affirm and what both recognize is the reason for his fear.

from the Holy Spirit—The messenger uses the same preposition, "from," that was used in the genealogy whenever the mother's role was mentioned in begetting. It is as if the Spirit plays a mothering role to match Mary's role. The Father begets the Son "from" the Spirit, with Mary's consent, and not without Joseph's paternity.

And you shall give him the name—Joseph also takes on the human office of the father, because he imposes the name and thereby claims guardianship. *Nota bene*: Jesus's divinely given name itself, which gives the purpose of the Incarnation, is his second credential.

Observe then this disparity between Luke and Matthew. Luke is not interested in credentialing, as Matthew is. Therefore, Luke tells of the ancestors and birth of the Lord from Mary's point of view. For Matthew, in contrast, the father and his public office are paramount.

> **22 The whole of this took place so that what was said by the Lord through his prophet might be fulfilled:**

The whole of this—All three, (1) pregnancy, (2) bearing a son, and (3) his name.

> **23 "Attend! The virgin will carry in her womb, and she will bear a son, and they shall give him the name 'Emmanuel'"—which when translated is "Among us—God."**

Joseph would have been well aware of the prophecy (Isaiah 7:14) and have seen the correspondence. Matthew takes the language of the prophecy from the Septuagint, where it is specifically a "virgin" not merely a young woman who conceives.

Matthew the tax collector, we propose, would have thought of the text from Isaiah as creating a literal obligation toward the human race with these three specifications, which were written by God into the codex of the household of Israel, with Isaiah serving as the recording clerk. Now at last, Matthew is saying, that obligation has been paid in full.

"Attend!" in the prophecy is of course "behold." One cannot rule out that Matthew, who takes himself to be imitating Isaiah (see the postscript), has learned from Isaiah how to use "behold."

> **24 Getting up from his sleep, Joseph did as the messenger of the Lord instructed him. He received his wife—25 and he had no relations with her through to the time she did bear a son—and he gave him the name "Jesus."**

Getting up from his sleep—The order of words implies that he got up immediately after the dream. What could he have done that very night, however, except change his intention? Well, might he not have gone romantically to his betrothed in the darkness, from sheer joy, and brought her back to his house—as he licitly could do? For such romanticism, see the poem "The Dark Night of the Soul" by Saint John of the Cross. Its first lines are "On a dark night / with disquietude, though inflamed with love / O blessed grace! / I went forth without being noticed / while my house most assuredly was at rest."[3]

Joseph did as the messenger of the Lord instructed him—Joseph shows himself to be a good banker. He accepts the Deposit, he exercises a fiduciary trust through maintaining a certain distance, and this trust proves fruitful. He does the proper accounting, so to speak, by applying the name that confirms the value of the Deposit—that is, a name that signals that for which the Deposit was to be spent.

she did bear a son—This is one of the three things the angel predicted and therefore is part of what the angel instructed him to do. Of course, Joseph as the husband cannot bear a son. But he can do his part. If it were a merely human son she was to bear, his part would have been to have relations with her. But as it is a divine son of the Father, his part is precisely the opposite during this time—that is, *not* to have relations with her. Joseph begets Jesus and enjoys real paternity *precisely by his abstaining from relations with Mary.* And this is why Matthew brings in the fact of abstention. There is no other purpose—that the child is from the Holy Spirit is already taken as a fact.

The first confirmation of the Deposit and first credential was his genealogy; the second was his name, Jesus. Now the third, we see that kings recognize Jesus as a king:

---

3 *En una noche oscura / Con ansias en amores inflamada, / ¡Oh dichosa ventura! / Sali sin ser notada, / Estando ya mi casa sosegada.*

2:1 After Jesus was born in Bethlehem of Judaea in the days of Herod the King, astonishingly, magi from the East arrived in Jerusalem.

Born in Bethlehem of Judaea in the days of Herod the King—In the ancient world, to date an event required mapping it to a regime. Our *Anno Domini* has the same rationale. Matthew the accountant straightaway records the place and date of the birth.

astonishingly—"Behold."

magi from the East—For an enlightening discussion of these mysterious figures, see Dwight Longenecker, *Mystery of the Magi* (Washington, D.C.: Regnery History, 2017).

2 "Where is the one born King of the Jews?" they said. "Because we saw his star at its rising, we have come to adore him."

to adore—To approach with great humility, bending low and kissing the hands or feet, the way dogs lick the hands of their master. As mentioned, count the willingness of these strange authorities to submit themselves in this way to Jesus as the third credential noted by Matthew.

3 Hearing this, King Herod was highly agitated, and all Jerusalem with him. 4 Gathering together all of the high priests and scribes of the people, he inquired of them where the Christ was to be born.

highly agitated—a "panic." There were crises and panics in the ancient world also, most notably a financial panic in 33 AD under Tiberius, which Tacitus (*Annals* 6.17) refers to similarly as an "agitation" (*commotus*).

scribes of the people—Observe how the former public tax collector, Matthew, takes pains to indicate that these are specifically religious scribes (of the Jewish people), rather than scribes from Herod's administration.

where the Christ was to be born—But the magi had not used this word "Christ"! Credit Herod, then, with inferring long before Peter that this King was the Christ—which shows the strength of the Messianic expectations of the time. Count Herod's testimony, then, as a fourth credential tallied up by Matthew.

> **5 "In Bethlehem of Judaea," they said to him, "since**
> **thus it was written through the prophet: 6 'And you,**
> **Bethlehem, land of Judah, are hardly least among the rulers of Judah, because from you a ruler will come forth who will shepherd my people Israel.'"**
>
> **7 Then Herod, summoning the magi in secret, ascertained from them the exact time of the star's appearance.**
>
> **8 Sending them to Bethlehem, he said:**
>
> **"Go on your way and inquire exactly about the child. When you have found him, report back to me, so that I too may go and adore him."**

Matthew is describing here, in somewhat technical language, what he recognizes as a standard way for a public authority to deal with a problem, in three stages:

- First, consultation—the chief authority gathers together the relevant general authorities and consults with them. Thus, Herod convenes a meeting with the high priests and scribes.
- Second, fact-finding—the chief authority "ascertains" from the relevant particular authorities the more exact details of the situation. Thus, Herod interrogates the magi.

- Third, due diligence—the particular authorities carry out their own careful inquiry in order to report back to the chief authority. Thus, the magi are instructed to confirm the details exactly.

Then Herod, summoning the magi in secret—Pay attention to Matthew's use of this slight word, "then" (Greek, *tote*), which would be very easy to miss. It is his favorite word for putting together the pieces of his narrative, and this is distinctive of him. See in the early chapters: 2:16, 2:17, 3:13, 4:1, 4:5, 4:11. It was a common opinion among the early Christians that Mark was not very careful about putting things into the correct chronological order, whereas Matthew was. Of course, bookkeepers take pains to mark the dates of transactions.

Observe next what I have called Matthew's "business Greek":

> **9 And they, after hearing out the king, went on their way.**
> **And, amazingly, the star which they saw at its rising went**
> **before them, until it came and stood above where the**
> **child was. 10 Seeing the star, they rejoiced heartily, with**
> **great joy. 11 Coming into the home, they saw the child**
> **with Mary his mother. Falling prostrate, they paid him**
> **homage. Opening their treasure boxes, they offered him**
> **gifts of gold, frankincense, and myrrh. 12 Having been**
> **warned in a dream not to go back to Herod, they escaped**
> **to their own country by another route.**

amazingly—"Behold." Matthew's own emotion, which he wants you to share in, breaks out in the midst of his business-Greek account.

Coming into the home—The good banker, Joseph, has made it so that there is a home at all, a place of safekeeping. A true home is always a safe.

they saw the child with Mary his mother—In the first appearance of the Lord he is explicitly identified as being with his mother. After birth, just as much as before birth, the mother and child are a pair, not autonomous individuals. They are "the child and his mother": see verses 13, 20, 21. Note that although *we* certainly know her name, Matthew takes pains to say here "Mary his mother." He is taking the magi's point of view, and they would have met her just then, as well as the child.

Falling prostrate—Matthew is keen on documenting appropriate action. An appropriate action is one that matches that to which it is directed, and these magi fall to the ground immediately upon seeing Jesus with his mother. This disposition of Matthew is an expression of his accountant's mind, since accounting aims to render apt representations of truth and to indicate worth accurately, precisely through those representations. That the magi are mysterious figures who come from nowhere and seem beholden to no one makes their representation disinterested and therefore more trustworthy.

Opening their treasure boxes, they offered him gifts of gold, frankincense, and myrrh—Likewise their gifts are representations of the worth of the recipient. Matthew would be aware that the gold was shortly to prove valuable to cover the expenses of the family's flight to Egypt and sojourn there. Very quickly the gold would be disbursed in the manner of an instrumental good. But not so the other gifts: the lasting "value" of the child was in his being the Savior who would offer his life as a great high priest, as signified by frankincense and myrrh.

Having been warned in a dream not to go back to Herod—This time Matthew does not say that it was an angel who appeared in the dream. Was it the child, then, they had just pledged fealty to and whom they recognized as having a higher authority than Herod in that jurisdiction?

13 After they had escaped—look!—an angel of the Lord appeared in a dream to Joseph:

> **"Get up and take the child and his mother and flee into Egypt. Stay there until I tell you. Herod is about to search for the child, to destroy him."**
>
> **14 And he, getting up, took the child and his mother during the night and escaped into Egypt, and he was there until Herod met his end. This was to fulfill what was spoken by the Lord through his prophet who said,**
>
> **"Out of Egypt I called my son."**

during the night—We have our stories of central bankers staying up late at night to find ways to forestall bank runs and crises. Here, the good banker, after learning of risk from a reliable authority, deals with it immediately, throughout the night and into the next day without sleep.

he was there—That is, Joseph. Just as the infant Jesus is inseparable from Mary, so the child is inseparable from Joseph. Matthew refers to Jesus by referring to Joseph.

"Out of Egypt I called my son."—Another credential: not many Jews could claim to have sojourned in Egypt and then returned to Judea, in recapitulation of the exodus of the Israelites. Thereby, too, a literal obligation is paid in full.

> **16 Then Herod, seeing that he had been made a fool of by the magi, became intensely enraged. Sending his henchmen, he eliminated all the boys in Bethlehem and in its surrounding districts two years of age and younger, based on the time as he had determined it precisely from the magi. 17 Then was fulfilled what was spoken through Jeremiah the prophet, who said,**
>
> **18 "A voice in Ramah was heard—weeping and great mourning—Rachel, crying for her children. And she refused to be comforted, because they are no more."**

Saint Augustine interprets the slaughter as a test of faith: "O blessed infants! He only will doubt of your crown in this your passion for Christ, who doubts that the baptism of Christ has a benefit for infants. He who at His birth had Angels to proclaim Him, the heavens to testify, and Magi to worship Him, could surely have prevented that these should not have died for Him, had He not known that they died not in that death, but rather lived in higher bliss. Far be the thought, that Christ who came to set men free, did nothing to reward those who died in His behalf, when hanging on the cross He prayed for those who put Him to death."[4] From the start, Saint Augustine says, we are invited to believe in a distinct divine economy.

In economics, the value of a thing is revealed in what you are prepared to spend, or give up, for it. Herod had referred to this child (Jesus) as the Christ. Now in a perverse way he reveals the worth he assigns to the child. And this persecution, too, credentials Jesus—not many of us were deemed so important by the highest civil authority in our area that he would wipe out an entire age range of human beings to stop us from living.

based on the time as he had determined it precisely from the magi—Herod's rage is depicted as irrational. It does not follow that because the star appeared two years ago then the boy had to be two years of age or younger. Herod knew this, because he asked the magi to inquire and report back to him. His rage comes from malice and spite.

19 After Herod met his end—look!—an angel of the Lord appeared in a dream to Joseph in Egypt:

4 St. Augustine, Sermon 373, as quoted in St. Thomas Aquinas, *Catena Aurea*, vol. 1, part 1, (Oxford: John Henry Parker, 1841), 82.

**20 "Get up and take the child and his mother," he said,
"and go into the land of Israel. They are now dead, the
men who sought the life of the child."**

Now another passage follows with much business Greek:

**21 And he, getting up, took the child and his mother and
went into the land of Israel. 22 But having heard that
Archelaus ruled as king over Judaea in place of his father,
Herod, he was afraid to return there. Having been warned
in a dream, he escaped to the area of Galilee. 23 Going
there, he dwelt in a town called Nazareth. Thus was
fulfilled what was said through the prophets, that he shall
be called a Nazarene.**

in a dream to Joseph in Egypt—Matthew hereby connects this Joseph with the patriarch. The patriarch had prophetic dreams and could interpret them, and this Joseph receives messages in dreams; also, both were skilled stewards of a king's household.

And pay attention to the example of that great patriarch. During the seven years of famine, he never gave away even a single grain from Pharaoh's storehouses. No free lunch with that Joseph—he only *sold* grain, for something in exchange. When the people ran out of money, he sold it to them first for their land and then for their liberty, such that, by the end of the famine, Pharaoh had become owner of all the land of Egypt, and all the people had sold themselves to him as his slaves (see Genesis 47). Surely in this way Joseph the Patriarch shows that God rejects what Dietrich Bonhoeffer called "cheap grace."[5]

---

5 And yet Bonhoeffer seems to keep stumbling when he tries to explain "costly grace" because he is intent above all on avoiding the unavoidable language of merit. Dietrich Bonhoeffer, "Costly Grace," chap. 1 in *The Cost of Discipleship*, 2nd ed. (New York: Macmillan, 1959)," 45–60.

he was afraid to return there. Having been warned in a dream—Like a good banker, Joseph shows prudential caution.

he shall be called a Nazarene—Nazareth was a tiny, inconsequential village in the outer districts. As a result, the label "Nazarene" (John 1:47; 7:52) was used by Jesus's contemporaries as a term of contempt, much as we say, "a hick."

So far, Matthew has given the following credentials of Jesus:

- His genealogy and its division into three parts
- His name itself, "Jesus"
- The fact that magi came and adored him
- Herod's esteem for him as the Christ
- The slaughter of the innocents as representing his preciousness
- His exodus from Egypt

Next we have John the Baptist, who was "officially" tasked by God with credentialing the Christ, as he was foretold through the prophet as the one who would point to the Christ. We might say that he was the accredited accreditor.

We said that the divine economy depends on notions of credit, debit, reward, punishment, and due compensation. If John is the accredited accreditor, then his teaching on these matters would set down principles for accepting the Christ. And this is what we find: he teaches that good trees are left to stand, that the wheat is harvested, that the chaff is burned, and that trees that produce no fruit or bad fruit are cut down.

3:1 In those days comes John the Baptist preaching in the wilderness of Judea, 2 saying,

"Repent, for the Kingdom of Heaven is near."

3 For this is the one spoken of through Isaiah the prophet
when he said, "A voice crying in the wilderness, prepare
the way of the Lord, make straight his paths."
4 John himself would take his clothing from camel hair,
and a belt of leather around his waist. His food was locusts
and wild honey.
5 At that time, Jerusalem and all Judea would go out to him,
and the entire district of the Jordan, 6 and they would be
baptized in the Jordan river by him, confessing their sins.

In the postscript, I will suggest that there was a Petrine tradition of the life and miracles of Christ, which the Apostles would have relied on in preaching, before the Gospels were written down. This "oral catechesis" would have been largely memorized, although they probably would have used notes on tablets as aids. A thumbnail sketch of John the Baptist would surely be included in this tradition. What might such a thumbnail have looked like? It would be composed of smaller essential points, which one might call "articles," like the articles of a creed. In parentheses, I give an estimate of the number of Greek characters that would be necessary for each point, based on the commonalities among all four Gospels. They sum to 460, which is about what can fit on a typical wax tablet.

- He was prophesied (requires ~72 characters)
- He lived in the wilderness (~36 characters)
- Everyone went to him (~63 characters)
- He preached
    - ❑ repentance for forgiveness of sins (~35 characters)
    - ❑ the one coming after him (~110 characters)
- He baptized (~66 characters)
- He was austere in: his appearance and his food (~96 characters)

I include this outline and calculation as an example of the sort of thing that can be done with many of so-called pericopes in the Gospels.

7 But seeing many of the Pharisees and Sadducees coming for his baptism, he said to them,

"Brood of vipers! Who warned you to flee from the impending anger? 8 Produce fruit, then, as valuable as repentance."

"as valuable as"—Repentance is itself of value (Greek, *axion*), which should show itself in the production of further value.

9 "And do not think to say among yourselves, 'We have Abraham as our father.' Because I say to you that God has power to raise up children for Abraham from these stones.

10 "Already the axe is laid at the root of the trees. Every tree, then, which fails to produce good fruit is cut down and thrown into a fire.

11 "Although I baptize you in water for repentance, the one coming after me is greater than I am, whose sandals I am not worthy to carry.

"He will baptize you with the Holy Spirit and with fire—12 whose winnowing fork is in his hand, and he will clear the threshing floor, and he will gather his wheat into the granary, but the chaff he will burn with an unquenchable fire."

13 It was at that time that Jesus comes to John the Baptist, from Galilee to the Jordan, to be baptized by him. 14 But he forbids it, saying,

"It is I who need to be baptized by you, and you are coming to me?"
15 **But Jesus says to him in reply,**
"Allow it now, because it is fitting for us to fulfill justice in this way."

Only Matthew records this exchange. Can we find an explanation in Matthew's being a tax collector?

The word "fitting" (*prepon*) in Greek carries the suggestion of "fitting for outward appearances and as a public expression." Moreover, it is fitting "for us," because Jesus cannot be baptized without John's help. Thus, the meaning of John's role must be considered also. If the baptism is fitting "for us," then it is a win-win interaction, and understandably Matthew the tax collector would be particularly drawn to this idea.

But how was it a win-win? John's baptism anticipated Christ's baptism and is therefore fulfilled in it. Thus, one thing fittingly expressed in this act, which is fitting for John and therefore to his good also, is just this fact that his baptism cedes its place to the Lord's baptism.

But from the point of view of the Lord, it would be fitting and a good also, because in submitting himself to that which he could have rejected by right, he is not claiming his rights, but rather in friendship is taking a position of solidarity with sinners. It was a common idea in the ancient world that the most refined expression of justice is found when someone refuses to stand on his rights in order to realize his equality with another—it being assumed that the essence of justice is to make us equal in our relations to others. That attitude, of not standing on one's rights in order to be equal with others, was called *epieikeia*, or "equity," which was regarded as very close to love and friendship. Jesus is saying, then, that he can realize a better equality with sinners if he puts aside his own claim of right and with John's permission is baptized by John.

Then he allows him. 16 Jesus having been immersed,
immediately he came up from the water and, amazingly,
the heavens were opened, and he saw the Spirit of God
coming down upon him as a dove and alighting on him,
17 and—look!—a voice from heaven was saying,
"This is my son, my beloved, in whom I am well
pleased."

Amazingly . . . look!—"Behold."

Now we see the credential of the Father's public recommendation, just as the descent of the dove is the credential of the Spirit's recommendation.

I said in the introduction that the most natural way to organize a piece of writing is to divide it in half, and then each half in half, and so on. I said that, on such a plan, the first half of Matthew is concerned with the Incarnation, which he conceived of as like a deposit, and the second half with the Passion, which he conceived of as like an expenditure, as in a *codex accepti et expensi.* I said that the first half in turn was divided into two halves, the first concerned with recognizing the Deposit, its existence and value, and the second as if clarifying the "account" to which this Deposit so recognized was to be assigned.

However, we need to get a little more precise about the section dealing with recognition. It is itself divided into two parts. The first part deals with *credentialing*, as we have been calling it—that is, with the attestation by an external authority of the reality and value of the Deposit. But then there is also second part (beginning in the next chapter), which deals with direct valuation—that is, with the attestation of value provided by Jesus's words and deeds themselves.

To review, the following list makes this structure clear:

Matthew as a codex accepti et expensi

I. The Deposit (Chapters 1–16:16)
   1. Recognition of the Deposit (Chapters 1–9:8)
      (i) Confirmation and Credentialing by Third Parties (Chapters 1–4:16)
      (ii) Attestation from Jesus's Own Words and Deeds (Chapters 4:17–9)
   2. Crediting of the Deposit to an Account (Chapters 9:18–16:13)

II. The Payment (Chapters 17:1–27:66)

Now we come to the temptation of Christ, which we count as the last text in I.1.(i). Here the external authority that attests to the value of the Incarnate Son of God is the devil. The devil attests to that value indirectly, by his attempts to subvert it.

In the account of the three temptations that now follows, Matthew introduces the first and second temptations with his typical temporal phrase, "At that time" in verse 1 and likewise in the transition to the second temptation in verse 5. However, the third temptation is not introduced with a temporal word. Rather, Matthew ties together the second and third temptations with the word "again" in verse 8. I interpret this language to mean that for Matthew the three temptations have a structure like this:

turn stones into bread
hurl yourself down and prostrate yourself before me

That is, he sees the second two as more closely related to each other than each is to the first. And indeed, the second two have basic similarities: each requires a transposition to a place; each occurs on a high place; each involves a power (the temple stands for religious power, and a mountain stands for worldly power). It seems that Matthew wanted to keep the temporal relationship of these two temptations indistinct. For all we know, in some mystical way, they took place "at the same time," as we think of time.

Matthew and Luke differ in the order in which they present these last two temptations. But Luke in his account uses no words of temporal sequencing like "then." He has a different expository order, but he makes no claim about their temporal order.

4:1 At that time Jesus was led out into the wilderness by
the Spirit to be put to the test by the devil. 2 And when he
had fasted forty days and forty nights, later he was
hungry. 3 And the Tester, approaching, said to him:

> **"If you are Son of God, tell these stones to become bread."**

The Fathers say that, as this Spirit was the Lord's own spirit, he led or persuaded himself to be subjected to these tests.

4 He said in reply,

> **"It is written: Not on bread alone will man live, but on every word coming forth from the mouth of God."**

5 At that time the devil brings him to the Holy City. And
he stood him upon the pinnacle of the temple 6 and tells
him:

> **"If you are Son of God, hurl yourself down. It is written, after all:**

"He will command his angels concerning you
And they will lift you with their hands,
Lest you strike your foot against a stone."
7—Jesus said to him:
"Again it is written, you shall not put the Lord your God to the test."
8 The devil brings him again, to an extremely high
mountain, and he shows him all of the kingdoms of the
world and their glory. 9 And he said to him:
"All of these things will I give to you, if you fall down prostrate and adore me."

This third temptation is different from the first two because it alone involves a deal, a quid-pro-quo. "Turn these into bread" and "Hurl yourself down" are dares. This one, however, is more like "would you like to sell your soul?" The devil proposes a trade, where all earthly wealth is on the table, and Jesus turns down this trade. It makes sense that Matthew the tax collector would see this proposal as the most serious of the three tests and place it last.

10 Then Jesus says,
"Be gone, Satan! It is written, after all, You shall do homage to the Lord your God and him only shall you serve."
11 Then the devil leaves him, and—look!—angels drew
near and ministered to him.
12 When he heard that John had been handed over, he
returned to Galilee. 13 And leaving the village of
Nazareth, he came and made his home in Capernaum,
along the sea, in the districts of Zaboulōn and

Nephthalim, 14 so that what was said through Isaiah the
prophet might be fulfilled, when he said,
15 "Land of Zaboulōn and Nephthalim,
pathway of the sea, beyond the Jordan,
Galilee of the Gentiles,
16 "The people sitting in darkness
have seen a great light,
and to those sitting in a land and under a shadow of death,
a light has dawned for them."

Matthew lived in Capernaum. He therefore is keen to explain how Jesus happened to move to his own hometown. Now that Jesus has moved to his village, we should understand everything that follows as what Matthew was able to verify directly.

17 It was from this time that Jesus began to proclaim and say:
"Repent, for the Kingdom of Heaven is at hand."
18 When he was walking along the sea of Galilee, he saw
two brothers, Simon called Peter and Andrew his brother,
casting a net into the sea. For they were fishermen. 19 And
he says to them,
"Come behind me, and I will make you fishers of men."
20 They immediately leaving their nets followed him.

Matthew unmistakably emphasizes and continues to wonder at their unhesitating response. One sees in his language (repeated in verse 22) the outlook of a prudent and conservative accountant who was fascinated by their daring. Perhaps, when he first heard about them, he started asking himself whether he was capable of doing something similar.

21 And going forward from there he saw two other brothers, James the son of Zebedee and John his brother, in a boat with Zebedee their father, mending their nets, and he calls them. 22 They immediately leaving the boat and their father followed him.

Presumably they leave with their father's approval. He says goodbye to them gladly, which looks like an even more puzzling phenomenon than leaving their father against his will.

23 And he was going about the whole of Galilee teaching in their synagogues and proclaiming the good news of the kingdom and healing every sickness and every kind of debility among the people. 24 And the report about him went out through all of Syria; and they brought him everyone who was badly off with diverse illnesses and painful conditions, troubled by demons and lunatics and paralytics, and he healed them.

Here is a fascinating detail. In verse 23, Matthew mentions "every sickness and every kind of debility," and then in verse 24 he gives a more precise accounting of five distinct conditions. This reveals an accountant's sensibility: accountants prefer to list items separately when doing so clarifies the value. In comparison, in the closest parallel passages, Mark writes simply "all who had diseases" (3:10) and Luke, although a doctor, refers only to "their diseases" (6:17). Once again, Matthew's accountant's sensibility shines through.

25 And large crowds followed him from Galilee and the Decapolis and Jerusalem and Judea and from beyond the Jordan.

Matthew's use of the plural "crowds" rather than the singular "crowd" (as in Mark 3:10, Luke 6:17), represents what might be called a distributed sum. Again, it reveals an accountant's sensibility. His language reflects how someone who was used to computing sums from various distinct accounts would think. What he means is a large crowd composed of a crowd from Galilee and a crowd from the Decapolis and a crowd from Jerusalem, and so on. He cannot see the crowd without seeing how the crowd breaks out into its sources.

(ii) Attestation from Jesus's Own Words and Deeds (Chapters 4:17–9)

The Sermon on the Mount

Now Matthew gives confirmation of the reality of the Deposit by Jesus's own words and deeds—and first, by words, through the Sermon on the Mount. Matthew's final comment on the Sermon is telling: the crowds were astonished at his teaching "because he was teaching them as someone who held authority, and not as their scribes" (Matthew 7:29). But who holds authority over happiness, the moral law, and the tradition of the prophets? Only God. Matthew is conveying too his own astonishment at Jesus through the common device of reporting the astonishment of others.

At the start, Matthew's business Greek is on display here, in sharp contrast with Jesus's own language that follows:

> **5:1 Seeing the crowds, he went up the mountain. Sitting down, his disciples came to him. 2 Opening his mouth, he taught them,**

In verse 4:17 just prior, Matthew had said that Jesus went around proclaiming, "Repent for the Kingdom of Heaven is at hand." Surely that sentence gives only the theme and summary of his teaching. We may interpret the Sermon on the Mount as an extended account of what that sentence was meant to summarize. If so, then the Sermon aims at inculcating both (1) repentance and (2) receptivity toward the Kingdom of Heaven. Let us take these two ideas as keys for understanding the Sermon.

Repentance in Greek is *metanoia*, which means a change in mind and heart, especially in how we view our past and future life. As for the Kingdom of Heaven, Matthew's book will ultimately reveal that it is established by the sacrifice of Jesus, in his Passion, undergone to buy back his people, as their Savior. This precisely is what is "at hand." Therefore, to be receptive to this Kingdom is to look for and desire a Savior. Therefore, one purpose of the Sermon on the Mount is to convict listeners of their deep and true need of a Savior.

If so, it would be misguided to say, as some do on the basis of the Sermon on the Mount, that "Jesus is a great moral teacher." The Sermon, rather, is intended to help the listener realize the extent of his own poverty and sin and to lead him to think that it would hardly be surprising if something truly extraordinary was necessary to pull him out of it—something as world-altering as a redemptive death on our behalf by a Messiah.

As this Sermon precedes Matthew's own call to follow Jesus (in chapter 9), we should presume that Matthew heard the Sermon and that his recounting of it here forms part of his own conversion story—that is, it helps to explain why he fell so deeply in love with Jesus, that he too immediately responded to his call. The Sermon inculcated repentance and an expectation of the Kingdom in him, and he wants to re-create that effect for you and for me.

On the economic interpretation we have been developing, it makes good sense that Matthew includes this Sermon here. We have said that the first half of his book records the Deposit of the

Incarnation, certifies it with credentials, verifies its value, and designates its beneficiary. However, nothing *has value* in economics unless it *is valued.* Something may have objective value, but it will not be understood to have a role in a trade, unless subjectively it is valued. Therefore, to establish the economic value of the Deposit, Matthew must highlight its subjective value. The value to us of freedom from sin is exactly the value we will place on a Savior from sin.

saying:

3 "Happy are the poor in spirit: because theirs is the Kingdom of Heaven.

4 "Happy are they that mourn: because they shall be comforted.

5 "Happy are the meek: because they shall possess the land.

6 "Happy are they that hunger and thirst after justice: because they shall have their fill.

7 "Happy are the merciful: because they shall obtain mercy.

8 "Happy are the clean of heart: because they shall see God.

9 "Happy are the peacemakers: because they shall be called children of God.

10 "Happy are those who suffer persecution for the sake of justice: because theirs is the Kingdom of Heaven.

11 "Happy are you when they revile you, and persecute you, and speak every kind of evil against you, for my
sake. 12 Be glad and rejoice, for your payment in heaven is very great. They persecuted the prophets who were before you in just the same way.

The Greek word for "happy" is *makarios*, the same word used at the start of Psalm 1 in the Septuagint: "Happy is the man." "Happy" had various senses then, as it does now. To call someone "happy" would mean:

a. He is on the path to his ultimate good
b. He is enjoying right now a joy that anticipates substantively the ultimate good he will enjoy
c. He is already enjoying fruits related to the fact that he is on a good path
d. He enjoys a certain immunity from evils that could block him from attaining his ultimate good

The Beatitudes themselves inculcate repentance and readiness for the Kingdom. Each puts someone in a position to rethink what is most important for him. A close relative dies suddenly, and you mourn—you see how you need to change your life. Or you suffer persecution for doing the right thing—you are trying to stay innocent, and you are being obedient, and yet you face mockery and opposition. Why? What is at work here?

From the point of view of the divine economy, the Beatitudes give an inventory of spiritual wealth:

- *Belonging to the Kingdom of Heaven*: enjoying its rights and privileges, its peace, its protection from evil, its eternal duration, its wise governance
- *Possessing the land*: a claim to creation as it was intended and a new creation
- *Fullness of justice as a personal virtue*: holiness
- *Mercy*: forgiveness of sins and the grace to avoid sin

- *See God*: possession of God through friendship and ultimately in the beatific vision
- *Children of God*: divine filiation, being an adopted son or daughter of God, and therefore divinization as well

The Beatitudes therefore also give the tradeoffs that are offered in Christian discipleship: in exchange for various sorts of renunciation, you are promised these spiritual goods. The phrase "payment in heaven" (verse 11) comprises all of the promised spiritual wealth—holiness, vision of God, friendship with God, and so on. The Greek term for "payment" here is *misthos*, a favorite word of Matthew. Its primary meaning is wages paid for labor. To translate it as "reward" is to soften and take away from its bracing economic sense.

13 "You are the salt of the earth. But the salt, suppose it should become dull—with what will it be salted? It is no longer good for anything, except thrown down, to be trampled under by men.
14 "You are the light of the world. It is not possible for a city
set on a mountain to be hidden 15 Neither do they light a
lamp and put it under a basket, but upon its lamp stand: and
it shines out to all that are in the home. 16 In that very way,
let your light so shine out before men, that they may see your good works and give glory to your Father who is in heaven.

Two great distinctions running throughout the Sermon are deeds versus words, and law versus prophets. Of these, deeds correspond to the law, because the law instructs us how to act, and words correspond to the prophets, because to be a prophet is to be someone through whom God speaks. Similarly, here, salt represents deeds and the law, while light represents words and the prophets.

**17 "Do not think that I have come to abolish the law, or
the prophets. I have not come to abolish, but to fulfill. 18
For until heaven and earth pass away—amen I say to
you—not one jot, not one tittle of the law shall pass away,
until everything shall come to be.**

Now begins an exegesis of the requirements of the law (through 6:18), which functions as an extended examination of conscience. Anyone who reflects upon this exegesis should see that, no, *I do not meet these requirements,* and furthermore, *I see no way of meeting them!*

In passing we might ask how likely it is that someone who was engaged in a project of unfolding the full demands of the law, as Jesus was here, even using the language of "jot" and "tittle," would have failed to make *any* provision to have someone record these full demands. Moreover, how could an accountant have heard this language of "jot and tittle" and not have been prepared to take up his stylus? How can we rule out that Matthew had taken down a draft of Jesus's set sermon even then, before he was called to follow him? What could have blocked him? Why wouldn't he have done so for his own profit?

One way of avoiding some demand of the law would be to say that it has been abolished (verses 17–18); another would be to say that parts of it, because they are minor, can be ignored (verses 19–20). Jesus has just blocked the first dodge, and now he blocks the second:

19 "Therefore, anyone who relaxes one of the least of these commandments, and teaches others likewise, will be called least in the Kingdom of Heaven. But anyone who follows that least commandment, and teaches it—he is the one who will be called great in the Kingdom of Heaven.

20 For—I tell you—unless your justice abounds beyond that of the scribes and Pharisees, you shall never enter into the Kingdom of Heaven.

He wants to eliminate wiggle room in his hearer's examination of conscience. Yet another dodge would be to fulfill the law only in appearance, or only when being watched, or only according to what is expected by human conventions, or only in the grossest way. Therefore, he next addresses dodges like these:

21 "You have heard that it was said to those of old: 'You shall not kill. And anyone who kills will need to answer for it in the judgment.' 22 But I say to you, that anyone who is angry with his brother will need to answer for it in the judgment. And anyone who says to his brother, 'Raka,' will need to answer for it to the council. And anyone who says, 'You fool!' will need to answer for it, with a view to the fire of hell!

A precept of the natural law such as "do not kill" is merely a starting point for righteousness. The meaning of that command is not fulfilled unless one banishes from one's heart even the slightest impulse of violence toward another. (And yet why is that impulse within you? How can you remove something so closely entwined with your own heart?)

23 "Therefore, if you happen to be offering your gift at the altar, and you remember there that your brother has something against you—24 leave your offering right there before the altar, and go first to be reconciled with your brother and at that time come to offer your gift.

> **25 "Reach an agreement with your adversary promptly,
> while you are still en route with him, so that the adversary
> does not hand you over to the judge, and the judge hand
> you over to the officer, and you are thrown into prison. 26
> Amen I tell you, you will not get out of there until you
> repay the very last penny.**

The Sermon on the Mount is marked by a strict notion of accountability, as must be the case if its goal is to provoke truthful repentance. To repent implies accepting that our bad actions place us in debt, which then leads us to look for a recourse—how can this huge mountain of debt be written off?

After discussing the commandment against murder, Jesus turns to the commandment against adultery and the associated commandment against lust:

> **27 "You have heard that it was said: 'You shall not commit
> adultery.' 28 But I say to you, whoever looks at a woman to
> desire her has already committed adultery with her, in his
> heart.
> 29 "If your right eye causes you to stumble, pluck it out
> and toss it away from you, because it is expedient for you
> that one of your members should perish and that your
> whole body not be cast into hell. 30 And if your right
> hand causes you to stumble, cut it off, and throw it away
> from you, because it is expedient for you that one of your
> members should perish and that your whole body not be
> cast into hell.
> 31 "It has been said, 'If anyone should divorce his wife, let
> him give her a bill of separation.' 32 But I say to you, that
> whoever divorces his wife—a case of fornication is**

excepted—makes her commit adultery, and whoever marries her once she is divorced commits adultery.

"Expedient" (*sumpherei*) is an economic term denoting what a good banker would trade for what. By trading away a part, he saves the rest; by not trading anything, he loses the whole.

a case of fornication is excepted—That is, he is not validly married to her, but cohabiting, even if others believe they are married. Herod and Herodias would be a good example: when John the Baptist preached that they should separate, he was not preaching that they should be divorced because they were not married in the first place but living in fornication.

Jesus passes over the commandment against stealing and the associated commandment about covetousness because he is going to deal with possessions at length later.

The precept against giving false testimony in a judicial proceeding is again simply a starting point for the virtue of truthfulness. He addresses oath-taking first because it presupposes lack of truthfulness in ordinary conversation:

33 "Again you have heard that it was said to those of old,
'You shall not swear falsely, but you shall keep your oaths
to the Lord.' 34 But I say to you do not swear at all,
neither by heaven, for it is the throne of God, 35 nor by
the earth, for it is his footstool, nor by Jerusalem, for it is
the city of the great king. 36 Neither shall you swear by
your head, because you have no power to make one hair
white or black. 37 But let your word 'yes' be yes, and your
word 'no' be no. Anything beyond these is from the evil
one.

Now he looks at other rationalizations we use to avoid acting justly. One is that we are simply doing to another the harm that he did to us. But the principle "never harm anyone" is not abrogated because someone harms us. More than this, we shouldn't fail to act with positive goodwill toward someone simply because he harmed us:

> **38 "You have heard that it has been said, 'An eye for an**
> **eye, and a tooth for a tooth.' 39 But I say to you not to**
> **resist evil. But if someone strikes you on your right cheek,**
> **turn to him also the other. 40 And if someone wants to sue**
> **you and take away your coat, let him have your cloak also.**
> **41 And if someone forces you to go one mile, go with him**
> **two. 42 To him who asks of you, give, and if someone is**
> **looking to borrow from you, do not avoid him.**

Another rationalization involves taking the world as divided between friends and enemies, and supposing that "never harm anyone" applies only to the first class.

> **43 "You have heard that it was said, 'You shall love your**
> **neighbor and hate your enemy.' 44 But I say to you, love**
> **your enemies, and pray for those who persecute you, 45 so**
> **that you become sons of your Father who is in heaven,**
> **because he causes his sun to rise upon bad men as well as**
> **good, and he sends rain to just men and also to the unjust.**
> **46 For if you love those who love you, what compensation**
> **do you have? Do not even tax collectors do the same? 47**
> **And if you greet your brothers only, what extra are you**
> **doing? Do not even the pagans do the same?**

To love only those who love you, only to the extent that they love you, is to seek no compensation in the exchange beyond what those others offer—that is to say, no spiritual wealth would be gained from it. But if spiritual wealth is to be gained from an exchange, God must somehow become a party in it. Such would be the case if even our compensated exchanges proceeded from the sort of goodwill and love of humanity we show when we love our enemies. To gain spiritual goods, there must be something extra proffered by us in the exchange that is for God and that therefore will be compensated precisely by Him.

The detail about tax collectors is strictly not necessary, as it would have sufficed to mention simply what "the pagans" do. But we are supposing that Matthew heard this teaching or one like it before he was called, and naturally this detail would have leapt out at him.

There are two or three great commandments in the Sermon on the Mount that seem to encapsulate much or all of Jesus's teaching, and this section ends with one of them, which is the formula for holiness:

> **48 "Therefore, you are to be perfect, as your Father in heaven is perfect.**

This command is a future imperative, like "Be good bankers."

It is impossible for anyone to hear this and not think, first, *I have not been perfect*, and second, *There is an order to creation as shown in such things as sunshine and the seasons which, as it were, "expects" me to be or somehow "calls" me to be perfect, in relation to which I am "liable to pay the price" for my shortcomings.*

It would also be difficult to hear Jesus's teaching and not think, *I have had glimpses of a heavenly reward that I am meant to enjoy, but I know full well that, on the contrary, I am deeply in debt, I cannot repay this debt, and over time I will acquire even more debt.* To engage in such an examination is a lot like drawing up a balance on a balance sheet.

So far Jesus has given an examination of conscience regarding the second table of the decalogue, which concerns our relationship with our neighbors. Now he turns to the first table and our relationship to God. He calls a right relationship with God "justice" ("righteousness"). He begins with a clear warning about how to be a good banker in such matters:

> **6:1 "Take care not to do your acts of justice before men, to**
> **be seen by them, or you will have no claim to payment**
> **from your Father who is in heaven.**

A model of such justice has already been presented by Matthew in Joseph, that good banker, who communed with God through dreams and through prompt and faithful action, the meaning of which was seen primarily by God.

Jesus now applies this general principle to alms-deeds, prayer, and fasting:

> **2 "Therefore, when you do an alms-deed, do not sound a**
> **trumpet before you, as hypocrites do, in the synagogues**
> **and in the streets, that they may be honored by men. Amen**
> **I say to you, they have received their payment. 3 But when**
> **you do an alms-deed, let not your left hand know what**
> **your right hand is doing, 4 that your alms may be in secret.**
> **And your Father who sees in secret will repay you.**

I use "do an alms-deed" rather than "give alms" because the latter suggests, wrongly, that only giving money away is at issue here.

Rather, an alms-deed, properly speaking, is any act of mercy done to relieve a need of your neighbor.[1]

Any alms-deed requires that the doer give up something. Therefore, it may be regarded as a trade. You give up something to get something in return. There are two choices: you can do the alms-deed "horizontally" (let us call it) to get something in return from other human beings. Or, you can do it "vertically" to get something in return from God. But human beings can give us only counterfeit goods, such as fame or attention, or genuine but lower-level goods, such as advancement and preference. God can give us higher-level goods. Therefore, a good banker, who shrewdly aims to grow value, will do an alms-deed vertically.

Saint John Chrysostom comments most perceptively that when we do an alms-deed vertically, we make God our debtor:

> Sometimes you show mercy to the poor. I know it as well as you. But even in this again great is the mischief. For you do this either in pride or in vainglory, so as not to profit even by your good deeds. What can be more wretched than this, to be making your shipwreck in the very harbor? To prevent this, when you have done any good action, seek not thanks from me, that you may have God as your debtor. . . .
>
> You have your Debtor: why leave Him, and require it of me, a poor and wretched mortal. What? Is that Debtor displeased, when the debt is required of Him? What? Is He poor? Is he unwilling to pay? Do you not see his

---

1 See the traditional list of seven corporal and seven spiritual acts of mercy: Joseph Delany, "Corporal and Spiritual Works of Mercy," in *The Catholic Encyclopedia*, vol. 10 (New York: Robert Appleton Company, 1911), http://www.newadvent.org/cathen/10198d.htm.

> unspeakable treasures? Do you not see his indescribable munificence? Lay hold then on Him, and make your demand; for He is pleased when one thus demands the debt of Him. Because, if He sees another required to pay for what He Himself owes, He will feel as though He were insulted, and repay you no more. . . . For although man received [your alms], it was God who commanded you to bestow; and His will is to be Himself, and in the original sense, debtor, and surely, affording you ten thousand occasions to demand the debt of Him from every quarter. . . . "He who has pity upon the poor lends to God" (Proverbs 19:17). You have lent to God; put it to His account.
>
> "But He doth not repay the whole now." Well, this too He does for your good. For such a debtor is He: not as many, who are anxious simply to repay that which is lent: whereas He manages and does all things with a view of investing likewise in security, that which has been given to Him. Therefore, some, you see, He repays here: some he assigns in the other place.[2]

No finer statement can be found of the divine economy. Saint John Chrysostom gives one of the first economic interpretations of the gospel.

It is not faith but hopelessness that is shown in disclaiming any such repayment from God; it is not high-mindedness but pride. If there were no payment from God for doing an alms-deed, then there would no opportunity cost in not doing it. If you were to buy a gadget instead of giving to the poor when you might have done so, you lose

---

2 John Chrysostom, *Homilies on the Gospel of Matthew*, trans. George Prevost (New York: Charles Scribner, 1888), homily X, n13, 226–27. I have modernized the English of the translation.

nothing—there was no reward, no payment, no benefit that you turned down. On the economic interpretation of the gospel, to have faith is to trust that God will compensate you—even though you do not see that compensation, you have no security for it, and (of course) you have no judicial recourse.

> **5 "And when you pray, you are not to be like the hypocrites. Because they love to pray in synagogues or standing on street corners so that they might be seen by men. Amen I say to you, they have received their payment. 6 But you, when you pray, enter into your room, and having shut the door, pray to your Father who is within what is hidden. And your Father who sees within what is hidden will repay you.**

you are not to be—Another future imperative, which, as we saw, commands us to realize progressively a wide range of actions, using good judgment to do so. There is no implication that we should not pray publicly (in churches), but only that we should not do so with a view to the trade implicit in *to be seen by others.*

Chrysostom comments here:

> Pay attention, I ask you, to the lovingkindness of God, in that He promises to bestow on us a reward, even for praying for those good things which we ask of him. . . .
>
> He said not, if you pray in secret, "[God] shall freely give you a gift," but, "shall repay you": yes, for He has made Himself a debtor to you, and even from this has honored you with great honor. For because He himself is invisible, He would have your prayer be so likewise.[3]

---

3 Chrysostom, *Homilies on Gospel*, homily XIX, n4, 293. I have made some light revisions in the translation.

The saint rightly identifies a consistent mistake of Christians. It is easier for us, as it implies a lesser commitment to God, a restricted basis of trust, and a lesser motive to sacrifice other goods, to say that we have no relationship of service to God such that God binds himself to repay us for our loving service to him. The language of "it is all a free gift"—which we like to use—looks noble, to be sure, but it is selfish, because it enables us to claim control of our lives and to avoid making tradeoffs with God as the counterparty. The free gift indeed was the gift of the Savior and his Passion. But once that gift is given, then a divine economy is established, and Christians in the service of God are in debt. Likewise they can merit repayment—they can make God a debtor too—as Jesus says here.

> **7 "And when you are praying, do not babble on as the**
> **pagans do. For they think that in their great quantity of**
> **words they will be heard. 8 You are not therefore to be like**
> **them, because your Father knows what things you need**
> **before you ask him.**

babble on—Stutter on, stammer, babble, repeat nonsense. The pagans use prayers as if they are incantations or spells. They also tend to think of the gods as distant, in the sense that they have no concern for human affairs and have difficulty receiving any message. Prayer then becomes an attempt to capture the power of the gods and compel it. In contrast, God the Father knows each of our thoughts immediately (see Psalm 139) and cares for us (see Psalm 8).

> **9 "Therefore you are to pray in this manner:**
> **Our Father, in heaven,**
> **May your name be held holy.**
> **10 May your kingdom come.**
> **May your will be done on earth as it is in heaven.**

11 Give us this day our substance-covering bread.
12 And forgive us our debts, as we also those in debt to us.
13 And do not lead us into temptation.
But deliver us from the evil one.
14 For if you forgive men their trespasses, your heavenly
Father will forgive you also your trespasses. 15 But if you
will not forgive men, neither will your Father forgive your
trespasses.

in this manner—Not simply "in these words," because the Lord's Prayer gives a pattern for all prayers, rather than a replacement for all prayers.

substance-covering—The curious term that Matthew uses here is used by Luke also in the same place in the Lord's Prayer (11:3). The word is *epi-ousios*. The prefix *epi* typically means "upon." *Ousia* is the Greek word for substance. *Ousia* is the "really real thing" (as Plato called it), the deep and true reality of something. Hence, *epiousios* would be "upon the substance" and "*ep-iousios* bread" would be "that bread that is placed upon and matches that bread that is really real"—one might call it "substance-covering bread." Older translations rendered the term as "supersubstantial." The word *epiousios* is found nowhere else among all extant Greek texts. That it means "daily" is unlikely, because several other expressions could have been used to express the mundane idea of the quotidian. Origen (who was fluent in Greek) speculated that the evangelists made up the word. But I regard it as more likely that the Jesus (who knew Greek, it seems safe to say) coined the word and instructed his disciples to use it when conveying the Lord's prayer in Greek.[4]

4 A fuller discussion would be out of place here, but see Michael Pakaluk, "The Lord of Substance," The Catholic Thing, June 7, 2023, https://www.thecatholicthing.org/2023/06/07/the-lord-of-substance/.

forgive us our debts—Luke in the same place uses "forgive us our trespasses." Unsurprisingly, Matthew prefers the financial imagery of debts. To forgive a debt is to write it off. Such imagery also makes the underlying logic of the petition extremely clear. If we are bankrupt, such that anything that others may owe us, we already owe to our creditor, then we must deal with our debtors as our creditor would deal with them—since the capital is really his. And if our creditor is pleased to write off our debts, then we must infer he is pleased to write off the debts of our debtors as well. On the other hand, if we do not wish to write off the debt that another in fact no longer owes to us, then we cannot rationally ask that our debts be written off by the one to whom they really are owed.

The Lord's Prayer has traditionally been said to consist of one line of address ("Our Father") followed by seven petitions. Many fine books have been written about the prayer as construed on this pattern. No doubt like all divine speech, it admits of many diverse interpretations, all truthful. No doubt, Jesus taught it on many occasions in many contexts, and even in different forms. (Luke's form, also authentic, is slightly different.) But in the present context of the Sermon on the Mount, which I am interpreting as a call to conversion (*metanoia*), so that its hearers will be prepared to accept the Kingdom of God as revealed in the Passion—I wish to interpret the Prayer as both suited *retrospectively* to the "examination of conscience" that Jesus has been undertaking here, and also as *prospectively* training the desire of his listeners to become adapted to the Kingdom that he is going to found. The Lord's Prayer as positioned, then, in the very middle of the Sermon on the Mount marks and expresses the change in heart and will that the Sermon is meant to provoke.

16 "And when you fast, you are not to become like the hypocrites. For they disfigure their faces, so that they may

appear to men to be fasting. Amen I say to you, they have received their payment. 17 But you, when you are fasting, anoint your head and wash your face, 18 so that it is not by men that you are seen to be fasting, but by your Father who is in secret. And your Father who sees in secret will repay you.

hypocrites—For us, this word means someone who says one thing and does another, or who appears to be one thing but in reality is another. La Rochefoucauld famously said that "hypocrisy is the tribute that vice pays to virtue."[5] But the word in the ancient world meant originally an actor who played a part on a stage and wore a mask. We must not lose sight of this meaning. There is a part to play in a religious culture of the pious, holy, or upright man, and the hypocrite plays this part, and perhaps he plays it very well, as if he were a good actor portraying a holy man on a stage. And from this acting, he gets what he desires for his compensation, which is the applause of his audience. But there is an opportunity cost. He could have played the role simply for God, in the presence of God, and for that he would have been richly rewarded.

We must resist the modern tendency to understand the error of the hypocrite to be a lack of authenticity or sincerity. Also, his error is not that he is fundamentally untruthful. Rather, Jesus's criticism of the man is that he is foolish. He is not a good banker. He throws away true value, which he could easily have gained, to gain instead nothing of lasting value.

The next verses will complete Jesus's discussion of the law by returning to the second table of the law and dealing in a general way

---

5 François La Rochefoucauld, *et Réflexions Morales* (London: A. Dulau et Co., 1799), n. 223, p. 55.

with covetousness. This discussion was prepared for by his reference to payment and rewards. He does not need to convince people that they fail to keep this commandment in its full meaning, as that is all too obvious to us. He merely needs to draw attention to the anxiety that we all feel.

We may be so entranced by the beauty of Jesus's teachings on greed, wealth, and worry in Matthew 6:19–34 that we may forget that this is the longest discourse on these topics preserved in any of the Gospels. The discourse's length is understandable on the thesis that it was attended to and recorded by a tax collector, whose profession was to assess and handle wealth. Tax collectors in popular culture stood for greed, and in their work, they were students of human greed.

It's difficult to figure out the logic and structure of these verses. Each is compelling and powerful. But how do they relate?

The first consideration seems a classic argument about wealth. We look for wealth in part because of the security we think it affords, but wealth in the ordinary sense is insecure. On the other hand, there is a type of wealth that offers the security we are looking for.

> **19 "Do not fill with treasure for yourselves treasure boxes on earth, where rust and moth consume and where thieves break through and steal. 20 But fill with treasure for yourselves treasure boxes in heaven, where neither rust nor moth consume and where thieves do not break through, nor steal. 21 For where your treasure box is, there your heart will also be.**

The relevant Greek word here, *thêsauros*, means originally a treasure box, and by extension the valuables kept in a treasure box (compare our "safe" and "savings"). Jesus's thought can therefore be rendered as either that we should store up heavenly treasures or that we should fill up heavenly treasure boxes. The second idea is more concrete; also, it draws attention to the mode of safe-keeping rather than what is kept safe. Jesus, with his mention of rust, moths, and thieves, clearly places emphasis on the mode of safe-keeping. So the second interpretation seems better. If so, then the meaning of "heart" changes also. Jesus is saying that if you fill a heavenly treasure box with treasure, then your heart too becomes a treasure box in heaven, not on earth.

We would expect a tax collector like Matthew to be very concrete about how wealth is stored and safeguarded; he would know that conserving an asset's value over time is dependent on recognizing the type of value that it holds.

> **22 "The light of the body is the eye. If the eye is single, the whole body will be illuminated. 23 But if the eye is evil, the whole body will be darkened. Therefore, if the light that is in you is darkness, how great is the darkness!**

This teaching seems to be true in many contexts. But if we understand it as offered here by Jesus in relation to covetousness, then its meaning would be that greed leads to a blindness to higher goods. Dickens teaches this truth in his story of Ebenezer Scrooge: the three spirits mainly help him to see the higher goods that his greed had blinded him to. At the end, Scrooge sees even the knocker on his door in a new way: "'I shall love it, as long as I live!' cried Scrooge, patting it with his hand, 'I scarcely ever looked at it before. What an honest expression it has in its face! It's a wonderful knocker! . . . Merry Christmas!'"[6]

---

6 Charles Dickens, *A Christmas Carol* (New York: Hodder & Stoughton, 1913), 128.

24 "It is not possible for a man to be in the service of two masters. For either he will hate the one and love the other, or he will cling to the one and despise the other. It is not possible for you to be in the service of both God and mammon.

The positive and negative attitudes in the two cases are not symmetric. If it is God we serve out of love, then we hate mammon—that is, money—conceived as an idol, when there is a conflict with that love. On the other hand, if mammon has us in its grip, with the result that we lose our freedom, then we do not hate God so much as despise him. To despise is to dismiss as of little value as if from a higher position. Matthew would know the contrast well, if, when he responded to Jesus's call, he changed from serving mammon to serving God.

But solicitude, anxiety, excessive preoccupation with wealth, domination by a fear of material loss, lack of confidence in God's providence—all of these place us at risk of serving mammon. Jesus after all does not speak about greed as something that affects only those other people—say, the Romans, tax collectors, the wealthy, the landowners, Herod and his court—but rather as a malady deeply rooted in the human condition, which threatens everyone. And this is as we should suspect, because greed is capable of diverting anyone's attention from the divine economy to the merely material economy.

Next, Jesus counsels his followers to trade goods of the body for goods of the soul:

25 "For this reason I say to you, as regards your soul, do not worry over what you will eat or drink, and as regards your body, do not worry over what you will wear. Is not

> **the soul superior to the food, and the body to the clothing?**
> **26 "Look to the birds of the air, because they do not sow, nor reap, nor gather into barns. And your Father in heaven feeds them. Are not you of far greater value than they? 27 Who among you, by worrying, can add to his stature by one cubit?**

Worrying is different from doing what a creature is naturally suited to do, and it is useless besides. By implication, a human being should, instead of worry, exercise reasonable prudence, engage in hard work, and practice thrift—not neglecting worship, prayer, and love of neighbor. In God's providence, these can be relied upon as sufficient.

> **28 "And why do you worry about clothing? Consider the lilies of the field, how they grow. They do not toil, and neither do they spin. 29 I say to you, that not even Solomon in all his glory was arrayed as one of these. 30 But if the grass of the field, which exists for a day and tomorrow is tossed into the oven, God so clothes; will he not much more clothe you, you little-faiths.**

Jesus here promises eternal glory for beings like us who in contrast with flowers and grass, are not transient. This is similar to his promise of compensation and reward for service rendered to the Father.

> **31 "Therefore, do not be worried, saying, 'What shall we eat? or What shall we drink? or With what shall we be clothed?' 32 It is the pagans, after all, who seek after all**

> **these things. For *he* knows—your heavenly Father does—that you need all these things.**

Worry is an attitude of those who lack faith. Here Jesus diagnoses someone's attention to the material economy solely as evincing fundamentally a lack of faith. Materialism is a negation, a falling way from attention to all the goods in play.

> **33 "But you, seek first the kingdom of God and his justice, and all these things shall be added to you.**

There is a hierarchy of goods in the divine economy. Although it is not possible to serve both God and mammon, it is possible to order wealth to God. Such an ordering will often require the sacrifice of material interests, yet doing so will make God a debtor. For instance, not to work on the Sabbath is a sacrifice, yet in faith one may be confident that this service will be compensated with divine goods, while also, in general and in the long run, it will bring greater material prosperity.

> **34 "Therefore, do not worry as to tomorrow. Tomorrow, after all, will worry for itself. A day has more than enough evil of its own.**

A final argument against worry: it is an attitude that supposes a control of the future. But when worry is restricted to what is properly before us, it becomes prudent solicitude, the outlook of a good banker.

We are understanding the Sermon on the Mount to be presenting anew the law and the prophets in a complete and compelling way, so as to provoke to conversion and lead its hearers to see that they need a Savior. What we have seen so far has given a challenging interpretation of the law, while the theme of "be good bankers" has been present throughout.

The rest of the Sermon, then, presents what it means truly to speak in the manner of the prophets. Doing so requires first of all a correct custody of our language:

> **7:1 "Do not judge, so that you are not judged. 2 For with**
> **the judgment by which you judge, you will be judged, and**
> **the measure by which you measure will be applied as a**
> **measure to you.**
> **3 "Why is it that you see the speck that is in your brother's**
> **eye, but the beam in your own eye you fail to notice? 4 Or**
> **how is it that you say to your brother, 'Let me remove the**
> **speck from your eye'—and look, a beam in your eye!**
> **5 Hypocrite! Remove first, from your own eye, the beam.**
> **And then you will see your way through to removing the**
> **speck from the eye of your brother.**

The first thing that can cause our zeal to go in a wrong direction is that we focus on the faults of others. The teaching "judge not" sets down a progressive standard. As you attain greater clarity about yourself, you will attain greater clarity about your neighbor. But then your attitude will have changed from judging in order to condemn to judging in order to help.

> **6 "Do not give what is holy to dogs nor cast your pearls before swine, so that they not trample them under their feet, and turning upon you, tear you to pieces.**

And yet you would not be a good steward of that wealth that is greater self-knowledge and of that clearer insight into the flaws of others—likened here to "pearls"—if you offered a correction to someone so mired a sin—and therefore a "swine"—that he is not open to reason.

Next, Jesus tells us that living in the spirit of the prophets requires constant, confident, and filial perseverance in prayer:

> **7 "Ask and it shall be given to you; seek, and you shall find; knock, and it shall be opened to you. 8 For every one who asks, receives, and he who seeks, finds, and to him who knocks, it shall be opened.**
> **9 "Or who among you, a mere man, if his son asks him for bread, will hand him a stone, 10 or if he asks him for a fish, will hand him a snake?**
> **11 "Therefore, if you, although you are bad, know how to give good gifts to your children, how much more will your Father who is in heaven give good things to those who ask him?**

Verses 9–11 depend on a contrast between how a mere human being will act and how God the Father in heaven can be relied upon to act. In verse 9, Jesus specifically addresses us as human beings, using the Greek word *anthrôpos*. The older translations capture this as "Or what man is there of you" (KJV). But the modern ones, in the interest of being inclusive, leave this out—for example, "Which of you" (NAB). Therefore, they fail to capture the relevant contrast.

The phrase "although you are bad" (verse 11) reveals that Jesus expects by this point in the Sermon that his listeners will have been convicted of their own badness.

Thus, humble self-knowledge and filial constancy in prayer are necessary, and now we have a summary:

12 "Therefore, everything whatsoever that you would will that men should do for you, do you in the same way for them. For this is the law and the prophets.

The Golden Rule is also a progressive standard. It becomes more and more refined in what it requires, as we become more refined in following it. It also leads to increasingly greater reciprocity among a community of disciples trying to put it into effect in the divine economy.

The standard is not what we feel or want or would like, but rather what precisely we *would will*, where "will" means a deliberate choice for what we reasonably conceive of as good, in circumstances of knowledge that are in some sense ideal. Suppose, for example, that I am going astray in some serious way and that I am at least vaguely aware that I am. I certainly would not "like" to be corrected by a friend—I would not find that pleasant at all, or aligned with what I am pursuing—moreover, in the moment, I may not even "will" to be corrected, since I do not clearly grasp that that would be to my own good. Yet I "would will" that my friend correct me. Despite my irritation and anger, my friend with his better insight can be confident that in correcting me he is doing what he "would will" if he were in my circumstances.

13 "Enter in through the narrow gate, because wide is the gate and broad is the path that leads to destruction, and many there are who are going in through it. 14 How narrow is the gate and how constricted the path that leads to life, and few there are who are finding it!

Complacency is yet another temptation that would render Jesus's words fruitless. Consider the material economy as a model for the divine economy. What teacher ever regarded it as prudent to tell a young person that he will be successful at what he does and able comfortably to support a family if he takes it easy and follows what everyone else is doing? And why shouldn't it be the case that the world is so designed that we need to strive even harder for what is more valuable?

Yet the quickest way to become a false prophet oneself is to follow one:

> **15 "Be on guard against false prophets who come to you**
> **clothed as sheep, but inwardly they are ravening wolves.**
> **16 "From their fruits you will know them. Do people**
> **gather grapes from thorns, after all, or figs from thistles?**
> **17 "Just so, every good tree produces good fruit, while a**
> **rotten tree produces bad fruit. 18 A good tree is not**
> **capable of producing bad fruit, and neither is a rotten tree**
> **capable of producing good fruit.**
> **19 "Any tree that fails to produce good fruit is cut down**
> **and cast into the fire.**
> **20 "You shall know them, then, by their fruits at least.**

Jesus implicitly gives a warning here. The fact that someone has not produced good fruit will be taken as a sign that he is not capable of producing it, which would mean that he is not a good tree, and therefore he is to be cut down and thrown in the fire. In the divine economy, mere words mean nothing:

> **21 "Not everyone who says to me, 'Lord, Lord,' will enter**
> **the Kingdom of Heaven, but only the one who does the**
> **will of my Father who is in heaven. 22 Many will say to me**
> **on that day, 'Lord, Lord, did we not in your name**

prophesy, and in your name cast out demons, and in your name do many miracles?' 23 And then I will say to them openly, 'Never did I know you. Away from me, you evildoers!'

The emphasis here is on "in your name." Someone can draw upon the power of the Lord and yet personally not follow his will. Many corrupt priests, bishops, and pastors have been like this.

24 "Therefore, everyone who hears these words of mine,
and does them, will be similar to a prudent man who
built his house on the rock. 25 And the rain fell, and the
floods came, and the winds blew, and they beat upon that
house, and it did not fall because its foundation was the
rock.
26 "And every one who hears these words of mine and
fails to do them will be similar to a foolish man who built
his house on the sand. 27 And the rain fell, and the floods
came, and the winds blew, and they beat upon that house,
and it fell. And great was its fall."
28 And it happened, when Jesus finished these words, that
the crowds would be astonished at his teaching 29 because
he was teaching them as someone who held authority, and
not as their scribes.

Matthew's words in verses 28–29 are written in the manner of an eyewitness ("it happened") who had seen Jesus give this sermon or others like it on multiple occasions ("the crowds would be astonished").

Matthew's Apologia Pro Vita Sua

I interpret the section of Matthew's Gospel that begins with the Sermon on the Mount (5:1) and leads up to Matthew's calling (9:9) as additionally giving an *Apologia Pro Vita Sua* as to why Matthew abruptly got up from his tax collector's table, immediately left everything, and began following the Lord as his disciple. This section, in telling us about Jesus, indirectly tells us also something about Matthew.

The crucial question is this: Suppose someone had heard the Sermon on the Mount and was deeply moved by it. He sees it as coming from someone who has genuine authority and who can make reliable promises about the most fundamental realities. What further steps would such a person have needed to take, interiorly, in order to leave everything on an instant and follow this person, if he was invited?

This section tells us those steps. The first step is that Matthew sees the example of others who—apparently simply on the basis of the Sermon on the Mount—boldly approach Jesus with full confidence in his power to heal. Truly, it was an extraordinary step of inference! What is the connection between preaching the Sermon on the Mount and having the power to heal? Yet these people see such a connection. They desire healing on this basis, they go after it boldly, and they attain it. Matthew observes or hears about this, admires these others, and perhaps even envies them. He asks himself what he is doing that is similar: he sits all day in a tax collector's booth, collecting duty on hauls of fish.

It would not be surprising if he identifies with these suppliants. One of them is a leper—but leprosy (as everyone understood) stands for sin. It would not be surprising if after hearing the Sermon on the Mount, Matthew became deeply convicted of his own sin (as Peter was by Jesus's teaching: "Depart from me, Lord, because I am a sinful man," Luke 5:8). Another is a public official who describes himself as located within a hierarchy of authority, under the authority of some but also having some under his authority. Yet Matthew as a public official was also embedded in such a structure. He had to follow the orders of the Roman occupiers; he presumably had authority over more junior tax farmers under him; and at very least he had authority to order around the subjugated Jews. This centurion had an intuition in faith that there was a higher structure of authority, and he appealed to it. But what about Matthew? What might he do to translate himself into this other structure, this "Kingdom of God"?

Tax collectors and prostitutes were grouped together in the public imagination at the time. Both types, it was believed, by open choice were dedicated to sinful and disreputable action in order to make a profit. Neither did honest work. To be sure, in principle, one could be an honest tax collector without resorting to extortion or fraud. But it was hardly profitable to be like that, and it seemed too lucrative not to be. We have no reason to think that Matthew was that exceptional, honest case. Therefore, if this section is an *Apologia*, it is the closest thing one can find in the New Testament to a sinner's confession—a form of writing and speaking common today. We know that prostitutes and tax collectors left their work to follow Jesus. When they did so, *why* did they do so? No prostitute wrote a conversion story; it would have been unseemly to do so. But a tax collector's journey? That could be explained, discretely, and in an understated way. This is what I think we find here.

This section also completes Matthew's intent to give the credentials of the Lord. The Sermon on the Mount, as we said, established Jesus's authority on the basis of the inherent power of his words; this section does so on the basis of the inherent power of his deeds.

In the following verses and throughout, I have tried to capture Matthew's business Greek as much as possible. Look for the construction participle + finite verb.

8:1 As he was coming down from the mountain, many
crowds followed him. 2 And—this is remarkable—a leper
approaching adored him, saying:
"Lord, if you should will, you have the power to make me clean."
3 And Jesus, stretching out his hand, touched him, saying:
"I will. Be made clean."
And instantly his leprosy was made clean. 4 Jesus says to
him:
"See that you tell no one, but go, show yourself to the priest, and offer the gift, which Moses commanded, to give witness to them."

this is remarkable—"Behold."

adored him—The attitude of the magi, bending the knee, possibly even prostrating himself, possibly clinging to his feet—although as a leper, he would have regarded himself as forbidden from touching him.

touched him—Jesus will not heal sin except by touching sin himself. Matthew sees this principle at work right away in this healing. But also see verse 17 below.

This healing takes place in accordance with principles from the Sermon on the Mount. The leper's request, "Lord, if you will," invites the Lord to take his own place and precisely to remove his leprosy out of a pity that comes of solidarity. The Lord does unto the leper as he would will to be done unto him. On the other hand, "tell no one" conforms to the instruction to do alms-deeds in secret. There were people watching, of course, but the Lord, insofar as he can, takes pains to do this act of mercy *not* so as to be seen and admired for it.

5 As he was entering into Capernaum, a centurion
approached him, entreating him 6 and saying,
"Lord, my servant is struck down in my house,
paralyzed and tormented with pain."
7 Jesus says to him:
"I will come and heal him."
8 The centurion replying said:
"Lord, I am not worthy that you should enter under my
roof, but only say the word, and my servant will be
healed. 9 I am a man subject to authority, after all,
having soldiers under me, and I say to this one, 'Go,'
and he goes, and to another, 'Come,' and he comes, and
to my servant, 'Do this,' and he does it."
10 Jesus, hearing this, marveled and said to those
following him:
"Amen I say to you, I have not found so great a faith among
anyone in Israel. 11 I tell you that many shall come from the East
and the West, and they shall recline at table with Abraham, and
Isaac, and Jacob in the Kingdom of Heaven. 12 But the sons of the
kingdom shall be cast out into the outer darkness, where there
shall be weeping and gnashing of teeth."
13 Jesus said to the centurion:
"Go. Let it be done to you as you have believed."
And the servant was healed in that very hour.

Readers should pause and read Luke's account of this healing (Luke 7:1–10). It's not plausible to regard the two accounts as reporting two different healings. Luke's account is more detailed. In his account, the centurion does not go to Jesus but stays in his house, saying he is unworthy even so much as to meet him. In Luke, the whole exchange takes place between Jesus and intermediaries sent by the centurion.

Does Luke's account, then, contradict Matthew's account? It's not necessary to think that, and here's why. First, the whole event probably took place over a couple of hours, and it is possible that, first, only intermediaries went to Jesus and then, later, the centurion changed his mind and went out also. Second, we can take Matthew to be supposing that what we do through intermediaries we do ourselves. Actually, this principle is stated in the story itself and was presupposed by everyone at the time, including Jesus. So it is misguided to assert that Matthew wouldn't be supposing it.

Also, Matthew likely did not witness this miracle because it preceded his calling. He likely heard of it by report, and common people would have abbreviated the story in just the way that we find it in Matthew—because common people always say that "this authority did this," when it was the officials of the authority who did it, on his command. Naturally, in the context of giving his *apologia*, Matthew would relay the story in much the same form as he heard it himself, since it was the story *under that telling* that had its effect on him.

Therefore, there clearly is no contradiction between the two accounts.

a centurion went to him—Note what Matthew does *not* say. He does not say that the centurion knelt before him, or prostrated himself, as one would expect to have happened if it was the centurion himself who approached Jesus rather than his intermediaries.

14 Jesus going into Peter's house saw his wife's mother
struck down and suffering from a fever. 15 He touched her
hand. The fever left her. She arose and saw to their needs.

16 Evening having come, they brought to him many who were demon possessed. He cast out the spirits with a word. All who were sick he healed, 17 so as to fulfill what was spoken by the prophet Isaiah, saying:

"He took our infirmities, and bore our diseases."[53:4]

This is yet another passage that avers that there were many healings. The great multiplicity of healings would have raised an interesting question at the time: Precisely which healings should the Apostles select to preach about? Most healings would not be very interesting to recount. "He was sick, Jesus touched him, and he was healed." Indeed, the healing of Peter's mother-in-law contains little of interest except for the fact that it was Peter's relative and an early miracle. Presumably only those healings would be selected that were dramatic, contained striking details, or somehow represented important truths.

Tellingly, Matthew does not regard a healing as without a cost. It is as if Jesus removes a sickness by taking on the sickness himself. Of course Jesus did not contract leprosy, become a paralytic, and fall ill with a fever when carrying out these healings. We must therefore understand Matthew as implying that these cures were "paid" for later on by the Passion. Matthew is saying that we are seeing the retroactive application of those graces won later on.

18 Jesus, seeing the crowd around him, gave instructions to depart for the other side of the lake. 19 And, approaching, a certain scribe said to him:

"Teacher, I will follow you where ever you go."

20 Jesus tells him:

"The foxes have holes, and the birds of the air nests, but the Son of Man has nowhere to lay his head."

21 Another of the disciples said to him:
"Lord, permit me first to go away and see to my father's burial."
22 Jesus tells him:
"Follow me, and let the dead bury their own dead."

let the dead bury their dead—The Greeks took the word for "corpse" and applied it to the person as dead. What this phrase strictly says, then, is "let corpses bury their own corpses"—shocking language! But again Jesus gestures to a hierarchy of goods and of economies—a mere corpse is embedded in the lowest economy.

The first man is a scribe—that is, someone who, like Matthew, makes his living by making records. He is also apparently someone who is looking for a secure and predictable position. The second wants permission to do something that memorializes what took place in the past—just as Matthew the tax collector is concerned with documenting and taxing completed business activity. It is not unreasonable that these two are mentioned because Matthew saw himself in them.

These two men declined to continue to follow Jesus just before the three incidents recounted next. (It would seem, at least, that Matthew's order of exposition is meant to relate the two groups of events.) Consider what those incidents are: first, a storm at sea, which Jesus calms by his command; second, strange demon-possessed men among the tombs on a dark coastline in strange land, with the utterly bizarre but terrifying sight of a herd of pigs hurling themselves into the sea; and, third, a contest that Jesus wins against the self-righteous and self-satisfied religious authorities of the time. All of these events would have appeared fascinating and tremendously exciting to an ambitious young man.

Now, consider again Matthew the tax collector. He works in a small customs booth next to an unimportant lake in an insignificant provincial town. He is paid by the occupying powers. He is detested by his fellows. His future must look bleak. "Corpses burying corpses" would strike him as a very apt description of his own life. He is caught in the lowest-level economy.

And then, he can identify with these two men and see what they gave up when—from fear, conventionality, or lack of imagination—they turned down Jesus. Economists speak of "opportunity cost," which is what we pay in pursuing a certain path, because we gave up the gains available in taking a different path. These two men who walked away paid the opportunity cost of not witnessing those three extraordinary events. Understand Matthew, the accountant, to be looking on and calculating the costs of their decision.

23 And as he entered into the boat, his disciples followed
him. 24 And, right then, a great squall arose in the sea, so
that the boat was swamped with waves. But he was asleep.
25 And going to him they woke him up, saying:
"Lord. Save us. We are perishing."
26 And Jesus says to them:
"Why are you afraid, you of little faith?"
Then getting up, he rebuked the winds and the sea, and
there came a great calm. 27 The men wondered at it,
saying:
"What manner of man is this, that even the winds and the sea obey him?"

right then—"Behold."

he was asleep—Humanly speaking, it would not be possible that anyone be asleep in the circumstances. After the fact, the disciples realized this, of course, and therefore realized also that the whole episode was designed to give them an example. The one who could calm the wind and the sea had also willed that the squall arise just then.

Many have seen in this miracle a living parable of their own lives. They think of themselves as at sea and in distress. Indeed, as was said in the introduction, in the ancient world, rescue from distress at sea was the paradigm of salvation. But if this section of Matthew's Gospel, as we are supposing, is giving his *apologia*, then Matthew too saw himself in this way. It may be a mistake to suppose that he was some kind of mild-mannered functionary, like a boring and bourgeois bank clerk. What if, like a lot of young men, he was turbulently troubled? By what? By politics, by his supervisors, by some serious wrong he had done, by boiling emotions, by contradictions between what he wanted and what he had, by temptations and compulsions and addictions—why not one or more of these, like just about everyone else?

28 After coming to the other side of the lake, to the region
of the Gadarenes, two demon-possessed men met him,
coming out from the tombs, very violent, keeping anyone
from passing along that path. 29 And—consider this—
they shouted out saying:
> **"What is it between us and you, Son of God? Have you come here to torment us before the time?"**

30 Far off from them there was a herd of many swine,
feeding. 31 The demons entreated him, saying:
> **"If you cast us out, send us out into the herd of swine."**

32 He said to them:
> **"Go."**

They, after coming out, went into the swine. And
amazingly the whole herd hurled itself down a steep bank

into the sea. They perished in the waters. 33 The men feeding them fled. Leaving for the city, they explained everything and what happened with the demon-possessed men. 34 And right then the whole city went out to meet Jesus. Seeing him, they implored him to leave their area.

consider this . . . amazingly . . . right then—"Behold."

Each of the miracles in this group involves some kind of amplification. Here, we see an amplification of matters that are typically not observable: the power of demons, their pointless malice, and their destructiveness. Sadly, these evils are clearer in the phenomenon of hundreds of pigs hurling themselves over a cliff into the sea than in a human being who has lost his mind.

Many persons who converted to Christianity felt before their conversion as if they were going mad or could go mad and that their conversion saved them and made them of whole mind again. Others when newly converted, from the stress and strain that still reached to them from their prior life, felt that but for Christian discipleship they would go mad. We may, if we wish, read Matthew's inclusion of the story here, before the account of his calling, as a declaration that he was like this too. (By "inclusion . . . here" I mean that either it did occur then, and Matthew selected it as relevant to tell for this reason, or it occurred later, but Matthew took it to represent well the sort of thing that served as one of his reasons for getting up from his table, and so he placed it here.)

9:1 Getting into a boat, he crossed the lake. He went to his own town. 2 And now look what happened: they brought him a paralytic lying on a pallet. Jesus, seeing their faith, said to the paralytic:

"Take courage, child, your sins are forgiven."

3 And consider this: some of the scribes said to
themselves, "This guy is blaspheming." 4 Jesus, knowing
their thoughts, said:

> **"Why do you think evil things in your hearts? 5 Which**
> **is the easier task, after all, to say, 'Your sins are**
> **forgiven,' or to say, 'Get up, and walk?' 6 But so that**
> **you may know that the Son of Man has authority on**
> **earth to forgive sins. . . ."**

(Then he says to the paralytic,)

> **"Get up, take your pallet, and go to your house."**

7 He got up and went to his house. 8 The crowd, looking
on, were filled with fear. They glorified "the God who had
given such authority to men."

now look what happened—"Behold."

consider this—"Behold."

this guy—They refer to him in a contemptuous manner.

knowing their thoughts—He did not hear them but did not need to hear them.

had given such authority to men—An extraordinary phrase. Matthew does not write, "to a man" or "to Jesus," but "to men," as if to indicate that some standing power to forgive sin has been established among the human race.

Now comes the calling of Matthew. There is little reason for this call of this disciple to be located here, except for its interest to the author. Also, the manner in which Matthew responds is clearly meant to stand in contrast with the two who declined to follow:

9 Jesus, passing on from there, saw a man sitting at the tax
collector's booth, named Matthew. He says to him,
"Follow me." He got up and followed him.

What, then, does the preceding section of Matthew's Gospel tell us about Matthew, if, as I have been suggesting, it gives an *apologia* for why he followed Jesus and an explanation of how he could have gotten up immediately to follow him?

It tells us that this Gospel was written by a young man who was deeply idealistic and easily aroused to hope in the truth of what he sensed had to be true. He was drawn to bold, heroic, adventurous, and competitive exploits, like other young men. He was wary of losing out on these things because of caution. He saw that caution would merely imprison him in a world of "corpses burying their corpses." He hated his lack of freedom as a minor public official in the Roman empire. He hated his lack of solidarity with the heritage and covenants of his people. He learned quickly from the example of others. He realized that nothing good comes without risk and without a cost. He probably began to pray for a way out. Perhaps he prayed to be called. And when he was called, he got up from his secure table, put down his books of account, got up, and walked away—just as the paralytic got up from his pallet and walked away.

We add as a kind of coda the reception at Matthew's house later:

10 It happened, as he was reclining at table in the house—
get this!—many tax collectors and sinners, having come,
were reclining at table along with Jesus and his disciples.
11 The Pharisees, looking on, intervened with his
disciples:
"Why is your master eating with tax collectors and
sinners?"
12 Jesus, hearing it, said:
"It is not the healthy who need a physician, but those
who are ill. 13 Go and learn what this means: 'I desire

> **mercy and not sacrifice.' For I have not come to call righteous men but sinners."**

get this—"Behold." This rendering risks being a little too colloquial, but it gets the spirit across. The term reveals that the author found the matter ironic.

those who are ill—How Matthew views himself, like the leper and the paralytic.

I desire mercy and not sacrifice—The verse from Hosea 6:6 echoes the Beatitudes, "Blessed are the merciful," and also Jesus's teaching on not judging others. To look for sacrifice is to look to extract repayment of debt, while to show mercy is to remit debt. It is a counsel to be on the correct side of a transaction involving a sinner. Only Matthew includes this verse. We take the verse and its connection to the Beatitudes to reveal how Matthew linked the Sermon on the Mount to the forgiveness he had received from Jesus. It confirms our view that he presents the Sermon on the Mount as part of his *apologia*. This feast, then, correspondingly expresses Matthew's gratitude and joy.

In Luke's telling of this event (Luke 5:29–32), Matthew (who is referred to as Levi) hosts a "reception" (Greek, *dochē*) in his own home, apparently right after he accepts the Lord's call, and a "great crowd" of tax collectors was present. The scope of the reception or feast implies that Matthew was not poor, and therefore he had not been one of the few honest tax collectors. Painstaking, precise, everything according to the book—these do not necessarily imply being honest. Did he throw this big reception precisely to begin spending down what he had? Matthew seems savvy, too, in recognizing that he will be more successful at introducing his fellow tax collectors to Jesus if he pleases them with a feast.

Second Part of the First Part: Crediting of the Deposit to an Account (Matthew 9:18–16:13)

We said that the simplest way to organize a piece of writing is by dichotomy—to divide it in half and then, if needed, each half into halves again. We said that Matthew divides his Gospel in half. The dividing point is Peter's confession. The first half deals with the Deposit, which is the Incarnation, and the second with the Payment, which is the Passion. In doing so, he works on the pattern of the standard record book at the time for a large household's use of wealth, a *codex accepti et expensi*.

But that first half is divided in half again. Matthew's call serves as its dividing point. Until that point, as we have seen, Matthew is concerned with confirmation and credentialing. Jesus's genealogy, the nature of his birth, the prophecies about him, the magi, John the Baptist, the temptations, and then the inherent authority of his teaching and deeds—these confirm that someone who believes in Jesus, like the leper and the centurion, is doing so on a solid basis. Matthew thereby accounts for the reality and worth of the Deposit: Jesus reliably is the promised Savior. Such accounting is what a good banker does. However, for the remainder of the first part (chapters 9–15), its second half, Matthew is mainly concerned with something else. But if so, with what?

We said that he is mainly concerned with the change in the account to which the Deposit should be credited—or, rather, the change in the household to which the Deposit is assigned. Jesus explains this change using the image of wineskins. New wine, he says, is to be placed in new wineskins. If one were to attempt to put the new wine into the old wineskins, the skins would tear, and both they and the wine would be lost. The new wine corresponds to what we have been calling the Deposit, and the wineskins to the household to which the deposit is credited. In this next section (chapters 9–15), then, Matthew is also telling us what these new wineskins are. He is telling us in effect about the new household that Jesus has been calling the Kingdom of Heaven.

About this new household:

- It has a new structure of authority, consisting of The Twelve who are authoritative representatives of the King, and other disciples who are apparently under these Twelve in turn (chapter 11).
- It has a new posture of being sent to proclaim the good news of the Kingdom of God and to do works of mercy (chapter 11).
- It involves a new mode of teaching and of reception of that teaching, as exemplified in parables (chapter 13).
- It invites a new range of persons to become members of its household, as it reaches outside of Israel, extending to all the "nations" without restriction (chapter 15).
- It has its own form of sustenance, akin to manna, as shown in the feeding of the five thousand, which is offered to the Gentiles as well in the feeding of the four thousand (chapters 14, 15).

All of these characteristics are sharply different from what was found in Israel beforehand. As if to underline the discontinuity, Matthew in this section also places an account of the passing of John the Baptist (chapters 12, 14).

Finally, a theme that runs throughout this section is how the Pharisees, Sadducees, and scribes in general reject this new system and reject Jesus as establishing it. They stand for how the old skins really cannot stretch to hold the new wine without tearing (chapters 12, 15).

9:14 At that time the disciples of John approached him, saying:
"Why do we and the Pharisees keep fasts, but your disciples do not?"
15 Jesus said to them,
"Are the sons of the bridal chamber even capable of grieving, so long as the bridegroom is with them? But days are coming when the bridegroom will have been taken away from them. And at that time they will keep fasts."

the sons of the bridal chamber—This is his literal language. It was an idiom that meant either the groomsmen or the wedding guests who would escort the newly married couple to the bridal chamber. But the literal language is important for three reasons. First, because it uses the term, "bridal chamber," which is a discreet way of referring to the consummation of the marriage. Therefore, the idiom in its deeper meaning points to the Incarnation, which is the one flesh union in Christ of divine with human nature. Second, because the idiom uses the language of "sons" or "children" and therefore indicates how his disciples through baptism will also become sons and daughters of God. They are children "of" this act of consummation. Third, because the idiom brings in joy at the consummation and not simply the joy of the wedding celebration. (See Tobit, 6:14, which uses the same Greek term *numphôn*.)

Now comes the foundational principle for this next part of Matthew's Gospel:

> **16 "No one sews a patch of raw cloth onto an old garment—because the repair pulls away from his garment, and a worse tear is the result.**
> **17 "But neither do they put new wine into old wine skins. And suppose they did? The wine skins will burst. The wine will pour out. The skins will be ruined. Rather, they put new wine into new wine skins. And both are conserved."**

Someone with care of the old takes care not simply to add the new to it; likewise, someone with care of the new should take care not simply to add it to the old. Rather, each seeks something conformable to what he has. The old looks to be matched with the old; the new seeks to be matched with the new.

both are conserved—We naturally read this phrase as meaning that both the new wine and the new wineskins will be conserved. But what it actually means, in the context, is that both the new wine and the old wineskins will be conserved. The image seems to be a proposal about how the new and the old can exist side by side.

What follows next are four healings that Matthew narrates as having happened all in a bundle. The healings are deliberately presented as happening one after the other. Matthew clearly considers it remarkable that things unfolded in this way. Also, Matthew takes pains to say that the reports of these miracles were spread far and wide. Why does he do this? We will see why, below.

18 As he was saying these things to them, right then, a certain ruler came and adored him, saying:

"Lord, my daughter has just died. But come and place your hand on her, and she will be alive."

right then—"Behold."

Astonishingly, the ruler has no doubts that Jesus can bring life to his daughter. But observe that his language suggests not that he thinks he will revive her—the ruler does not say "she will come back to life"—but rather that life itself will be conveyed through the touch of Jesus—"she will be alive."

19 Jesus, getting up, followed him; his disciples also.
20 And—then look!—a woman who had been bleeding for twelve years, approaching from behind, touched the hem of his garment.
21 For she was saying within herself: *If I only touch his garment, I will be made whole.*
22 Jesus, turning and seeing her, said:

"Take courage, daughter; your faith has made you whole."

And the woman was made whole from that hour.

then look—"Behold."

The woman was ceremonially unclean because of her flow of blood. She was not permitted to touch anyone (Leviticus 15:25). In humility, then, she tries to approach unseen and to touch simply Jesus's clothing, which she is confident will be sufficient.

I will be made whole—Literally, "I will be saved," or even "I will be rescued." She sees her affliction as impossible for her to escape; she needs assistance from above, a Savior.

Note that the Apostles would needed to have interviewed her later to learn what she was thinking (unless Jesus knew it and revealed it to them). But having interviewed her, wouldn't they have written the matter down? Surely a professional record-keeper like Matthew would have done so.

23 And Jesus, coming into the house of the ruler and
seeing the flute players and the distressed crowd, 24 said:
"You may leave. The girl is not dead. She is sleeping."
They mocked him. 25 But when the crowd had been
removed, going in, he took her by the hand. The girl got
up. 26 This report went out into the whole of that land.
27 As he was passing on from there, two blind men
followed Jesus, crying out and saying,
"Have mercy on us, O Son of David."
28 As he was entering the house, the blind men
approached him. Jesus says to them,
"Do you believe that I am able to do this?"
They say to him,
"Yes, Lord."
29 Then he touched their eyes, saying,
"Let it be done to you according to your faith."

He asks them about their faith, both to elicit an act of faith to their good and for them to give witness to their faith for the good of others around them.

30 Their eyes were opened, and Jesus sternly charged
them, saying,
"See that no one knows this."

31 But they, going out, spread reports about him in the whole of that land.
32 As they were leaving—consider this—they brought him a dumb man, demon-possessed. 33 Once the devil was cast out, the dumb man spoke. The crowds were astounded, saying,
"Never has anything like this been seen in Israel."

consider this—"Behold."

The crowds had followed him around and seen the series of miracles in succession, culminating in this dramatic exorcism. They exclaim about the total impression. But the exclamation is important for Matthew's narrative, because it conveys the sense that what is happening is something entirely new.

34 But the Pharisees kept saying,
"It is by the prince of demons that he casts out demons."
35 Jesus went around all the towns and the villages, teaching in their synagogues and preaching the good news of the kingdom and healing every sickness and every infirmity.

Here is yet another verse that says that there were a great number of miracles. But Matthew picks out these four because they are paradigmatic, and because when taken altogether, they conveyed newness.

A New Structure of Governance

Here, things that presumably happened once are presented by Matthew as having standing significance. On one occasion, Jesus was looking out at the crowds and presumably told his disciples how they appeared to him and how he felt. On that occasion, he asked them to pray for workers. On one occasion, he summoned the Twelve disciples and sent them out as Apostles. And yet this constellation represents the standing condition of this new thing he was founding in relation to the world.

36 Seeing the crowds, he had compassion on them, because they were disturbed and scattered, like sheep that had no shepherd.
37 At this time, he says to his disciples:
"Although the harvest is great, the workers are few. 38
Therefore, earnestly beg the Lord of the harvest, that he send out workers into his harvest."

had compassion on them—Literally, he felt for them in his gut; he had a visceral reaction.

disturbed and scattered—These are very strong words in Greek meaning literally "flayed" and "jettisoned." There is no pretense that the human condition of itself is peaceful and tranquil. Think of a restless, troubled group of sheep, moving pointlessly this way and that, some exhausted and stretched out on the ground, all of them brooding, anxious, haunted, dazed.

10:1 And after summoning his Twelve disciples, he gave them power over unclean spirits, to cast them out and to heal every kind of illness and every kind of infirmity.

summoning—The Greek word means not a casual calling together (like ringing a bell for dinner) but rather a deliberate act in view of their standing as the Twelve (like a legal act that convokes an assembly).

his Twelve—This is the first mention of them as the Twelve. Early Christians did not need to be told that there was a specially chosen group of Twelve. This would have been familiar to Matthew's readers. Yet the tax collector must give an accounting by a list of their names.

power over unclean spirits—Throughout the Gospels (and even in the immediately preceding section) power over supernatural spirits was regarded as the most noteworthy expression of divine power, much more than power over mere nature and mere corporality. It should continue to startle us that such a power was conferred by Jesus on the Apostles together.

2 Of the Twelve Apostles, the names are these:
first, Simon, who is called Peter,
and Andrew, his brother, and James, the son of
Zebedee, and John, his brother;
Philip and Bartholomew;
Thomas and Matthew the tax collector;
James the son of Alpheus and Thaddeus;
4 Simon the Cananean and Judas, the Iscariot, the one
who also betrayed him.
5 These Twelve Jesus sent,

first, Simon—Simon is always listed first in the New Testament, just as Judas is last. But then a group of four, consisting of two pairs of brothers, is picked out as having special status. On many occasions, Jesus draws them aside separately. The other pairs are perhaps how they went out two by two (Luke 10:1), or maybe they simply represent a mnemonic. If the former, then we must be alert as to how Thomas and Matthew may have influenced each other.

Matthew the tax collector—Every other Apostle had a profession before he was called. But James and John are not identified as "the fishermen." Therefore, we have some confirmation that Matthew continued to think of his tax collector background as entering into his role as an Apostle. Also, if the label "Matthew the tax collector" was meant to impugn him by identifying him as a former public sinner, then it is more likely that Matthew himself is the author, deprecating himself in humility, rather than someone else. (He is not identified as "the tax collector" in the lists in Mark 3:18, Luke 9:15, or Acts 1:13.) It would be unseemly for others to deprecate him.

A New Stance towards the World

First, he gives definite instructions for this particular sending forth:

> **5 instructing them, saying: "Avoid any road to the Gentiles. Do not enter any town of Samaritans. 6 But go, rather, to the lost sheep of the house of Israel.**
> **7 "Preach as you go, saying, the Kingdom of Heaven is at hand.**
> **8 "The sick, heal. The dead, raise up. Lepers, make clean. Demons, cast out.**

This sending forth is to the lost sheep of Israel, but because they reject the Kingdom, as through compulsion it gets extended to all the nations.

> **"A gift you have been given: a gift freely give.**
> **9 "Do not carry any gold or silver or copper in your money belts, 10 or, for the road, a purse, an extra shirt, or sandals or a staff—because a worker deserves his keep."**

They are workers sent into the harvest, but they are not to sell spiritual goods, although they require daily room and board. One might wonder why this needs to be said. On the interpretation proposed here, it is that Jesus has so clearly taught that discipleship is a kind of service for compensation—remember that he calls them "workers"—that he must be equally clear that they are not to seek compensation from human beings.

11 "Whatever the town or village you enter, inquire who
within it is deserving, and stay there until you leave.
12 "As you are entering the dwelling, greet it. 13 If the
dwelling is deserving, let your peace come to it. But if it
happens not to be deserving, let your peace return to you.
14 "When they do not receive you, or even bear to listen to
what you say, as you depart from that dwelling or from
that town, shake the dust from your feet. 15 Amen, I say
to you, it will go more tolerably for the land of Sodom and
Gomorrah in the day of judgment than for that town."

deserving—Only Matthew uses this language of merit and deservedness (compare Luke 10:7). It would have been an honor and blessing to have hosted an Apostle, which would have had to be earned.

16 "Pay careful attention! I am sending you out as sheep
in the midst of wolves. Therefore, be clever, like serpents,
and innocent, like doves.
17 "Be on guard against men. They will hand you over to
judges, and in their assemblies they will have you
disciplined. 18 Even before governors and kings you will
be brought, for my sake, as a witness to them and to the
Gentiles."

pay careful attention—"Behold."

clever, like serpents—"Clever" translates *phronimoi*, which means "prudent men," or "men of practical wisdom." This term has the sense of astutely looking after one's own genuine interest. To be a good banker is to be astute, like a serpent, but also innocent, like a dove, because dishonesty is never contemplated and plain dealing is always offered.

Curiously, Jesus mentions all branches of government: judges, legislatures, and executives. What he has said so far applied to the Apostles, nearly all of whom were martyred. But next he speaks prophetically about the Church as apostolic, stretching into the future:

> **19 "But when they do hand you over, do not be anxious as to how you will speak or what you are to say, since it will be given to you, in that hour, what you are to say—20**
> **since you are not the ones doing the speaking but the Spirit of your Father, which is speaking in you.**
> **21 "Brother will hand over brother, to be put to death, and father son; even children will rise up against their parents and put them to death.**
> **22 "And you will be hated by everyone, because of my name. But the one who perseveres to the end—this is the one who will be saved.**

because of my name—In the ancient world, what was "in" someone's name was his whole personality and what he stood for. To say that the Christians were baptized "in the name of the Lord Jesus" did not mean that only the name of the Lord Jesus was used in the formula of baptism but that the baptism had the power of the Lord Jesus and identified someone spiritually with the Lord.

23 "When they persecute you in this town, flee into the next. Amen, I say to you, you will not have gone through all the towns of Israel before the Son of man comes.

This statement must be taken to mean that there will always be some safe place to flee to.

24 "A disciple is not above the master, nor a servant above his lord.
25 "It is enough for the disciple to become just like his master, and the servant just like his lord. If they have called the Master of the house Beelzebub, how much more the members of his household?

We have described the divine economy as the economy of a household, and here Jesus calls himself the Master of that household.

26 "Therefore, have no fear of them: because nothing is concealed, which will not be revealed; and nothing is hidden, which will not be made known.
27 "What I say to you in the dark, tell it in the light, and what you hear whispered in your ear, shout it out loudly from housetops.
28 "Have no fear of those who kill the body but have no power to kill the soul. Fear rather the one who has the power to destroy both soul and body in hell.

The parallel passage in Luke does not say anything about the soul (Luke 12:4). We have seen that Matthew likes the language of "soul" because it allows for a vivid explanation of the divine economy: bodily goods are to be traded for the goods of the soul, not the reverse.

> **29 "Two sparrows are sold for a penny, are they not? And one of them will not fall to the earth, without your Father. 30 Even your hairs on your head, all of them, have been fully accounted for. 31 Therefore, put aside fear. You are worth more than many sparrows."**

Luke, in contrast, has five sparrows being sold for two pennies (Luke 12:6). Actually, the coin was the Roman *assarius*, made of copper. It was the smallest unit of currency in the empire and therefore like our penny. But why the disparity in price between the two evangelists? Commentators like to explain away Luke's figure as representing a discount for buying in bulk, like "buy four get one free." However, retailers never offer such discounts for the very least expensive items purchased in the smallest quantities—precisely because such items are so cheap, no one expects a discount unless for buying in bulk.

A better explanation, in my view, is this: Matthew, having an accountant's sensibilities, believes it is most truthful to give the asking price for sparrows on the market at the time of his writing. He is not going to give the historic price, back when Jesus said what he said. Luke, on the other hand, as a historian, regards it as most truthful to give the price as quoted by Jesus, even if that is not the price of sparrows on the market when he writes. Thus, Luke's price is from about 33 AD, while Matthew's price is from the year he writes, whenever that is.

If we adopt this interpretation, the two numbers give us a way of estimating the date of Matthew's writing. In the period between 100 BC and 200 AD in the Mediterranean of the Roman empire, as various studies have indicated, prices were rather stable, with an annual inflation rate of about only 1 percent per year. At that rate, the number of years necessary for Luke's price to inflate to Matthew's price would be twenty-three—which would imply a date in the early 50s for the composition of Matthew's text. If five sparrows sold for two pennies in 33 AD, then, after inflation, a sparrow would have sold for a half penny at around 55 AD.

have been fully accounted for—A similar phrase is found in Luke. But Matthew uses a different construction, which is interesting and revealing. Luke uses simply a perfect tense of a verb, meaning: *the hairs of your head have been completely counted.* But Matthew uses, rather, a perfect participle together with a present tense of the verb *to be.* This construction, called a "periphrastic perfect," has the meaning *the hairs of your head are now in the state of having been completely counted.* To grasp the difference, consider this example. Suppose that a table has a certain number of blocks on it. Suppose someone looks carefully at the table and counts the blocks. The blocks then "have been completely counted." That is to say, someone has passed over them and counted them. *They have been the object of an act of counting.* This is Luke's idiom. But suppose now that someone counts the blocks and, in counting them, marks or changes them somehow, to indicate that they have been duly counted. Perhaps he flips each block over as he counts it. Or perhaps he affixes a number to it, to mark it, as if to declare that it has been counted. Then, when he is done, someone might survey the blocks and observe that *they are in a condition of having all been counted.* That is to say, we may have assurance that they have been counted; there is a permanent and standing correlate in the blocks of the action by which they were counted. The latter is Matthew's idiom. Of the two idioms, the second is what would be preferred by someone with an accountant's sensibilities, who wants to see not merely that something is counted, but also that there is confirmation and assurance of the fact that they were counted. In short, the phrase in Matthew does not mean merely that God has counted the hairs; it means, more strongly, that God, in numbering the hairs of your head, has registered, recognized, and accounted for them. They remained counted "in God."

> **32 "Therefore, everyone who makes a profession, in me, before men—I too will make a profession, in him, before my Father who is in heaven; 33 but everyone who would renounce me before men—I too will renounce him before my Father who is in heaven."**

a profession, in me, before men—This strange construction represents the literal language of the Greek. It is an idiom found only here, and nowhere else. What does it mean? Presumably, it is stricter than simply a profession "of me" because it must be well grounded, by someone who is truly following the Lord and abiding by his commandments ("in me"). Therefore, take it to be a public acknowledgement *of the Lord* by someone who is living *in the Lord*.

> **34 "Do not suppose that I came to impart peace to the earth. I did not come to impart peace but a sword—35 because I came to divide a man against his father, and a daughter against her mother, and a daughter-in-law against her mother-in-law."**

In verse 12, the greeting that an Apostle would have given upon entering a dwelling would have been "peace be upon this place." Jesus is saying that he did not come to the earth conveying a similar greeting to the earth.

> **36 "A man's enemies—those of his own household.**
> **37 "If someone loves father or mother above me, he is undeserving of me, and if someone loves son or daughter above me, he is not deserving of me.**

38 "And whoever fails to take up his cross and follow behind me, is not deserving of me.
39 "If someone finds his life, he will lose it; and if someone loses his life for the sake of me, he will find it."

A man's family is being treated here as an extension of himself. If he has to suffer violence himself rather than be unfaithful to the Lord, then he must accept division in his family, if the alternative is to offend the Lord. Verse 39 about crucifixion is what philosophers call an *a fortiori* argument—if you must take up your cross daily against your will, then, *a fortiori*, you must accept this cross of a divided family if it comes your way. The sequence of verses 36–39 shows how there is often a hidden logic in a sequence of assertions of Our Lord that at first can seem unrelated. It is left up to us to discover the connection, which is part of what reading the Bible means for an educated person.

40 "If someone receives you, he receives me, and if someone receives me, he receives the one who sent me.
41 "If someone receives a prophet in the name of a prophet, he will gain the compensation of a prophet, and if someone receives a just man in the name of a just man, he will gain the compensation of a just man.
42 "And whoever gives something to drink to one of these little ones—only a cup of cold water—in the name of a disciple—Amen, I say to you, he will not lose his compensation."

Verses 40–42 have no correlation in another Gospel. It is obvious how these sayings would have intrigued Matthew, the tax collector and good banker. How does someone who cooperates with an apostle, prophet, or just man, simply by welcoming or receiving him, become deserving of the same compensation (*misthos*) of the one who is received and who has done so much more? Jesus must mean either that that act of receiving him counts as an act characteristic of that person or that the act of will involved in receiving him, if one is faithful to it, implies a willingness to make sacrifices like those of the person one receives—as if you have become implicitly and virtually the person you receive, in receiving him. This implicit reference to the receiver's willingness to make sacrifices in imitation of the one received links verses 40–41 to the preceding three verses.

> **11:1 It happened when Jesus finished instructing his Twelve disciples that he moved from there to teach and preach in their towns.**

it happened when Jesus finished—Matthew uses this phrase at the end of four of the longer discourses in his Gospel. See 7:28.

A New Act of Conversion and Loyalty

New wine into new wineskins—the preceding sections showed the newness of the wine; this section presents the newness of the wineskins—that is to say, the definite act of conversion and loyalty to him personally, which Jesus requires as the only commensurate response to this new thing.

> **2 When John in prison heard the works of the Christ he said to him (through his disciples he had sent), 3 "Are you the one who is coming, or should we look for another?"**

Matthew writes that John said this to Christ, even though his emissaries did the speaking—which is an example of how what we do through others is what we do ourselves.

He also writes, literally, that John heard "the works" of the Christ, when strictly John heard reports of those works. That is, Matthew and John both take for granted the social nature of our knowledge of the world.

Then, Matthew describes this as "John heard the works of the Christ," not that he heard "the works of Jesus," which most naturally means that John believed Jesus to be the Christ who was doing these works.

It follows that John must have conveyed this question for the sake of his disciples, not for his own sake. Why? Because John's disciples must stop following him and start following Jesus—which would be difficult for them if they had followed John with great sacrifice for many years. He expects or perhaps even has been told by God that he will soon be put to death, and he wants his disciples to make the definite act of becoming now followers of the Christ.

> **4 Jesus in reply said to them: "Go and tell John what you**
> **hear and what you see. 5 Blind men are seeing again, and**
> **lame men are walking about. Lepers are cleansed, and**
> **deaf men hear. And dead men are up and about, and poor**
> **men are receiving good news. 6 And whoever takes no**
> **offense in me is happy."**

These verses are usually rendered with definite articles: "the blind see," "the lame walk," and so on. And one must do so if one wants to avoid using the word "men." And yet no definite articles are in the Greek (when they might naturally have been included; therefore, their omission is significant), and the terms, after all, are masculine plural. The way I have rendered it is the way it reads.[1] And the claim that results is slightly different: not "everyone with infirmities is healed," but rather "these are the things going on here."

But once these claims are rendered appropriately, it becomes clear that verse 6 is presenting a parallel claim. It is about the happiness that can be seen around Jesus and his followers. The sole condition for enjoying this happiness is not to manufacture an objection against him—which, as we shall soon see, the Pharisees most conspicuously were doing. Verse 6 is *not* presenting a warning to John to be careful not to doubt Jesus.

Jesus is echoing Isaiah here (see Isaiah 35:5–6; 42:18; and 61:1), and he knew that John and his disciples would perceive this. For Matthew, so keen on Isaiah also (about which, see the postscript), the echo is so obvious that he does not even suppose he needs to call attention to it. And now we see why Matthew was so intrigued by that occasion when several of these miracles were bundled into a continuous stream, in Matthew chapter 9. He recognized this confluence of wonders as a realization of what he knew from Isaiah. He was even careful to say, for some of these miracles, that the report of them went out to all the land (9:26, 31) because that would then explain how John in prison had come to hear about them.

7 When they went on their way, Jesus began to address the crowds about John.

"What did you go out into the desert to see? A reed tossed back and forth in the wind?

---

1 As there are no definite articles in Latin, the Vulgate gets this exactly right: *Cæci vident, claudi ambulant, leprosi mundantur, surdi audiunt, mortui resurgunt, pauperes evangelizantur.*

8 "But what did you go out to see? A man clothed with soft garments? There they are, men wearing soft garments—in the households of kings!
9 "But what did you go out to see? A prophet? Yes, I am telling you. And something more than a prophet.
10 "This is the man about whom it was written:

> **'Attend carefully! I am sending forth my messenger before your face, who will prepare your path in advance of you.'**

11 "Amen, I say to you, there has not arisen, among those born of women, anyone greater than John the Baptist. But take anyone less than another in the Kingdom of Heaven—he is greater than John.
12 "From the days of John the Baptist until this time
now, the Kingdom of Heaven is treated violently, and
violent men snatch it away 13 because all the prophets
and the law prophesied until John. 14 And if you
choose to receive it, he is 'Elias who is to come.'
15 "Let the man who has ears listen."

violent men snatch it away—John and other prophets in the tradition suffered violence precisely because they foreshadowed Jesus. Therefore, John excels among the prophets because his execution immediately indicates the Lord's crucifixion. Matthew understands this and deals with that execution accordingly.

16 "But to what shall I compare this generation? It is like
when children sit in the market place 17 and call out to
others:

'We piped your favorite tune, and you did not dance!
We sang a sad song, and you did not beat your breast!'

18 "After all:
John came neither eating nor drinking, and they say,
'He has a demon'
19 —the Son of Man came eating and drinking, and
they say: 'A glutton, he is, a bit too fond of wine,
friendly with tax collectors and sinners.'
"And wisdom is vindicated by her deeds."

In this lovely image, Jesus likens himself and John to children sitting in a marketplace playing a pipe. (I take it that they and not their critics are the pipers.)

20 He then began to castigate the towns in which the larger number of his powerful works were done, because they did not repent:
21 "Woe to you, Chorozin, woe to you, Bethsaida, because if in Tyre and Sidon the powerful works had appeared, which appeared among you, long ago they would have repented in sackcloth and ashes.
22 "Only, I tell you, for Tyre and Sidon it will go more tolerably in the day of judgment than for you.
23 "And you, Capernaum, will you be lifted up so far as heaven?—so far as hell you will go down. Because if in Sodom the powerful works had appeared, which appeared among you, it would have stood until this day.
24 "Only, I tell you, that for the land of Sodom it will go more tolerably in the day of judgment than for you.

Chorazin—Chorazin in the Holy Land is today a pile of stones strewn among plants by the side of the road.

lifted up to heaven—Antecedently, one might have thought that the city where Jesus lived would have remained a thriving and important pilgrimage site. But today Capernaum too is a pile of stones.

The Ones Who Made Themselves Unhappy

25 It was at that time that Jesus in response said: "I
praise you, Father, Lord of heaven and earth, because
you have hidden these things from experts and clever
men and have revealed them to little children. 26 Yes,
Father, for so it was pleasing in your sight.
27 "All things have been delivered to me by my Father.
No one knows the Son except the Father, and neither
does anyone know the Father except the Son and
anyone to whom the Son chooses to reveal him.
28 "Come to me, all you who labor and are heavily
burdened, and I will give you rest. 29 Take my yoke
upon you, and learn from me, because I am meek and
humble of heart, and you shall find rest for your souls.
30 For my yoke is easy and my burden light."

in response—No one quite knows what this means. Perhaps it is a Hebraism. It may simply mean indefinitely—"when giving a reply once to someone." Or it may mean "as a reply to the Father in prayer."

experts and clever men—There are no definite articles here in the Greek. It is not "the expert and the clever" or "the wise and the understanding." It is not that as a rule the gospel is hidden from those with expertise and intelligence. It is rather that sometimes it is so hidden, when one might have expected it never would be. "Expert" is literally "wise," (*sophoi*), but in the ancient world a wise man was anyone with special expertise. A sculptor or mathematician would be a wise man. "Clever" means someone who is intelligent, quick, and acute. It follows that human education and accomplishment can themselves give no assurance of insight into the most important truths. In particular, it in no way counts against these truths, if, for example, the entire faculty of Harvard University failed to acknowledge them.

give you rest—The Greek word (*anapausis*) means a rest that refreshes, not simply a cessation from labor.

> **12:1 At that time, Jesus took a path through the grain fields on the sabbath, and his disciples were hungry, and they began to pull off some grains and eat them.**

Matthew describes the event as something spontaneous and completely trivial, like what children or "mere babes" would do.

> **2 The Pharisees, seeing them, said to him:**
> **"Look, your disciples are doing something not permitted on the sabbath!"**
> **3 He said to them:**
> **"Have you not read what David did when he was**
> **hungry, and those with him also—4 how he went into**
> **the house of God and ate the loaves of the**
> **presentation—which it was not permitted for him to**
> **eat? And neither was it permitted for the men who**
> **were with him. It was permitted only for the priests. 5**
> **Or maybe you have not read in the law that on the**
> **sabbath days the priests in the temple break the**
> **sabbath and are blameless. 6 But I tell you that there is**
> **something greater than the temple here. 7 If you knew**
> **what this means, 'I desire mercy, and not sacrifice,' you**

would not have condemned the innocent. 8 For the Son of man is Lord of the sabbath."

Our tendency is to look for neutral principles to mediate disputes, but there is no neutral principle here. A judgment is necessary on a substantive matter of fact. Is Jesus the incarnate Son of God, such that his body is akin to the temple (as he taught in John 2:21)? Does he have a priestly office greater than that of the priests in the temple? Does he, as a king, enjoy prerogatives greater than David's? The Pharisees might have had the circumspection at least to suspend judgment until they were clear who Jesus was. But they condemned through their characteristic fault of wanting to exact punishment from others for violations of the law.

'I desire mercy and not sacrifice'—Scholars reckon up doublets like this (see 9:13) as if they are unusual editorial oversight on Matthew's part. That is doubtful. We have had lots of evidence of how carefully constructed Matthew's Gospel is. More remarkable is why there are so few repetitions, when surely Jesus repeated his sayings in different contexts.

9 After going on from there, he went into their synagogue.
10 And look!—a man having a withered hand. They asked him, saying,

"Is it permitted to heal on the sabbath?"

to have a reason to accuse him. 11 He said to them,

"Who among you will be a man who, if he has one sheep and this one sheep falls into a pit on the sabbath, does not take hold of it and pull it out? 12 How much more valuable, therefore, is a man than a sheep! It follows: it is permissible to do what is good on the sabbath."

13 Then he says to the man,
"Stretch out your hand."
He stretched it out. It was restored to health, just like the other. 14 The Pharisees, after leaving, began to plot against him, how they might destroy him.

Jesus's short speech in verses 11–12 reads like a legal defense given in advance. He sees they want to accuse him, and he defends himself against the accusation.

Matthew interprets this plot to destroy Jesus as the beginning, in God's providence, of a kind of expulsion of Jesus out of Israel toward the Gentiles. Here we see the concrete beginning of the specific historical process by which the Deposit of the Incarnation became credited to the whole human race.

15 Jesus, being aware of it, departed for another place. Many followed him. He healed them all. 16 He charged them not to make him a celebrity, 17 so that there might be a fulfillment of what was spoken by Isaiah the prophet, saying:

18 "Consider my servant, whom I have chosen,
my beloved in whom my soul has been well pleased.
I will place my spirit upon him,
and he will announce judgment to the Gentiles.
19 "He will not contend, nor will he cry out;
no one will so much as hear his voice in the streets.
20 "A bruised reed he will not break,
and smoldering flax he will not quench,
until he leads judgment to victory.
21 "In his name the Gentiles will hope."

Matthew presumably was at first surprised by the Lord's unwillingness to acquire renown given the extent of the miraculous healings—since wouldn't his fame spread the good news faster?—But then he understood the literal obligation created by these lines in Isaiah. The crucial verses are 18 and 21, referring to the Gentiles. From this point on, Matthew's account begins to pivot toward the Gentiles.

22 It was at that time that a demon-possessed man, blind and dumb, was brought to him. He healed him, so that the dumb man spoke and saw. 23 All the crowds were astounded. They kept saying,

"Is this 'the Son of David' then?"

24 But the Pharisees, hearing the report, said:

"This guy does not cast out demons except in Beelzeboul, Prince of Demons."

The Pharisees seem a little too familiar with demons, and perhaps they are also afraid, since they link Jesus to a god of the Philistines from of old, the "Lord of the Flies."

25 Jesus, knowing their thoughts, said to them:

"Every kingdom divided against itself will be brought to destruction. Every city or house divided against itself will not stand. 26 And if Satan casts out Satan, he is divided against himself; therefore, how will his kingdom stand?"

27 "And if it is 'in Beelzeboul' that I cast out demons, then, your sons—in whom do they cast them out? That is why they will be your judges. 28 But if it is in the Spirit of God that I cast out demons, then the Kingdom of God is right now upon you."

The accusation supposes that someone could expel demons only by a fundamental idolatry—that is, by conjuring false gods from the ancient traditions of the Philistines five hundred years earlier. But neither the Pharisees nor their disciples ("sons") actually accept this absurd idea. Notice that in this back-and-forth it is taken for granted on both sides that this god of the Philistines is actually a demon.

> **29 "Or how does anyone have the ability to go into the house of a strong man and take his possessions away, if he does not, first, tie up that strong man? Only then will he take his possessions away."**

The Pharisees are being naïve about the devil, whereas Jesus speaks from direct experience. The devil willingly lets no soul out of his grasp. The devil would try to destroy anyone who was going about freeing captive souls. But then this point immediately leads to a warning, because the direct implication is that, in opposing Jesus, the Pharisees have unwittingly aligned themselves with the devil and his interests.

> **30 "Anyone who is not with me is against me. And anyone who is not gathering up with me is scattering. 31 That is why I am telling you: Every sin and blasphemy will be forgiven men, but blasphemy of the Spirit will not be forgiven. 32 And whoever speaks a word against the Son of man, it will be forgiven him. But whoever speaks against the Holy Spirit, it will not be forgiven him—not in this world and not in the world to come."**

Matthew's typical word for what we call a miracle is a "powerful work," or more literally a "power'" (*dunamis*). A power has an effect and is an origin. The Son of Man casts out a demon—an effect—and they say "a word" against him—that is, they accuse him of being prideful or ambitious. This is to criticize the effect or application of that power. But suppose someone going further actually takes the origin of the good effect to be bad? What then? What could break through to such a person and provoke a change of heart? Not something else whose origin he also took to be bad. That is why the Lord next says:

> **33 Either make the tree good and its fruit good, or make the tree corrupt and its fruit corrupt; it is by the fruit that the tree is known.**

Now he finally turns to the character of the Pharisees and warns them, saying that the surprising thing is that they say anything good about anyone, not that they are saying something bad about him:

> **34 You brood of vipers, how are you capable of saying**
> **good things when you are bad?—as it is out of the**
> **abundance of the heart that the mouth speaks. 35 A good**
> **man from a good treasure box brings out good things,**
> **and a bad man from a bad treasure box brings out bad**
> **things.**
> **36 I tell you that for every ill-considered word that men**
> **shall speak, they will render an account of it in the day of**
> **judgment. 37 It is by your words that you will be reckoned**
> **as just and by your words that you will be condemned.**

You might have expected—and you would be right—that these last two verses, redolent of accounting language, have no correlation in any other Gospel. Each word we speak is as if an entry, and its valence as good or bad will ineluctably be accounted for. More than that, whether an "entry" counts as fraud, by making representations that cannot be supported, will be held against us.

Perhaps Our Lord's warnings had some effect, since Matthew takes care next to say that only "some" Pharisees pursue the next point:

38 It was at that time that some of the scribes and
Pharisees answered him, saying:
"Teacher, we want to see a sign from you."
39 He, in reply, said to them:
"An evil and adulterous generation seeks after a sign,
and a sign will not be given to it, except the sign of Jonah
the prophet. 40 Because as Jonah was in the belly of the
whale three days and three nights, so will the Son of
Man be in the heart of the earth three days and three
nights. 41 Men of Nineveh will rise in the judgment with
this generation, and they will condemn it because they
repented at the preaching of Jonas, and now look here:
something greater than Jonah! 42 A queen of the south
will rise in judgment with this generation, and she will
condemn it because she came from the ends of the earth
to listen to the wisdom of Solomon, and, consider here:
something greater than Solomon!"

Nineveh repented because of preaching alone; the Queen of the South became a disciple of Solomon because of his wisdom alone. Neither Jonah nor Solomon worked any miracles. The Sermon on the Mount ought to have been enough for these men to repent—as we saw, the leper who approached Jesus after that Sermon was not looking to be cured as a *proof* of anything; in faith he had intuited already that Jesus had the power to heal him.

And note that the miracles of Jesus do essentially come to an end in Matthew's account, from here on. Matthew reports him as working only two more in Jewish regions (the demon-possessed boy in chapter 17 and the two blind men in chapter 20), as if to clear the way for "the sign of Jonah."

43 "When an unclean spirit has gone out of a man, it goes
through dry places seeking rest. It fails to find it. 44 Next
it says: 'To my home I will return—whence I came out.'
Coming, it finds it vacant, well swept, and attractively
decorated. 45 Next it goes forth. It brings along with it
seven other spirits more evil than itself. Entering in, they
take up residence there. The last troubles of that man
become worse than the first. So it will be, also, for this evil
generation.

This warning is addressed both to individuals and to institutions. We say correctly "the corruption of the best is the worst," but sometimes something additional is at work, something demonic, an evil force from the outside, which takes over and seems actively to twist and pervert the life of an individual or the workings of an institution. There are many examples: Germany under Nazism is only the most startling. Jesus's "so it will be" looks like a prophecy of how things will turn out in a post-Christian West.

46 While he was still speaking to the crowds, right then,
his mother and his brothers took a place outside, as they
were looking to speak with him. 47 Someone said unto
him:

"Look, your mother and your brothers are standing outside, looking to speak with you."

48 He, replying, said to him:
"Who is my mother? And who are my brothers?" 49
And stretching out his hand toward his disciples, he
said: "Look: my mother and my brothers—50 since
whoever does the will of my Father who is in heaven,
that is the one who is my brother, and sister, and
mother."

Jesus likely made such a demonstration at various times, in various circumstances, and to make slightly different points. Matthew notices that on this occasion it explains the extension of the preaching of the Kingdom of Heaven to the Gentiles. Jesus's family represents the blood relationships among the people of Israel—exactly the sort of thing that was invoked at the beginning of Matthew's Gospel with the genealogy. But that family can grow to include anyone who simply becomes his disciple, like the disciples there.

A New Mode of Correspondence to Teaching: The Significance of Parables

We are understanding this part of Matthew's Gospel to be an account of how the Deposit of the Incarnation was applied to the account of the human race, and indeed the parables that come next are about receptivity to a deposited word.

A parable is a comparison formed by placing an image alongside the reality one wants to illuminate. Jesus constantly taught in such images: salt of the earth, children piping in the marketplace, the sign of Jonah. What marks out the comparisons here as special is that they are all completely general in relation to the human race and are meant to explain our human condition. They are about the world, the devil, angels, the course of history, and a final judgment. Moreover, they all concern a common good, the Kingdom of Heaven, which is no longer defined by a series of covenants with a specific people, as Israel was.

These parables are puzzles. Those who heard them would have wanted to figure out what they meant—as the disciples show us. Therefore, they also challenge those who hear them later, like us, to look for interpretations of them in their own lives. In this sense, they propose a new mode of discipleship. Discipleship for a follower of Christ is not a matter of learning a legal code and carrying out its instructions. Rather, it is about intelligently discerning, in one's own facts and circumstances, how a generally true analogy is to be realized. Remember again the future imperative form of that other parable "Be good bankers." The parables are a mode of teaching suitable for a new kind of follower, who is meant to be repeatedly taking an initiative.

13:1 At that time, Jesus, after leaving his house, sat beside
the sea. 2 Many crowds gathered around him, so that,
getting into a boat, he sat down. The entire crowd stood
on the shore. 3 He spoke many things in parables, saying:

> **"Attend! A sower went out to sow. 4 As he sowed, some**
> **fell along the road, and the birds of the air came and**
> **consumed it.**
> **5 "Yet other seeds fell on rocky ground, where they did**
> **not have not much earth, and they sprang up**
> **immediately, because they had no depth of earth. 6**
> **Once the sun rose they were scorched, and, as they had**
> **no roots, they withered up.**
> **7 "Yet others fell among thorns: the thorns grew up**
> **and choked them.**

8 "Yet others fell on good ground, and they produced fruit, some a hundred, some sixty, and some thirty. 9
Let him who has ears listen."

It takes about thirty-five seconds to speak the above words. If said only once, no one could memorize them, grasp them, or be in a position to decode them. No one would be able ponder the parable later. Even someone who was paying careful attention could not profit from it. We presume otherwise because the words are written down for us and familiar. One must conclude, then, that the parable had to have been taught in such a way that the crowds would memorize it. Perhaps the disciples went out among the crowd and repeated and reviewed it among smaller groups. If so, they would likely have been assisted by outlines of the parables on wax tablets, the composition of which Matthew would have overseen.

10 The disciples came up and said to him:
"Why do you speak to them in parables?"
11 Replying, he said to them:
"Because to you it has been given to know the mysteries of the Kingdom of Heaven, but to them it has not been not given."

A first reason Jesus gives is to distinguish between the Twelve and his followers among the crowd, in the way they receive his teaching.

12 "For whoever has, to him it will be given, and he will be superabundantly supplied, but whoever does not have, even what he has will be taken away from him."

A second reason is to highlight that when following Christ, one is either building upon past progress and moving forward quickly, or losing ground at an increasing pace because of a matching retraction of grace.

> **13 "I speak to them in parables for this reason, that although they see, they do not see, and although they hear, they do not hear, nor do they understand."**

A third reason is that his teaching in parables is itself a parable. It shows that resourcefulness, application, and love of truth must be brought to bear in grasping his teachings. Parables show this because they are originally hidden and reveal their meaning only through our efforts. It has always been the prerogative of divinity to speak obscurely.

> **14 "And the prophecy of Isaiah is completely fulfilled, which says:**
>
> **'In listening you will listen and you will not**
> **understand,**
> **and when you look, you will look and you will not see.**
> **15 For the heart of this people has become obese,**
> **and with their ears they hear only muffled sounds,**
> **and they have closed their eyes shut,**
> **lest they should see with their eyes,**
> **and hear with their ears,**
> **and understand in their heart,**
> **and they should convert, and I should heal them.'"**

completely fulfilled—The Greek term here is used in business contexts to connote "paid in full." It means more than simply to fulfill. It means to fulfill in such a way as to match exactly what was expected or due. This is the only occurrence of this word in any Gospel. The prophecy (Isaiah 6:9–10) is completely fulfilled because people had indeed made themselves stupefied when in the presence of God himself, to block themselves from hearing him and needing to convert. Implicit in Jesus's use of this phrase, then, is an assertion of his divinity.

> **16 "Happy are your eyes, because they see, and your ears,
> because they hear. 17 Amen I tell you, many prophets and
> just men have yearned to see the things you are beholding,
> and they did not see them, and to hear the things that you
> are hearing, and they did not hear them."**

"Happy" is *makarios*, just as in the beatitudes—a foreshadowing of the beatific vision. But to those who have, more shall be given:

> **18 "You—therefore—hear the parable of the sower. 19
> When anyone hears the word of the Kingdom and fails to
> understand it, the evil one comes and snatches away what
> was sown in his heart. This is the one sown along the road.
> 20 The one sown on rocky terrain—this is someone who
> hears the message, and immediately with joy receives it. 21
> Yet he lacks roots within him—he is, rather, ephemeral—
> and when troubles come, or persecution, because of the
> word, he immediately spurns it. 22 As for the one sown
> among thorns, this is someone who hears the message, yet
> the cares of this world and the deceit of wealth choke the
> word. He fails to produce fruit. 23 But the one sown on
> rich soil—this is someone who, after he hears the word and
> understands it, bears fruit and produces, as the case may
> be, a hundred, sixty, or thirty."**

The next parable is recorded only by Matthew:

24 Another parable he put before them saying,
"The Kingdom of Heaven is like a man who had sown
good seed in his field. 25 When his men were sleeping,
along came his enemy, and he oversowed weeds among
the wheat, and he went away. 26 When the crop had
sprouted, and after it had produced fruit, then there
appeared also the weeds. 27 The servants of the master
of the house came to him and said: 'Lord, didn't you
sow good seed in your field? What caused it to have
weeds?' 28 He said to them: 'A hostile man has done
this.' The servants say to him, 'Then do you want us to
go out and collect the weeds?' 29 He says, 'No, so that
in collecting the weeds you don't uproot the wheat
along with them. 30 Leave them to grow together until
the harvest. When it is harvest time, I will tell the
harvesters, "Collect first the weeds and bind them into
bundles to burn. As for the wheat, gather it together
into my barn."'

is like—This is actually a past tense in Greek ("has been like"), which is used in prophecies sometimes to emphasize the utter certainty of what is being said.

bind them into bundles—That is, the weeds lose both their freedom and their individuality.

31 Another parable he put before them, saying,
"The Kingdom of Heaven is like a grain of mustard seed,
which a man took and sowed in his field. 32 Although it is
smaller than any other seed, when it has grown, it is

greater than any plant, and it becomes a tree, so that the birds of the sky come and make nests in its branches."

any plant—The mustard tree (*Salvadora persica*) a berry-bearing evergreen that can grow over twenty feet tall, is highly versatile—its small branches can be used as toothbrushes, its leaves are edible, and its oil is useful as a detergent.

33 Another parable he told them: "The Kingdom of
Heaven is like leaven, which a woman took and concealed
in three measures of flour, until the whole was leavened."

concealed—Yeast (really sourdough starter) is visible only when it is on its own. Once it is mixed in with the moistened flour, it disappears. It is essential to the operation of the yeast that it disappear. If it remained separate, it would not be doing its work.

34 All these things Jesus spoke in parables to the crowds.
He would say nothing to them without a parable, 35 so
that what had been said through the prophet might be
fulfilled, when he said:

"I will open my mouth in parables;
I will utter things hidden from the foundation of the world."

36 Then, dismissing the crowd, he went into his house,
and his disciples came to him, saying:

"Make the parable of the weeds of the field clear for us."

37 Replying, he said,

"The one sowing the good seed is the Son of Man.
38 The field is the world. The good seed—these are the

> **sons of the Kingdom. The weeds are the sons of the evil**
> **one. 39 The hostile man who has sown them is the**
> **devil. The harvest is the end of the world. The**
> **harvesters are angels. 40 So then, just as weeds are**
> **collected and burned with fire, so it will be at the end**
> **of the world: 41 the Son of man will send his angels;**
> **they will collect from his Kingdom everything that**
> **gives scandal and those who act lawlessly. 42 They will**
> **cast them into the furnace of fire, where there shall be**
> **weeping and gnashing of teeth. 43 Then the just will**
> **shine out like the sun, in the Kingdom of their Father.**
> **Let him who has ears listen."**

To explain a parable, then, one assigns referents for each of its elements, and then one assigns analogous actions among those referents. How would we interpret, then, the next two parables, which are recorded only by Matthew? The first clause in each gives the elements, the next the actions.

> **44 "The Kingdom of Heaven is like a treasure concealed in**
> **a field, which a man, after having found it, conceals, and**
> **out of joy leaves it and sells all that he has, and he buys**
> **that field.**
> **45 "Again the Kingdom of Heaven is like a man who is a**
> **merchant looking for fine pearls, 46 who when he had**
> **found one pearl of great value, went and sold all that he**
> **had, and he bought it."**

Both involve someone who finds something of great value and then leaves it to sell all that he has in order to buy it, coming back to it now as something that belongs to him—indeed, as the only thing that belongs to him. In the first, finding it is incidental to his purpose; in the second, he finds the very sort of thing he was looking for. In the first, he has to hide it because everyone else will recognize its value if they see it; in the second, we presume, only he has recognized its extraordinary value. In both cases, someone makes a trade; in both cases, he improves his position markedly by the trade. In both cases, someone must act decisively and take a risk, even risking everything.

> **47 "Again the Kingdom of Heaven is like a net cast into**
> **the sea, pulling into it things of every kind, 48 which,**
> **when it was full, after drawing it up upon the shore and**
> **sitting down, men collected the good kinds of things into**
> **vessels, while the rotten kinds they threw out. 49 This is**
> **how it will be at the end of the world. The angels will go**
> **out, and they will mark off the bad men from the just**
> **men. 50 They will throw them into the furnace of fire,**
> **where there shall be weeping and gnashing of teeth."**

weeping and gnashing of teeth—We saw this phrase before (Matthew 8:12; 13:42). Matthew uses it three other times (Matthew 22:13; 24:45; 25:30), and Luke only once (Luke 13:28). The phrase is nowhere found in the Old Testament. We are inclined to interpret "weeping" to mean sorrow and "gnashing of teeth" to mean regret, or perhaps seething anger, and yet it seems likely that the gnashing, from the usage of the term in the Septuagint, is displayed rather by the tormenters of these unfortunates than the unfortunates themselves. See Job 16:9, Lamentations 2:16, and Sirach 51:3.

> **51 "Have you understood all these things?"**
> **They tell him,**

"Yes."
52 He said to them:
"That is why every scribe instructed in the Kingdom of
Heaven is like a man who is a master of a house, who
brings out of his treasure box new things and old."
53 It happened, when Jesus had finished these parables,
that he moved on from there.

The Full "Crediting" of the Incarnation to the Gentiles

It is a striking phenomenon of the Gospels that in places their narrative pace quickens toward a conclusion. In these last episodes of Part One of Matthew's Gospel, before Peter's profession, all of the trends of this section accelerate. Jesus's final rejection begins with his hometown.

54 Coming to where he grew up, he was teaching them in
their synagogue, with the result that they were
overwrought, and they said,
"How did he get this special knowledge and these
powers? 55 Isn't he the carpenter's son? Isn't his
mother called Mary, and James, Joseph, Simon, and
Jude his brothers? 56 Aren't all his sisters with us? So,
how did he get all these things?"
57 They started to take offense at him. Jesus said to them,
"A prophet is not without honor—except where he
grew up and in his own household."
58 He did not do many powerful works there because of
their lack of faith.

where he grew up—Literally, his "fatherland"—Nazareth, a tiny rural village.

were overwrought—Literally, they were driven out of their senses.

what is the source—They apparently fear demonic influence; perhaps the Pharisees had played on these fears.

brothers and sisters—Typical language for an extended family.

14:1 It was at that time that Herod the Tetrarch heard the report of Jesus.
2 He told his servants:

> **"This guy is John the Baptist. John himself has risen from the dead. That is why divine powers are at work in him."**

This guy—He refers to him contemptuously.

Herod believes the reports of the miracles, but he spins a superstitious story to account for them, born of a guilty conscience. What next follows explains the guilty conscience. Matthew's formulation of it has the tone of a memorized, formulaic account of the episode, common to the early Church:

**3 It was because Herod had arrested John, tied him up,
and locked him away in a prison, because of Herodias, the
wife of Philip his brother. 4 This was because John kept
saying to him: "It is not permissible for you to have her." 5
Although he wanted to put him to death, he feared the
people, because they held him up as a prophet. 6 But at a
celebration of Herod's birthday, the daughter of Herodias
performed a dance among them, and she ingratiated
herself to Herod, 7 which led him to promise, on an oath,
to give her whatever she might ask. 8 Prompted by her**

mother, she says, "Give me on a platter the head of John
the Baptist." 9 And, although distressed, the King on
account of his oaths and dinner guests, ordered that it be
given, 10 and he sent and beheaded John in prison. 11 It
was brought to him, his head on a platter, and it was given
to the girl, and she brought it to her mother. 12 And his
disciples came and took the corpse and buried it. And
they came and told Jesus about it.

Matthew shows little concern with the personal details of this episode compared with Mark (6:17–29). For him, John's violent death and his disciples coming to Jesus are the important facts. As mentioned, John's death stands for the point of transition of the crediting of the Deposit to the account of the human race as a whole.

13 Jesus, after he heard them out, withdrew by boat to a
desolate place on his own. The crowds, after hearing of it,
followed him on foot from their towns. 14 After getting
out of his boat, he saw a great crowd, and he felt
compassion for them. He healed their sick. 15 With
evening approaching, his disciples came to him, saying,

> **"This place is desolate, and the day has already gone by. Tell the crowds that they may go, so that by departing for the villages they can purchase food for themselves."**

16 But he said to them,

> **"There is no need for them to depart—you give them something to eat yourselves."**

17 They tell him:

> **"We don't have anything here, except five loaves and two fish."**

18 He said:
"Bring them to me, here."
19 After instructing the crowds to sit down on the grass, taking the five loaves and the two fish, and looking up to heaven, he blessed the loaves, broke them, and gave them to his disciples, and the disciples to the crowds.

blessed, broke, and gave—The language suggests a repeatable ceremony.

After verse 17, the other synoptics portray the disciples as wondering how they might go out and purchase bread; in Mark, they even calculate that two hundred denarii would be needed (Mark 6:37; see also Luke 9:13). One might have supposed that Matthew the tax collector would have been interested in their calculations about purchasing bread and would have conveyed these details also. But it is telling that he doesn't—because the proposed purchase of bread was fantastical and unrealistic. It is exactly the sort of thing that a "man of business" like Matthew would dismiss and omit. He was there, and he witnessed it, but he found their ideas embarrassing.

20 And they ate, all of them. They ate until they were full. And they picked up the leftover bits, twelve baskets full.
21 Those who ate, the men alone, were about five thousand in number, not counting women and children.
22 Jesus immediately told his disciples that they must get into the boat and go before him, until he sent the crowds away, to the other side.

The walking on water, which comes next, is obviously a deliberately crafted miracle. There was no other reason why the Lord did not get into the boat with them, except to display this power. But why did he do it just then? It seems that he wanted to link the feeding of the five thousand with walking on water, but why? And how would he have linked them?[2]

> **23 And after he sent the crowds away, he went up to the mountain alone, to pray. When evening came, he alone was there. 24 But the boat was already many stadia distant from land, tossed about by the waves (as there was an opposing wind).**

he alone was there—Therefore, he is the source of this account, and therefore he can be the source of much of what is in the Gospels. As explained in the preface, it is an interesting question regarding which details of Matthew's Gospel were put there upon the explicit instruction of Jesus.

stadia—A stadium was 600 feet. So, one would think, the boat was at least a mile from where it left the shore.

> **25 In the fourth watch of the night, he came to them walking upon the sea. 26 The disciples, when they saw him walking upon the sea, were in a panic and said, "It is an apparition!" They shrieked in terror.**

shrieked—The Greek word was meant to imitate the cry of frogs and birds, like our word "croak"—that is to say, the disciples screamed like animals in sheer terror.

---

2 The examination of these questions is not relevant here. But see Pakaluk, "Lord of Substance."

27 Immediately he spoke to them and said:
"Be of good courage. It is I. Do not be afraid."
28 Peter said in reply,
"Lord, if it is you, command me to come to you upon the water."
He said,
"Come!"
And coming down out of boat, Peter walked upon the water and went to Jesus.

It is I—Literally, "I am" (Greek *egô eimi*), the name of God (see Exodus: 3:14).

if it is you—Literally, "if you are"; possibly, "if you are real and not a phantom."

coming down out of the boat—And perhaps down a steep slope of water too if the boat was on the crest of a wave.

30 But when he saw the wind, he was afraid, and as he started to drop in, he shrieked and said:
"Lord, save me!"
31 Straightaway Jesus stretching out his hand took hold of him. He says to him,
"Small-faith man. What was your point in doubting?"
32 And after they had gone up into the boat the wind
faded away. 33 The men in the boat paid him homage,
saying:
"Truly, you are Son of God."

saw the wind—Saw the waves made by the wind. In violent storms waves can reach up to ten feet tall there.

drop in—The words suggest he was plunging down fairly quickly, like someone thrown in.

what was your point—Jesus uses a stronger expression than "why?" He asks a question about practical rationality and "good banking" even in extreme situations.

34 After crossing to the other side, they came to the land
of Gennesaret. 35 The men of that place, recognizing him,
sent out word to that entire area. They brought him
everyone with infirmities. 36 What they did was to
implore him simply to be able to touch the hem of his
garment. Whoever touched it was healed.

simply to be able to touch the hem of his garment—Perhaps the story of the woman healed of a hemorrhage had reached them, and they thought to imitate her.

Now, Matthew gives another important step in the opening up of the Gospel to the pagans, the nullification for them of the Jewish dietary laws:

15:1 It was at that time that scribes and Pharisees came to
him from Jerusalem and said,
2 "On what basis do your disciples violate the tradition
of the elders? Because they fail to wash their hands
when they eat bread."
3 Replying, he said to them,
"On what basis do you also violate a commandment of
God because of your tradition? 4 For it was God who
said, 'Honor your father and your mother' and 'Let the
one who curses father or mother meet his end with
death.' 5 But you say, 'Once someone has told his father

or mother, "It is gifted—whatever you might have been
owed from me," he must not honor his mother and
father.' You cancel the word of God, on the basis of
your tradition. 7 Hypocrites! Rightly did Isaiah
prophecy about you when he said, 8 "These people
honor me with their lips, but their heart keeps far from
me. 9 In vain do they worship me, when the teachings
they teach are the dictates of men.'"
10 Calling the crowd to him, he said:
"Hear and understand. 11 It is not what goes into the
mouth that defiles man, but what comes out of the
mouth—this defiles man."
12 Then his disciples approaching, said to him,
"Do you realize that when the Pharisees heard this
statement they found it offensive?"
13 Replying, he said,
"Every plant that my Father in heaven has not planted
will be uprooted. 14 Leave them alone; they are blind
guides. If a blind man guides a blind man, both will
fall into a pit."

a blind man guides a blind man—The first blind man here would be the disciples, since they wanted to correct the Pharisees, and yet they did not even understand what the Lord had taught.

15 Peter, replying, said to him,
"Lead us through this parable."

Lead us—Peter uses a word that originally meant "showing the way" and came to mean "explain." He has grasped that he is blind and needs a sighted person to lead him. His question is not absurd, since it would be natural for him to think that "what comes out of the mouth" meant spittle. But how does spitting defile a man?

16 He said,
"At this point do even you lack sense?"

Jesus uses here an interesting word meaning "at this decisive moment," *acmê,* which indicates that they have reached a crucial time. Note how "even you" testifies to Peter's special role among the Twelve. The phrase sets the scene for Peter's profession, which comes soon after.

17 "You fail to see that everything that goes into the
mouth makes its way into the gut and is discharged
into a latrine? 18 But the things that come out of the
mouth proceed from the heart, and these defile man.
19 Because from the heart proceed evil plans, murders,
adulteries, fornications, thefts, false testimonies,
slanders. 20 These are the things that defile man, but
eating with unwashed hands does not defile man."
21 Jesus left there and withdrew toward parts of Tyre and
Sidon.

withdrew—That same word used of the magi and of Joseph, which connotes escaping danger. Tyre and Sidon are major Gentile cities; as we said, as if by force, the Gospel now comes to the Gentiles. Matthew keeps accelerating the pace of his narrative:

22 And consider this—there was a Canaanite woman from
those districts who kept shouting out, saying,
"Have mercy on me, Lord, son of David! My daughter is
badly affected by demons." 23 He answered her not a word.

This pagan addresses him as "Lord" and "son of David," in contrast with the Pharisees. But his disciples do not see this and are simply annoyed. He seems at first to agree with them, stating the original object of his mission, and yet then he gives the basis for its extension (as per Matthew 12:50):

His disciples coming began to implore him, saying,
"Tell her to go away, because she follows us shouting."
24 Replying, he said,
"I have not been sent except to the lost sheep of the house of Israel."
25 Coming, she adored him, saying,
"Lord. Help me."
26 Replying, he said,
"It is not good to take the bread of the children and throw it to the dogs."
27 She said,
"I agree, Lord. As for the dogs, they eat the morsels that fall from the table of their lords."

She agrees with him entirely but then states the alternative way in which the dogs, nonetheless, receive food: not from its being thrown to them, but from its falling; and not because it is taken away from the children, but because it comes directly from the table of its master or "lord." This pagan woman has articulated an accurate analogy of the way in which pagans would now have access to the Kingdom of Heaven.

Note that when she "adored" him in verse 25, she took the posture of a dog, crouching down and probably kissing his hands. As mentioned, that is what the Greek word for adoration originally meant.

28 Then Jesus, replying, said to her,
"Dear lady, your faith is great. Let it be done to you just as you wish."
Her daughter was cured from that hour.

dear lady—Literally, "O woman," but the addition of "O" here expresses delight and surprise, which must be conveyed, and the term for "woman" in the context is highly ennobling. Compare what this woman says to Mary's fiat (Luke 1:38). There is a rough parallel. Mary's profession of faith was the occasion of the Deposit, while this woman's profession is presented as the occasion of the crediting of that Deposit to the Gentiles. And, therefore, Jesus addresses her as if she were his mother.

The active power of her faith is revealed here in the sense that, next, the morsels do fall from the Lord's table explicitly, in the feeding of the four thousand, which takes place in Gentile territory:

29 Moving on from there, Jesus went along the Sea of
Galilee. Ascending a mountain, he took a seat there. 30
Many crowds came to him with their dumb, blind, lame,
maimed, and many others. They strew them at his feet,
and he healed them.

31 *strew them at his feet*—The term means to toss and suggests a certain abandonment and even carelessness; the impression is that these pagan people were a bit rough with the sick, while also tending to show a certain abasement toward the person they regarded as a Great Lord.

The same miracles done among the Jewish people are now done among the Gentiles, and they—in contrast to the residents of Jesus's hometown, the Pharisees, and others—take a first step in converting:

31 Its effect on the crowd was that they were awestruck, seeing the dumb speaking, the maimed restored, and the lame walking and the blind seeing, and they gave glory to the God of Israel.

32 Jesus, summoning his disciples, said,

"I am moved with compassion toward the crowd, because it is three days now that they are staying here with me, and they do not have anything to eat. To send them on their way fasting—that is not something I want, as they might faint on the way."

33 His disciples say to him,

"How are we to acquire in a desert enough bread to satisfy such a crowd?"

34 Jesus says to them,

"How many loaves do you have?"

They said,

"Seven. And a few small fish."

35 And instructing the crowd to become seated on the
ground, 36 he took the seven loaves and the fish and,
giving thanks, he broke the loaves and kept giving them to
his disciples, and the disciples to the crowds. 37 Everyone
ate. Everyone was full. They picked up seven baskets full
of the surplus fragments. 38 Those who ate were four
thousand men, not counting women and children.

The Gentiles, then, because of their faith will receive the same graces and will be admitted to the Lord's supper.

kept giving them—Matthew's use of the imperfect tense here for continued past action points to the answer to a question that someone might have raised: at what point were the loaves and fish miraculously created? Not, from this language, as they were pulled out of the baskets by the people, but, rather, as the empty baskets were brought back to the Lord and then sent out again full.

39 Dismissing the crowds, he got into the boat. He went to the region of Magadan.
16:1 The Pharisees and Sadducees, coming to test him, asked him to show them a sign in the sky.

They want a display involving what was called at the time "meteorology"—some wonder in the heavens, like a comet or meteor, perhaps because the sky was regarded as intermediate between the divine and the terrestrial. Or perhaps they thought, especially now that he was in pagan territory, they could draw him out and expose him as assisted by demons, because the sky, in pagan religions, was often regarded as the realm of power of the evil one. Baal, after all, was a storm god. The name Lucifer is likely derived from a sky god.

2 Replying, he said to them,
"In the evening, you say, 'Fair weather, because the sky burns red.'
3 In the morning, 'A storm today, because a threatening sky burns red.' You know enough to discern the face of the sky. But you have no ability to interpret the signs of the times?
4 An evil and adulterous generation seeks after a sign, and a sign will not be given to it, except the sign of Jonah the prophet."

You know enough to discern—If they intended to draw him out, suspecting him of being a devotee of Baal, he brings them down to earth with prosaic examples of what we would call "science."

signs of the times—In its literal meaning, this means something easier in nature to forecast than daily changes in weather, such as seeing when winter is approaching. The change in "season" that Jesus alludes to is presumably what his followers will soon see, too, beginning with Peter's profession, with the start of those events that lead inexorably to the Passion, which is the sign of Jonah.

an evil and adulterous generation, etc.—This second statement confirms and seals the first.

5 His disciples, crossing to the other side, had forgotten to
bring bread. 6 Jesus said to them:

> **"Look out for and guard against the leaven of the Pharisees and Sadducees."**

7 They started puzzling among themselves, saying, "Is it
that we failed to bring bread?" 8 Jesus, knowing it, said,

> **"Why are you puzzling, you little-faiths, over your not**
> **bringing bread? 9 Do you still fail to understand—do**
> **you fail to remember the five loaves for the five**
> **thousand and how many baskets you picked up? 10 Or**
> **the seven loaves for the four thousand and how many**
> **large baskets you picked up? 11 How do you fail to**
> **comprehend that it was not about loaves that I said to**
> **you, 'Be on guard against the leaven of the Pharisees**
> **and Sadducees.'?"**

12 That was when they understood that he did not say to
be on guard against leaven for loaves of bread, but rather
against the teaching of the Pharisees and Sadducees.

This interesting exchange shows that the disciples have now learned to see physical bread, when referred to and used by the Lord, as a type and symbol of higher things, including teaching. It also shows that he anticipates that they will be playing a role with regard to the pagans, whose territory they are now leaving, analogous to that of the Pharisees and Sadducees in regards to the Jews. He does not want them in their ministry to the pagans to carry over the same hypocrisy.

This passage brings to a close this first half of Matthew's Gospel. The Deposit has been fully received and recognized in the appropriate account, and in conclusion Jesus warns, in effect, *exercise vigilance against yourselves, so that you do not permit this thing of value to become corrupted*. Be good bankers of this Deposit.

The Dividing Point: Announcement of the Passion (Matthew 16:13–28)

Now we come to the dividing point in Matthew's Gospel, in his account book of the household of God, between the pages dealing with the Deposit and the pages dealing with payables and indeed the Payment. As mentioned, we are at the exact halfway point of his account.

16:13 Jesus, coming into the parts of Caesarea Philippi, asked his disciples, saying,
"Who do men say that the Son of Man is?"
14 They said,
"Some say John the Baptist. Others, Elijah. Yet others, Jeremiah or one of the prophets."
15 He says to them,
"Who do you say that I am?"
16 Replying, Simon Peter said,
"You are the Christ. The Son of the Living God."

Peter's profession on behalf of the disciples settles the accounting of the Deposit. An analogy today would be a CEO's signing off on the financials.

17 Jesus, replying, said to him,
"Happy are you, Simon Bar-Jona, because flesh and blood have not revealed it to you, but my Father in heaven.

Matthew was not naïve about the ultimate basis of his careful credentialing. He understands that credentialing, or documented believability, in divine matters is not without divine assistance. It cannot be a mere human project. From the very start, after all, he proposed that we believe in Mary's word and believe the magi about the miraculous appearance of a star, and so on.

18 "And I say to you, that you are Peter, and upon this rock I will build my Church.

It hardly seems plausible, given the crucial point at which "you are Peter" is located in Matthew's Gospel and how it answers "you are the Christ," that Jesus's statement is not a solemn act with lasting consequences.

And the gates of hell will not prevail against it. 19 I will
give to you the keys of the Kingdom of Heaven.
Whatever you bind upon earth will be bound in heaven. If you loose upon earth, it will be loosed in heaven."

19 And then he commanded his disciples not to tell anyone that he was the Christ.

In no way did he want to appear to be drawing the Passion down upon himself by imprudence.

> **21 It was from that time that Jesus began to show his disciples that it was necessary for him to depart for Jerusalem and to suffer many things from the elders and chief priests and scribes and to be put to death and on the third day to be raised.**

"From that time," as we saw, is Matthew's own marker of the turning point in his Gospel. He is saying, now we turn the page, from receipts to expenditures. Recall that the commentator Bengel, in his *Gnomon*, observed that "from that time" divides the Gospel of Matthew in two.

> **22 Peter, taking him aside, began to remonstrate with him, saying,**
> **"All will go well for you, Lord! This will not happen to you."**

Peter's first act after Matthew turns the page in the ledger is a misunderstanding of God's providence and perhaps even an expression of softness and cowardice.

> **23 Turning, he said,**
> **"Get behind me, Satan! You are a stumbling block to me because you are weighing not the things of God but of men."**

Peter is not weighing divine goods in his assessment of what would be good for his Lord. He is being a poor banker.

24 Then Jesus said to his disciples,
"If anyone wishes to come after me, let him deny
himself and take up his cross and follow me.

The Lord then tells them, in contrast, what sorts of transactions they should engage in:

25 "Because anyone who would choose to save his soul
will lose it. And whoever would lose his soul for the sake
of me will find it. 26 For what good will it do for a man if
he should gain the whole world for the loss of his soul? Or
what will a man give in exchange for his soul?

To be good bankers, they should trade away the good of their biological life for the higher good of eternal life. And then he promises a final reckoning of their compensation:

27 For the Son of Man will come in the glory of his Father
with his angels, and at that time he will pay back to each
man according to what he did.

This economic reasoning, of losing one's soul to find it again, will govern Part Two of Matthew's Gospel. All of the expenditures that are required by Jesus's followers in ordinary life will display this reasoning.

Finally, Matthew reports a saying that leads directly to the Transfiguration. Jesus speaks of "some" because he will take only some of them up the mountain:

28 "Amen I tell you that there are some standing here who will not taste death before they see the Son of Man coming in his kingdom."

Therefore, the Transfiguration is to be interpreted as a pledge of this final compensation. Yet for all that, it is a pledge, too, that requires faith for its assurance.

PART TWO

The Payment (Matthew 17:1–27:66)

The value of the economic interpretation of Matthew's Gospel that I am proposing is found in three things: structure, logic, and details. First is the structure of the two halves of the Gospel according to Matthew, the Deposit and Payment, which correspond to the Incarnation and Passion, and then the halves within those halves. Second is the new insights it yields into the logic of Christian life when understood as a project of good banking. Third is in the small details of Matthew's writing that come to life when seen against his background of accounting and bookkeeping. These three differ in prominence for various passages in Matthew's Gospel.

Part Two of Matthew's Gospel is dominated by the Payment, the "Saint Matthew Passion," in which the Redeemer purchases back the human race from the debt of sin and slavery. One can quibble about where precisely the account of the Passion begins, but I shall take it to begin at Matthew 20:17, which is the third foretelling by the Lord of his Passion. (After all, three is complete.) I take this verse to mark the start of the second half of Part Two.

Here Matthew's goal as the narrator of the Passion, and mine as an interpreter, is to let the Passion speak for itself, so that it can play its intended role in the divine economy. An economy we said is transactional, dynamic, and progressive. We saw in the introduction that the Passion, which is a buying back (or "Redemption") by which we are saved, implies a threefold debt among those who are bought back. We called these a "debt of justice," a "debt of love," and a "debt of zeal." These sources of Christian "banking activity" and entrepreneurship going forward will become living motivation in someone to the extent that he recognizes the value of the Payment—remember what Peter and Paul said: "You were purchased at a great price." That value and that price are shown in the Passion itself. That is why my goal in interpreting the second half of Part Two of Matthew's Gospel must be to let the Passion speak for itself, so that the price is made clear.

But the first half of Part Two is different. Remember that on the interpretation proposed here the focus of Matthew's Gospel changes with Peter's profession. Matthew's Gospel is written on the pattern of a *codex accepti et expensi*. Part One of his Gospel is accordingly all about receipts: how the divine nature is deposited into the human nature and how that deposit becomes credited, not to the household of the Jewish people merely, but rather to a new household, the Kingdom of God, which embraces the Gentiles and indeed the entire human race. Correspondingly, Part Two is all about expenditures. It is dominated, as was said, by the Lord's redemptive expenditure of his life for our salvation. But remember that Part Two is introduced with the teaching of Jesus: "If anyone wishes to come after me, let him deny himself, and take up his cross, and follow me" (Matthew 16:24). That is to say, anyone who wishes to be his disciple must live a life consisting of similar expenditures. His followers are invited to join his project of purchasing back. They are to become, as is said in the Christian tradition, coredeemers with Christ. But how is this to be done? Some of his followers will indeed be crucified like him, or martyred in some way, but most will not.

Jesus explains how, in a sequence of teachings on marriage, accepting children, the use of the body and of wealth, the use of time, and the use of authority. Here, Jesus is instructing his followers how to be good bankers in the ordinary realities of daily life, by making sacrifices—payments—in imitation of him, to accrue true value. What is typically described by Christians as "taking up one's cross" under the economic interpretation becomes "making a payment of one's life" to attain genuine value, in imitation of the great Payment set down by Christ.

First Part of the Second Part: Payments Looked for in the Followers of Jesus (Matthew 17:1–20:19)

17:1 After six days, Jesus takes Peter and James with him,
and John his brother, and leads them up to a high
mountain by themselves. 2 His form became changed in
their presence. It beamed light—his face—like the sun.
His garments became brilliant, like light. 3 And
amazingly Moses and Elijah became visible to them,
speaking with him. 4 Peter, in response, said to Jesus,

> "Lord, for us to be here is a good thing. If you want, I will construct three shelters here: one for you, one for Moses, and one for Elijah."

5 While he was still speaking, amazingly, a shining cloud
cast a shadow on them, and, right then, a voice from the
cloud says,

> "This is my son, my beloved, in whom I am well pleased. Listen to him."

6 The disciples, hearing it, fell on their faces and were
extremely afraid. 7 Jesus went to them and, touching
them, said,

> "Get up, and do not be afraid."

8 Raising their eyes, they saw no one except Jesus himself,
alone. 9 While they were coming down from the
mountain, Jesus commanded them, saying,
"Tell no one this vision before the Son of Man has been raised from the dead."

Occurring just before the Passion, the Transfiguration shows clearly the great value of the price paid ("my son, my beloved") and his complete freedom in giving up his life as payment.

Tell no one—Since they had no idea of the occasion or time that they might tell it, it seems plausible that someone would have made a written record, right then. (With some guesses as to abbreviations, the record would come to about five hundred characters—a suitable length for a typical wax tablet.) Of the Evangelists, John is the only one who does not recount the Transfiguration, but he is also the only one who witnessed it and the only one to whom it was directly commanded, "Tell no one."

I interpret Matthew's inclusion of the next episode, following immediately upon the Transfiguration, as saying in effect that the disciples, approaching the Passion (see verse 22 below), are meant to preserve with faith and trust the clear vision that they had just enjoyed of Jesus's precious worth. Only in this way will they be able to discern the value of the Payment.

14 As they were coming to the crowd, a man approached
him, falling on his knees before him.
15 "Lord, have mercy on my son,"
he said.
"He is a lunatic and deeply disturbed. He often throws himself into a fire and often into the water.

16 I brought him to your disciples, and they lacked the power to cure him."
17 "What a faithless and twisted generation!" Jesus said in reply.
"How long shall I be with you? How long shall I endure you? Bring him here to me."
18 Jesus rebuked the demon. It went out from him. From that hour, the child was cured.
19 It was at that time that the disciples, approaching Jesus, said in private,
"Why did we lack the power to cast it out?"
20 He says:
"Because of the smallness of your faith. Amen I tell you, if you have faith as of a seed of mustard, you will say to this mountain, 'Move, from here to there!' and it will be moved. And nothing will be impossible for you.
21 [But this kind does not go out except in prayer and fasting.]"

faith as of a seed of mustard—A mustard seed is the size of a period at the end of a sentence. The phrase has been interpretated in two ways in the tradition. Some commentators say that Jesus is implying that the disciples had very little faith, since even faith as small as a mustard seed would have been sufficient. Others say that the littleness of a mustard seed stands merely for the hiddenness of any degree of faith.

Verse 21: Many of the earliest and most authoritative manuscripts omit this verse. Along with other scholars, I interpret it as apostolic commentary, not as quoted speech of Jesus.

22 Jesus said to them when they were all gathered together in Galilee, "Soon it will happen that the Son of Man is betrayed into the hands of men. 23 And they will kill him. And on the third day, he will arise." They were very deeply distressed.

24 As they were coming to Capernaum, the collectors of the two-drachma temple tax approached Peter and said:

"Your teacher doesn't pay the two drachma tax?"

25. Peter says,

"Oh yes, he does."

And as he was entering the house, Jesus anticipated him, saying,

"Simon, what is your view? The kings of the earth— from whom do they collect duties, or a poll tax? From their sons, or from strangers?"

26 Just as he was saying, "From strangers," Jesus said to him,

"Presumably, then, the sons are free. 27 But so that we give no cause for scandal, go to the sea, cast a line, and take the first fish that you catch. When you open its mouth, you will find a four-drachma coin. Take it and give it to them on behalf of me and of you."

As one might expect, this episode about taxation, with its precise language about different types of taxes and duties, is found only in the Gospel of Matthew. It is a humorous incident, characteristic of Peter—improvising, he tells the tax collectors that of course his Master pays the tax, and then he goes to Jesus to confirm whether what he said was true. We need posit no further reason for this episode's inclusion than that it took place at this time and that the tax collector evangelist found it fascinating. However, it does anticipate the answer to Pilate's question later on, "Are you the king of the Jews?" (Matthew 24:11).

18:1 At that time, the disciples came to Jesus, saying,
"So, who is greater in the Kingdom of Heaven?"
2 Calling to his side a little child, he stood him in their midst, saying:
"Amen I tell you, unless you turn and become like children, you will not enter into the Kingdom of
Heaven. 4 And so, whoever humbles himself, like this child—this is the one who is greater in the Kingdom of Heaven."

We can interpret Jesus to be setting down now some fundamental virtues for his followers that would enable them to be good bankers. He had just spoken about the importance of faith. Now he speaks about the importance of humility.

who is greater—The disciples mean "which of them is greater than which others?" They are violating that important principle in the spiritual life—do not make comparisons. But when the Jesus replies that "whoever humbles himself . . . is greater," he means instead that he is "greater than he was before made himself into a child." Jesus thereby explains what holy ambition, holy greed, looks like.

Now he turns to lessons about proper valuation.

5 "And whoever receives one such child in my name receives me."

That is, the value of any child is the same as his own value. If you love him and are his follower, you will value each child as you value him.

He uses a "child" here as his example, rather than any grown human being, because a child stands for each of us in God's original creation. This creation and this child are wrecked by sin, and the Savior came to save and re-create this wrecked world. He is setting forth the value of what he purchased back in paying the price of his life.

> **6 "But whoever should lead into sin one of these little ones who have faith in me, a better result for him would be for a large millstone to be hung on his neck and that he be drowned in the depths of the sea."**

He came to save from the wreckage of sin. So to induce to sin is to work against his purposes. It follows that, on a proper valuation of the goods in play, his followers should trade away any good rather than induce anyone to sin.

> **7 "Woe to the world because of its inducements to sin! For it is necessary that inducements to sin should come. But woe especially to the man through whom an inducement to sin does come!"**
> **8 "But if your hand or your foot should lead you to sin, cut it off and toss it away from you. It is better for you to enter into life maimed or lame than to be thrown, possessing two hands or two feet, into that fire that is everlasting.**
> **9 And if your eye leads you to sin, pluck it out, and toss it away from you. It is better to enter into life a one-eyed man than to be thrown, possessing two eyes, into the Gehenna of fire.**

As we saw, in the divine economy, bodily goods should of course be traded away without hesitation when this is necessary to avoid the loss of one's spiritual goods.

> **10 "Be careful that you do not despise one of these little ones. For I tell you that their angels in heaven are gazing continually at the face of my Father in heaven. 11 For the Son of man has come to save that which was lost."**

Children were despised as a rule in the ancient world because they were immature, ignorant, and unskilled. Jesus is affecting a transvaluation of values; he is aware that he is doing so, and he declares to his followers that he is doing so.

> **12 "What is your view? Suppose there is a man with one hundred sheep and one of them wanders off. Won't he leave the ninety-nine in the mountains and go look for that wandering sheep? 13 And if he finds it? Amen I tell you that he finds more joy in it than in the ninety-nine that had not wandered off. 14 In this same way, nothing could be found good in the sight of your Father in heaven that would result in the loss of one of these little ones."**

Through the economic interpretation, he is saying that he would gladly make the Payment, which is the Passion, to purchase back just one of us. It follows that each of us should look upon the Passion that is to come as undertaken for each one of us personally—from which will follow, for each of us, the aforementioned debt of justice, debt of love, and debt of zeal.

The foregoing parable of the shepherd looking for his lost sheep naturally raises the question of how equal brothers should look for a lost sheep who is one of their own. That is why Jesus next proposes what has become known as "fraternal correction" as the appropriate means. In this practice, "two or three together" have the authority of Jesus himself.

15 "If your brother should sin against you, go and—
between you and him alone—convict him of it. If he
listens to you, you have gained your brother. 16 If he does
not listen to you, take one or two with you, so that 'every
word might stand on the testimony of two or three
witnesses.' 17 If he will not listen to them, tell it to the
church. And if he will not listen to the church, he should
be to you as if a pagan or tax collector. 18 Amen I tell you,
what you bind on earth will be bound in heaven, and what
you loose on earth will have been loosed in heaven. 19
Again I tell you, that if two of you agree on anything that
they ask for, it will be done for them by my Father in
heaven."

as if a pagan or tax collector—That is, shunned and, more formally, excommunicated.

"For where two or three are gathered together in my
name, there I am in their midst."
21 This provided the occasion for Peter to go up and say to
him,

"Lord, up to how many times if my brother should sin against me should I forgive him? Up to seven times?"

If fraternal correction provided the occasion for Peter to ask a next question, then the cases must be different. In the former case, the corrected brother does not listen; that is, he does not repent and ask forgiveness, and so he is shunned. In this new case, he does repent when corrected and asks forgiveness.

> **22—Jesus says to him,**
> **"No, I am telling you, it's not as many as seven times.**
> **Rather, it's as many as seventy times seven times."**

Luke tells us that Jesus on at least one occasion taught us to forgive one another up to seven times (Luke 17:3–4). Seven is the perfect number and would mean "as often as necessary." Peter apparently remembers this teaching and repeats it, looking for confirmation.

In reply, Jesus strengthens that teaching, not by increasing the number (as seven was already perfect) but by changing the dimensionality. Seventy times seven is (7 x 10) x 7, or (7 x 7) x 10. Seven is a perfect number. A square number (which would have been pictured as a plane) represents solidity and stability. Multiplied by ten, it forms a rectangular prism. Take ten to represent the Ten Commandments. Seven represents fulfillment. (7 x 7) x 10, then, suggests a stable attitude of perfection of forgiveness, which testifies to the Ten Commandments precisely in our forgiving contrite brothers and sisters who have offended against these commandments.

This teaching and the parable that now follows are found only in the Gospel of Matthew:

> **23 "That is why the Kingdom of Heaven is comparable to**
> **a king who wanted to settle accounts with his servants. 24**
> **As he began reconciling them, one debtor to the amount**
> **of 10,000 talents was brought to him. 25 Because he**

lacked the means to repay it, the lord ordered that he be sold, and his wife and his children, and everything that he had, and that repayment be made. 26 The servant in response fell down, prostrated himself, and said, 'Show me forbearance, and I will pay everything back to you.' 27 Moved with deep compassion, the lord of that servant released him and forgave his debt."

settle accounts—The verb (literally, "to take up together") is used in this technical accounting sense only by Matthew and nowhere else in extant Greek.

that he be sold . . . and repayment be made—The king is contemplating a bankruptcy of his household and liquidation of all of its assets to satisfy creditors as much as possible.

A talent was the equivalent of 6,000 denarii, which was equivalent to about 6,000 days' wages. Therefore, he owed about 164,000 years of wages. Think of it as $32 billion, on the assumption that an average wage is $50,000 per year. It is a vast sum of money and a vast debt.

The servant in some sense wanted to repay it and said that he would. Nonetheless, he had no realistic hopes of doing so, and his plea that the lord be patient was effectively a plea that the lord accept whatever the servant could pay over an indefinite time.

There are many interesting, implicit details here; for example, since we are told that the lord released him, the servant must have already been bound and on his way to jail and enslavement when he fell to the ground to beg.

28 "But after he had left, that same servant located one of his fellow servants who owed him a hundred denarii. Taking hold of him, he started to strangle him: "Pay back whatever you owe!"

A hundred denarii was not an insignificant sum, about 100 days' wages. But it is the proportion which matters. He is strangling someone who owes him 1/600,000th of what he owed his lord.

located—Again, an interesting detail in passing—he did not simply stumble upon this debtor but sought him out.

whatever you owe—The Greek suggests that he did not even have a definite idea of what he was owed. He did not seek out this man because he had been involved in any process of settling accounts within his own household—nor could he have been, because he could not have been aiming to settle his own accounts in general without keeping in mind what had happened with his account with his lord. Matthew's language is very precise here!

29 "His fellow servant in response fell down and implored
him, saying, 'Show me forbearance, and I will repay you.'
30 He did not consent, but, leaving him, he had him
thrown into prison until he should pay back what he owed."

show me forbearance—This detail confirms that we are dealing here with the question of forgiving another when that person is contrite.

leaving him—Another fascinating and important detail—he must distance himself from his fellow to treat him in this way, and he goes away and hires someone to do this dirty work for him.

until he should pay back—If he ever does; the Greek leaves it open that maybe he never could make repayment and would stay in prison until he died. His creditor does not care.

31 "His fellow servants, seeing what had happened, were deeply distressed and came and explained clearly to their lord everything that had happened. Then, summoning

him, his lord says to him, 'You evil servant. That entire
sum that you owed me I forgave you, when you implored
me. 33 Was it not also binding upon you to show mercy to
your fellow servant, just as I had shown mercy to you?' 34
Filled with anger, his lord handed him over to the prison
torturers, until such time as he should repay the entirety
of what he owed."

prison torturers—Not just jailers, but jailers with the specific function of inflicting corporal punishment on prisoners.

until such time—He would be released if indeed he could pay, but he never could and never would.

35 "So also your Father in heaven will do to you if you do
not forgive, each his brother, from your hearts."

I have rendered this sentence literally so that you can see how interesting its construction is. It speaks to all his followers at once ("you" and "your hearts" are plural), but forgiveness is I-thou and personal, "each his brother." At the same time, someone who fails to forgive separates himself from the community.

This parable, unique to Matthew, wonderfully shows, then, how a new economy of forgiving and asking forgiveness in turn is established, once each person's own vast debt is remitted by Christ through his Passion.

Marriage naturally follows as a subject after forgiveness because in general the closer people are to each other, the more frequently they will offend each other and need to exercise forgiveness, and marriage is the closest human relationship. Remember we are interpreting the next section of Matthew's Gospel (chapter 19) as explaining how in ordinary life the followers of Christ will be asked to take up their cross—that is, as good bankers to undertake to make a payment of their lives, in imitation of him.

19:1 What happened when Jesus finished saying these things,

Most commentators make a big deal of the fact that Matthew uses the phrase here, "finished saying these things," which they say marks what he has just taught as one of the five discourses interwoven among accounts of deeds and of miracles. But they fasten upon something superficial and fail to locate correctly these teachings in the structure of Matthew's Gospel. These teachings, we have seen, are meant to convey attitudes of proper valuation among "good bankers." They convey facts about fundamental trades for value in the divine economy. Under the economic interpretation, we apprise them correctly by pointing out that they fall within the first half of Part Two, the Payment, and concern the Cross—that is, the payments assumed by the followers of Christ.

is that he left Galilee and came to the districts of Judea beyond the Jordan. 2 Many crowds followed him, and he healed them there.
3 Pharisees approached, testing him, saying, "Is each and every cause a valid one for divorcing one's wife?"

The question presupposes a preexisting list of causes. It is a trap because they think by taking a position he will inevitably make enemies.

4 Replying, he said,
"Have you not read that he who created 'in the beginning' 'made them male and female'?"

And he stated:

> **"It is for the sake of this that a man shall leave behind his father and his mother, and he shall become melded with his wife, and they shall be two in one flesh. 6 The result is that they are no longer two but one flesh. What, therefore, God has yoked together, let man not separate."**

Jesus gives the basis for why marriage for his followers will be a taking up of the Cross. Marriage involves a death to self. Recall, "if someone loses his life for the sake of me, he will find it" (Matthew 10:39). Marriage for his followers is a transaction in which at the price of one's former self one purchases a new reality, that is, the one flesh union. This death of self is "for the sake of" Jesus because the one flesh union that results is an image of the Incarnation and of his relationship to the Church.

in the beginning—The good available in marriage derives from the original creation; therefore, it is a divine good.

leave behind—The price of entering marriage is to "spend" the self and whatever interests it had prior to marriage.

in one flesh—This is the precious new reality purchased at the price of one's former self.

To be a good banker as regards one's own marriage is to see that it offers something very precious to be purchased, but that it can only be purchased at the price of one's own former self. The purchase is irrevocable if one's former self has truly been given up as the price of attaining it.

7 They say to him,

> **"Why then did Moses issue the command to give her a document of alienation and put her away?"**

8 He tells them,
"Because Moses, in view of the hardness of your hearts, yielded to you, to put away your wives. But 'in the beginning' it was not so. 9 And I am saying to you that anyone who divorces his wife—I except the case of fornication—and would marry another commits adultery."

yielded to you—He did not "permit" or "allow" it, as if it were blameless, but made a legal provision to minimize harm, given that they were set on something evil.

I am saying to you—He speaks from the point of view and with the authority of the Creator.

I except the case of fornication—See Matthew 5:32.

10 His disciples tell him:
"If the valid claim that a man can bring against his wife is like that, it is better that he not marry."

They are referring to "the case of fornication" as the only valid claim of separation.

They see clearly that marriage without recourse to divorce is of necessity a Cross; it requires a death to self, and they recoil from it.

Divorce as construed here is fundamentally a flight from the Cross, for at least one of the parties. Marriage conceived of as allowing for divorce is a relationship that never embraced the Cross. Similarly, a marriage with a prenuptual agreement would be very poor banking, as it would be a trade for no lasting value.

Jesus therefore immediately clarifies that the only reason he accepts a disciple's avoidance of the Cross of marriage is to accept another, more challenging Cross:

11 He said to them,
"Not everyone can find a place for what you say, but only those to whom it has been given. 12 There are eunuchs,
after all, who were begotten that way from their mother's womb. There are eunuchs, too, who have been made so by men. And there are eunuchs who made themselves so, on account of the Kingdom of Heaven. Let the man who can find a place for it, find a place for it."

from their mother's womb—Implicit in this language, of course, is that we exist already in the womb.

made themselves eunuchs—Dedicated celibacy in the service of God was unknown in Judaism. But the future practice of Christian celibacy is so settled in the mind of the Lord that he speaks of it as in the past already, the so-called prophetic past. Note that he desires it strongly.

13 This was the time when little children were brought to him so that he might place his hands on them and pray.
The disciples took them to task. 14 But Jesus said,
"Allow the little children to come to me and do not prevent them, because the Kingdom of Heaven consists of such as these."
15 When he had placed his hands on them, he departed from there.

Given the sequence here, marriage-celibacy-children, we ought to conclude that those followers of the Lord who are in a one-flesh union, precisely in imitation of the Lord, will welcome children and not prevent them. The welcoming of children, too, involves a Cross and a death to self.

the Kingdom of Heaven consists of—This is strong language that implies that to welcome a child is to welcome the Kingdom of Heaven. As we saw, it is to welcome Jesus. Being a good banker, then, as regards welcoming children in marriage, is a matter of making expenditures of time, money, and indeed of one's very self to acquire in one's own household the spiritual good that is to welcome the Kingdom of Heaven.

The sequence continues with a consideration of the next great item in ordinary life, material possessions:

16 Now look!—one man, coming up to him, said,
"Teacher, what good shall I do that I might possess eternal life?"
17 He said to him,
"Why do you ask me about the good? One there is who is good."

This is as if to say, "Do you understand what your question means when you pose it to me? Are you prepared to hear my answer to this question?" But Jesus tests him, gently:

"If you want to enter into life, keep the commandments."

To keep the commandments, Jesus had explained in the Sermon on the Mount, is to fulfill their spirit and purpose, not merely to meet a bare minimum. Yet the young man clearly does not understand this.

18 He says to him,
"Which ones?"

Jesus said,
> **"'Do not murder.' 'Do not commit adultery.' 'Do not steal.' 'Do not bear false witness.' 19 'Honor your father and your mother.' Also, 'Love your neighbor as yourself.'"**

Simply to enumerate which commandments is not to say what keeping them amounts to in its fulness. That matter is still left undecided.

20 The young man says to him,
> **"All of these I have kept. What do I still lack?"**

Apparently, he has "kept" them only in the sense of not violating them grossly. By the way, only now does Matthew identify him as a "young" man, presumably to emphasize that he is starting out in life. He has his whole life before him. The trade that will be offered him is a trade of his life.

21 Jesus said to him,
> **"If you want to be perfect, go and sell what you have and give to the poor, and you will have treasure in heaven, and come follow me."**

Jesus tests his disposition in keeping the commandments by offering him the ultimate trade. He places the pearl of great price right before him, as if to say, "If you have been keeping the commandments for the right purpose, then here is your chance. I myself am offering myself to you as your good. Show your prudent good sense, here and now, by trading away the whole world in exchange for me!" Note that the man had no reason to think that Jesus was making him a standing offer. For all he knew, he would have only this one chance to become a disciple.

**22 But the young man, after hearing this proposition,
went away distressed because he had many possessions.**

proposition—The Greek word is *logos*, which refers to the proposed *quid pro quo*. It is an accountant's use of the word. The proposition was to purchase the *One there is who is good*, the greatest good that exists, for funny money. But the young man declines.

23 Jesus told his disciples,
"Amen, I tell you, a rich man only with difficulty will
enter into the Kingdom of Heaven. 24 Once more, I am
telling you, it is easier for a camel to pass through a
needle's eye than for a rich man to enter into the
Kingdom of God."
The disciples, when they heard this, were greatly
amazed, and said,
"Who then is in a position to be saved?"
26 Jesus looked directly at them. He said,
"It is not something within the power of men. But with
God, everything can be done."

If the man had said yes to the proposition, he would rightly have attributed his decision to the grace of God breaking through, not his own will. To adopt the outlook of the divine economy is not to embrace Pelagianism, the view that we can save ourselves through our own efforts.

27 This was the occasion on which Peter said to him, in response,
"Look at us: we have left everything and have followed you. What, in consequence, will there be for us?"

Peter is alert to the question of compensation for service, expressed here and in other verses by the Greek word, *misthos*, and therefore he asks the Lord about it. Rather than rebuking him, Jesus affirms that he and the others will indeed be compensated. Tellingly, only Matthew's Gospel records Peter's question and this answer by Jesus:

28 Jesus said to them,
"Amen I tell you, you who have followed me: in the new creation, when the Son of Man will sit on his throne of glory, you too shall sit on twelve thrones and judge the
twelve tribes of Israel. 29 And everyone else who has
left houses or brothers or sisters or father or mother or children or fields for the sake of my name will receive a hundredfold and will inherit life everlasting.

will receive a hundredfold—The principle "seek first the kingdom of God, and his justice, and all these things shall be added to you" (6:33) applies not simply to how one sets priorities in life but also to choices, transactions, and sacrifices. These are blessed with greater wealth, in its proper context, than if one solely seeks wealth.

He wants his disciples to believe this truth and to undertake risks upon it in faith. But he immediately explains an important qualification about this compensation, which he teaches with a parable:

30 "But many who are first will be last, and many last who will be first.

> **20:1 "For the Kingdom of Heaven is like a man, the
> master of a house, who went out at the break of dawn to
> hire workers for his vineyard. 2 After he had gained their
> consent, on condition that they be paid a denarius for the
> day, he sent them into his vineyard.**

This parable with its details of work and compensation is given only by Matthew. Note Jesus's precise language for the terms of the agreement. Note that the workers are sent, just as apostles are sent ("apostle" means "sent man"). Therefore, all of his followers are sent and are apostolic.

> **3 "When he went out around the third hour, he saw other
> men standing there in the market, with nothing to do. 4
> He said to them, 'You go too into the vineyard, and I will
> pay you what is fair.' And they departed.**

The third hour is nine in the morning. The work day is well underway. If these men hadn't been hired yet, they could reasonably presume they would not get hired. Therefore, anything they receive in payment makes them better off than if they just stood around doing nothing. That is why the steward does not need to agree with these other men in advance on the precise wage but can leave things up in the air. The fact that they depart shows that they consent to leaving their compensation up to the steward and his sense of fairness. And he explicitly sends them into the vineyard, just as the first group, with "You go too."

> **"When he went out around the sixth and around the ninth
> hour, he did the same thing. 6 Around the eleventh hour,
> when he went out, he found other men standing around,**

> **and he says to them, 'Why have you been standing around here all day with nothing to do?' 7 They say to him, 'Because no one has hired us.' He says to them, 'Go into the vineyard, you also.'**

He seems to hire this last group more for their sake than because he needed the work. The eleventh hour is five o'clock in the afternoon, just one hour from the end of a typical twelve-hour work day.

> **8 "When evening came, the lord of the vineyard tells his steward, 'Call the workers, and pay them their compensation, beginning with the last and ending with the first.' 9 When the workers who had been hired around the eleventh hour came up, they received one denarius each. 10 When the workers who had been hired first came up, they expected to receive more, and they received the wage of one denarius each—they as well. 11 As they took it, they complained to master of the house 12 and said: 'These last ones have worked one hour. You have made them equal to us, we who have borne the burden of the day and its blazing heat.' 13 He said to one of them in reply, 'My friend, I do you no injustice. Did you not agree on one denarius with me? 14 Take what is yours and go. It is my wish to pay this last one as I pay you. 15 Am I not permitted to do as I wish with what belongs to me? Or is your eye wicked because I am good?'**
> **16 "In this way the last will be first and the first last."**

It is easy to see why Matthew the apostolic "good banker" would have been fascinated by this parable and why he took pains to preserve it for us. Let us note ten interesting details and implications of the parable:

- First, a new person is introduced near the end, the steward. In terms of narrative logic, there was strictly no need for this person to be introduced, since if it wasn't below the dignity of the master of the house to hire the workers in the first place, it wouldn't be so for him to give them their pay. Thus, this little detail shows Our Lord's bias, as it were, toward the use of intermediaries who are strictly speaking not necessary.
- Second, all the workers work in the employ of the master of the house. No one receives compensation who did not first work.
- Third, all of them receive payment *precisely in response to* the work that they did. They are all receiving compensation (*misthos*). What is at issue is simply the amount of that compensation. No one is described as being given a gift
- Fourth, the lord responds to the grumbling by addressing just one man among the first workers. He does not address them as a group. There is no collective bargaining. His words to this one man represent what he would say to each of them individually. Strikingly, he greets him in goodwill and even calls him "my friend."
- Fifth, consent and agreement as to what is fair in a market transaction is affirmed here as establishing a suitable standard of justice for such a transaction ("I do you no injustice").
- Sixth, the fruit of someone's labor is really his ("take what is yours").
- Seventh, private property ("what belongs to me") is a realm in which we promote and thereby express what we regard as good. Note in this regard that the master of the house expresses both

the good of compensation (that is, payment in return for service) and the good of equality, through his use of his property.

- Eighth, those who started to work last are called forward to receive their compensation first.
- Ninth, those who started to work first are presented as being tempted to grumble; they must be on guard against seeing things in a warped way, whereas those who started to work last have no such problem.
- Tenth, the parable gives us no reason to think that the master would hand out denarii to men who were standing idle in the market, so as to treat them as equal to those who worked, or to give a denarius to anyone who refused to go to the vineyard after he was told to go. That is to say, the logic of the parable is the logic of payment for services rendered, not of receiving gifts for doing nothing at all.

The obvious interpretation of the parable is that: both someone who starts to follow Jesus as a young man, undergoing many trials and persecutions over a long life, and someone who starts following him as an old man, maybe even on his death bed, would receive the same reward. They are both compensated for service, even though their service is unequal.

One might ask: "Where in this interpretation do we find room for the idea that, as seen in the parable, some receive their payment *before* the others?" It seems difficult to do so without introducing some such doctrine as a state of purgatory. If such a doctrine is introduced, then it could happen that those who began serving late in life entered immediately into heaven, while those who began serving early might need to spend time first in purgatory.[1]

1 Perhaps that follows on the grounds that someone who begins service late has less occasion for committing sins that would need to be purged.

So ends the first part of the Payment half of Matthew's Gospel on expenditures in ordinary life, the daily Cross taken up by the followers of Jesus. Now Matthew proceeds to enter the Payment into his ledger of the household of God.

Second Part of the Second Part: The Payment of the Redeemer (Matthew 20:19–27:66)

The Saint Matthew Passion begins here:

> **17 As he was going up to Jerusalem, Jesus took aside**
> **just the Twelve and said to them on the road, 18 "Pay**
> **attention now. We are going up to Jerusalem. The Son of**
> **Man will be handed over to the chief priests and scribes.**
> **They will condemn him to death. 19 They will hand him**
> **over to the Gentiles to mock him, to scourge him, and to**
> **crucify him. And on the third day, he will arise."**

pay attention now—"Behold." Observe that in a parallel passage, instead of "behold," Luke puts it as, "Let these words sink into your ears" (Luke 9:44). This suggests that Luke too saw that "behold" would have different senses depending upon the context.

What comes next is what I call a bridge passage because it deals with the use of authority. It can therefore be viewed as coming at the end of a sequence and completing that sequence:

marriage-children-wealth-time-honor-authority

It therefore bridges the two halves of Part Two of Matthew's Gospel.

As with all those other realities, so here, to be a follower of Jesus in the exercise of authority requires a death to self and an embrace of the Cross. One gives up or pays out "lording it over others," and its material rewards of wealth and power, in order to purchase the spiritual goods attained through humble service.

And yet the passage ties into Matthew's account of the Passion, because the reader (in his own ambitions) is meant to identify with the two brothers and say with them, "I am capable of drinking that cup." The passage is meant to elicit from the reader an act of will to join Jesus in his Passion.

20 Then the mother of the sons of Zebedee came to him
with her sons, doing him homage, to supplicate
something of him. 21 He said to her,

> **"What is it that you want?"**

She says to him,

> **"Make it so, with your word, that these two sons of mine will be seated, one on your right, and the other on your left, in your kingdom."**

She approaches in great humility and presumably thought she was doing him honor and showing their worthiness by her attitude. Her language sounds carefully prepared. She takes herself to be making a great act of faith ("with your word"). She assumes but does not say that the older son will be on the right.

22 Replying, Jesus said,

> **"You do not know what you are requesting. Are you capable of drinking the cup that I am about to drink?"**

They say to him,
"We are capable."
23 He says to them,
"My cup you shall drink—indeed. But to be seated at my right or at my left—it is not mine to give, but it is for those, rather, for whom it has been prepared by my Father."

you are requesting—Through the use of the plural "you," he takes the sons to be making the request, using their mother as an intermediary. The way that these Apostles act when they want something very much testifies to Jesus's fondness for intermediaries, seen many times already.

Are you capable—Jesus is presuming what might be called the "principle of compensation": no honor, no reward, without a paying of the price.

for whom it has been prepared by my Father—This seems a very polite way of saying that those places have already been assigned in God's providence. (Will they belong to Saints Peter and Paul? Or some great saints still to come? We do not know.)

24 The ten, when they heard this, were indignant at the two brothers. 25 Jesus called them over and said,
"You know that the rulers among the nations lord it over those nations, and their great ones give the orders.
26 It shall not be like that among you. Rather, whoever wants to become great among you will be a servant to all of you. 27 And whoever wants to be first among you will be the slave of all of you.—28 just as the Son of Man did has not come to be served, but to serve, and to give his life as a ransom in exchange for many."

The ten were "indignant at the two." The Lord himself shares the feeling of the ten that the brothers had erred in making their request, but then he speaks so as to include the ten in the same error. He could see their hearts directly, but to us their indignation is meant to serve as a sign that they have a similar ambition.

the ten—Matthew does not write simply "the others": that is, their offices are so important that any subset of them properly goes by the corresponding number ("the five," "the three," and so on).

their great ones give the orders—The Lord seems to be referring to a hierarchy of power, with rulers being ruled over in turn by "great ones" among them, the way that a Roman governor would be ruled over in turn by the great emperor. He proposes, instead, a descending hierarchy of service, where the lowest, who is the "greatest," would be "the servant of the servants of God."

to give his life—In this descending hierarchy, Peter, "the first," when he was martyred, must have viewed his death as "for" the other Apostles, and they, when they were martyred, as "for" the other followers of Christ.

as a ransom in exchange for many—Here, at the beginning of his section on the Payment, Matthew gives the basic exchange and basic form of exchange of the divine economy.

As Jesus is about to enter the city, the two apostles asking for seats of power, who do not see what they are asking for, are contrasted with two impoverished blind men, who are seated on a dusty road and ask only to see. They are granted the gift of sight. This incident, too, prepares the reader for the Passion. The reader is meant like them to ask to see what follows, in its depth and meaning:

29 As they were leaving Jericho, a great crowd followed him. 30. And look!—two blind men, seated by the side of

the road, hearing that Jesus was passing by, cried out, saying,

"Have mercy on us, Son of David!"

31 The crowd scolded them to be quiet. But they cried out all the more, saying,

"Have mercy on us, Lord, Son of David!"

32 Jesus, standing still, called out to them, saying,

"What is it that you want me to do for you?"

33 They say to him,

"Lord, that our eyes be opened once again."

34 Moved with great compassion, Jesus touched their eyes, and they regained their sight immediately, and they followed him.

One of the blind men was called Bartimaeus (Mark 10:46–52). His name would have been known if both became followers. Matthew alone mentions that there were two, presumably because he wanted to emphasize the parallel with the sons of Zebedee through giving the number two. Correspondences of numbers are more salient for him than for the other evangelists; moreover, like a good accountant, he likes to put pairs together and match them to each other.

Jesus's Passion, however, in the strict sense of actual suffering, begins with his entry into Jerusalem because he is immediately rejected by the authorities, which would have been extremely painful to him—for the indignity and injustice of it.

21:1 When they got near to Jerusalem and they came to Bethpage next to the Mount of Olives, that was when Jesus sent two disciples and said,

> **2 "Go into the village across from you, and straightaway you will find a donkey that is tied up and a colt along with her. Untie them and bring them to me. 3 If anyone says something to you, you will say that their lord has need of them and at once he will send them."**

4 This took place so that what was spoken through the prophet might be fulfilled when he said,

> **5 "Say to the daughter of Sion, see, your king is coming to you, meek and sitting upon a donkey and upon a colt, the foal of a beast of burden."**

6 The disciples went and did as Jesus directed them. 7
They brought the donkey and the colt. They laid their cloaks on them. He took a seat upon them.

upon them—"Them" can mean in the Greek either the cloaks or the animals. It seems absurd to say that he sat on two animals at once. So, interpreters have liked to insist that "them" must refer to the cloaks. However, it is just as absurd to say that he sat on various cloaks at once, if the cloaks were placed on two different animals. It is better to say, therefore, that the donkey and the colt, although distinct animals, are being counted as a single unit by Matthew simply on the authority of the prophecy. Remember that, for Matthew, a prophecy in the manner of a literal obligation has the power to bind things together, just from the fact that something was written down.[1] Jesus, of course, was physically seated on only one of them, the donkey, but the two were bound together by the prophecy.

---

1 Apparently, even a Hebraic poetic parallelism has this force if it is written down in the manner of a prophecy.

Note Matthew's careful accounting of the different crowds with different roles:

> **8 The greater part of the crowd laid their cloaks down on the road. Others cut down branches from the trees and laid them down on the road. 9 The crowds that went before him and that followed him kept shouting out and said,**
>
> **"Hosanna to the Son of David. Blessed is he who comes in the name of the Lord. Hosanna in the highest."**
>
> **10 Once he had entered into Jerusalem, the whole city was shaken and said,**
>
> **"Who is this?"**
>
> **11 The crowds kept saying,**
>
> **"This is the prophet, Jesus—the prophet from Nazareth of Galilee."**

Matthew uses the same verb that is used for earthquakes, "was shaken" ("turned topsy-turvy," we might say). There was a shock to the city's perception, such that it was as if the city as a whole was posing a question.

> **12 Jesus entered the temple. He threw out all the vendors and buyers in the temple. He overturned the tables of the money-changers and the chairs of the dove-sellers. 13 He tells them,**
>
> **"It is written, 'My house shall be called a house of prayer** [compare with Isaiah 56:7]**. But you make it a den of robbers** [compare with Jeremiah 7:11]**."**
>
> **14 Blind and lame men came to him in the temple, and he healed them.**

The language is precise. They are not a "den of thieves," because thieves steal secretly by deception, while robbers steal openly by coercion. The robbery in this case was the open taking by force by men, of the place, time, and attention that should have been devoted to God. They force bad trades. Pilgrims who had traveled to Jerusalem to offer sacrifices needed to buy animals and change their coins into the local currency. This business could have been conducted in the streets. Instead, it was monopolized and brought into the temple so that the priests could take a share of the profits. Presumably, they did so under the cover of devotion ("animals purchased in the temple itself will make better offerings," and so forth). Presumably, too, the priests and temple guards were aware that they were imposing something wrongly, out of greed, and suffered from bad consciences. Hence, when Jesus threw the merchants out, he was only imposing what their consciences were saying should be done.

Blind and lame men would spend their days in the temple because they could not do work. As if to make a point about what sort of "business" should take place in the temple, he heals them and of course does not charge a fee.

15 When they saw this, the amazing things that he did,
and the children shouting out in the temple and saying,
"Hosanna to the Son of David!" the chief priests and the
scribes were indignant. 16 They said to him,

> **"Do you hear what these children are saying?"**

Jesus says to them,

> **"Yes. Have you never read that 'out of the mouth of babes and nursing infants you have furnished yourself with praise'?"**

17 He just walked away from them and exited, outside the
city, to Bethany and stayed there.

I have tried to bring out three details of the Greek: First, Matthew emphasizes that now the chief priests and scribes have seen with their own eyes what they had merely heard, until now, from the reports of others. They themselves see the healing of the blind men, and yet they carp about the children.

Second, the adults seemed to have been cowed enough not to repeat these messianic words inside the temple, but the children continue to speak because they "don't know any better."

Third, Matthew was clearly impressed by how Jesus simply walked away from the persons there who held the highest authority, without asking their leave or being dismissed by them or anything like that, and yet in no way was that unseemly.

18 In the morning, as he was going back to the city, he was
hungry. 19 Seeing a lone fig tree along the road, he went
up to it and found nothing on it except leaves, that's all.
He says to it:

> **"May you not bear fruit from now on through eternity."**

And presently the fig tree withered away.

Here Jesus acts out rather than speaks a parable. The incident is a living parable. His curse, "through eternity," reveals that it is a parable, because fig trees do not last forever. This living parable requires that there be a leafy and healthy tree that nonetheless lacks figs.[2] So, Jesus approached a fig tree, knowing that it did not have figs and cursed it for not having them. What, then, does the parable mean?

2 Of course, it would have been bizarre if a leafy and healthy tree, in the season for figs, did not have any. That is why Mark believes he needs to explain—it was not the season for figs (Mark 11:13).

Perhaps his human hunger stands for his divine hunger for holiness in Jerusalem. Jerusalem was presumably flourishing admirably in a merely human sense: it had leaves but no fruit. But when the Lord came to visit it, it lacked the supernatural fruit it ought to have had.

The disciples seem to have grasped the parable, because they wonder not that he cursed the tree for not having figs then, but that his words affected the tree:

20 When the disciples saw it, they wondered at it and said,
"How did the fig tree become withered so quickly?"
21 Jesus said to them in reply,
"Amen I tell you, if you have faith and do not doubt,
not only will you effect a change in a fig tree, but if to a
mountain you should say, 'Be lifted up, and be hurled
into the sea,' it will take place. 22 Everything that you
ask for in prayer, if you have faith, you will receive."
23 After he went into the temple, the chief priests and
elders of the people came up to him as he was teaching

Mark says this happened while he was walking about in the temple (Mark 11:27); we may infer that, like Aristotle, Jesus liked to teach while he walked.

and said,
"By what authority are you doing these things? Who
has endowed you with this authority?"
24 Jesus said to them in reply,
"I will ask you as well, for my part, just this one thing,
which, if you tell me, I myself will tell you also by what
authority I do these things. 25 The baptism of

> **John—where did it come from? Was it from heaven, or from men?"**
>
> **They started debating among themselves and said, "If we say, 'from heaven,' he will say to us, then why did you not believe him? 26 While we need to fear the crowd if we say, 'from men,' because all of them take John to be a prophet."**
>
> **27 They said to Jesus in reply,**
>
> **"We do not know."**
>
> **And he himself, for his part, said to them:**
>
> **"Neither do I tell you myself by what authority I am doing these things."**

Usually, translators just have "Neither do I tell you by what authority." But the "myself" is marked in the Greek, which suggests, "My deeds witness, Scripture witnesses, the crowds know, the children say it, your eyes should tell you. I needn't tell you *myself*."[3]

What follows is yet another passage that mentions tax collectors and that is preserved solely by Matthew. We can interpret it as confessional. Matthew is revealing to us that it was because he first believed in John the Baptist that he was in a position later to believe in the Lord:

> **28 "What is your view? A man had two sons. Going to the first, he said: 'Child, go out today. Work in the vineyard.' 29 He said in reply, 'I don't want to.' But later, thinking better of it, he went out. 30 Going to the other, he told him the same. He said in reply, 'I will, sir,' and he did not go out. 31 Which of the two did the will of the father?"**

---

3 This is another perceptive observation offered by Eric Mader.

They say to him,
"The first."
Jesus says to them,
"Amen I tell you that tax collectors and prostitutes are
going into the kingdom of God before you. 32 Because
John came to you along the path of righteousness, and
you did not believe him. Yet tax collectors and
prostitutes did believe him. And you, when you saw
this, did not even think better of it later and start to
believe in him."

Now begins a series of parables that try to shock these religious authorities out of their animus against him:

33 "Another parable—listen to it. There was a man, the
master of a house, who planted a vineyard. He placed a
fence around it. He dug a wine press in it. He built a tower.
He rented it out to farmers. He left for another land. 34
When harvest time drew near, he sent his servants to the
farmers to take the fruit that was his. 35 The farmers took
his servants, and one they beat, another they killed, and
yet another they stoned. 36 Once more he sent other
servants, more in number than those at first, and they
treated them in the same way. 37 At last he sent his son to
them, saying, 'They will not dare show disrespect to my
son.' 38 But the farmers, when they saw the son, said to
themselves, 'This one is the heir. Come, let us kill him and
take possession of his inheritance.' 39 And they took him
and threw him out of the vineyard and killed him. 40
When the lord of the vineyard comes, what will he do to
those farmers in response?"

41 They say to him,
"He will utterly and badly destroy those evil men and rent out the vineyard to other farmers, who will render its fruits to him at their due times."
42 Jesus says to them,
"Have you never read in the scriptures, 'The stone that
the builders rejected has become the chief cornerstone.
This was from the Lord, and it is wonderful in our
eyes'? 43 This is the reason, I am telling you, that the
Kingdom of God will be taken away from you, and it
will be given to a nation that yields the fruits of that
Kingdom."

The next verse is omitted by some ancient authorities and therefore also in some translations. I think we must understand it as Jesus's pointing to himself, rather than referring back to "the chief corner stone." Think of him as pointing to himself while he says it. He says it to warn the chief priests and Pharisees, because he knows their plots:

44 "If someone falls upon this stone, he will be broken. And if it falls upon someone, it will grind him to powder."
45 When the chief priests and Pharisees had heard his
parables, they knew that he meant them. 46 Although
they were looking for a way to arrest him, they were afraid
of the crowds, since they accepted him as a prophet.

They were afraid of getting stoned by the people, which is why they tried to find a basis to stone him instead.

22:1 In response, Jesus again spoke to them in parables
and said,

> **2 "The Kingdom of Heaven is comparable to a man, a**
> **king, who prepared a wedding feast for his son. 3 He**
> **sent his servants to call those who had been invited to**
> **the feast. They did not want to come. 4 Again he sent**
> **other servants and said, 'Tell those who have been**
> **invited, "See, I have prepared my banquet. My oxen**
> **and fattened cattle have been slaughtered, and**
> **everything is set. Come to the wedding feast!"' 5 But**
> **they had no interest and went off, one to work his field,**
> **another to work his trade. 6 The rest, after seizing his**
> **servants, abused and killed them. 7 The king became**
> **angry. Sending his army, he destroyed those murderers**
> **and burned down their city. 8 After that, he tells his**
> **servants, 'The wedding feast is set. Those who had been**
> **invited were not worthy. 9 Go therefore to the main**
> **roads. Invite to the feast anyone you find there.' 10 And**
> **so, these very servants went out to the roads and**
> **brought together everyone they found, whether bad or**
> **good."**

Jesus gives special emphasis to "these very servants" because they stand for the Twelve and other disciples who are there listening to this parable and who are about to go out into the whole world in a similar way. The word for "brought together" is *synêgagon* and suggests the formation of a new type of assembly. But a warning is added for these new invitees:

"The wedding feast was filled with guests enjoying the
banquet. 11 But when the king came in to observe the

guests enjoying the banquet, he saw there a man not clothed in clothing for a wedding feast. 12 He says to him, 'Friend, how did you come in here not wearing clothing for a wedding feast?' He had nothing to say. 13 Thereupon the king said to the servers, 'Bind his feet and his hands and throw him out into the darkness outside,' where there will be the wailing and gnashing of teeth. 14 Because many are called, but few are selected."

This phrase "a man not clothed in clothing for a wedding feast" in Greek does not have an indefinite article, or indeed anything to indicate it is just one man, but in fact if the phrase were removed from the context, it would be construed as "man, as not clothed in clothing for a wedding feast." That is, it refers to those in general who were called on the main roads but who show up without proper clothing, howsoever many they are. In his commentary on the line, Origen says that Jesus refers to them as if they were one man, because in God's eyes they are all of a piece, as there is nothing worth distinguishing in them.[4] But who are they? The traditional interpretation is that the wedding garment is "the new man" (Ephesians 4:24) and consists of charity together with fulfillment of the moral law. If charity is shown in deeds of sacrifice, then "man, as not clothed" would be bad bankers who never traded for a wedding garment.

Next we see that his attempts to warn them have failed. In fact, they take the offensive against him:

15 Then the Pharisees went away and planned how to entrap him in his words. 16 They therefore sent to him two of their disciples, along with the Herod supporters, saying,

---

4 St. Thomas Aquinas, *Catena Aurea*, vol. 1, part 2 (Oxford: James Parker and Co., 1874), 746–47.

These two won't be recognized as from them, and they won't appear threatening. The Herod supporters (or "Herodians") were there as witnesses who would bring him to the authorities if he taught anything rebellious (see Luke 20:20):

> **"Teacher, we know that you are true. You teach the way**
> **of God in truth. You give no heed to anyone because**
> **you do not look for human respect. 17 Tell us therefore**
> **your view: Is it permissible to pay the imperial tax to**
> **Caesar, or not?"**
> **18 Jesus knew their malice and said,**
> **"Why are you testing me, you hypocrites? 19 Show me**
> **the coin for the tax."**
> **They brought him a denarius. 20 He says to them,**
> **"Whose image is this, and whose name is written on**
> **it?"**
> **21 They say to him,**
> **"Caesar."**
> **Then he says to them:**
> **"Return, then, Caesar's things to Caesar, and God's**
> **things to God."**
> **22 As they listened, they were amazed. They left him alone**
> **and went away.**

The denarius serves as a parable. After all, if the image and inscription on a coin meant that the money was actually Caesar's possession and therefore ought to be returned to him, then all Roman coins ought to be sent to Caesar in Rome, which is a silly idea. Taxation is not a partial reclaiming by the government of its possessions—as Matthew knows well. The conclusion of the parable might therefore be stated as that insofar as Caesar has a claim to something, and in that sense it belongs to him, then one ought to render it to him. It is a conclusion about what we owe in justice to governments who undertake justifiable expenses for the common good. It would certainly imply that it was not wrong to pay an imperial tax. But also it would certainly not imply that regardless of the amount of the tax, or the purposes for which a tax was used, the tax would be just.[5]

The parable mainly shows the hypocrisy of those setting the trap. Those two disciples of the Pharisees are arguing on the premise that the Romans are unjust occupiers and that therefore it is unjust to pay the tax. Their goal is to draw Jesus in and have him say something rebellious, on that premise. However, these disciples and the Pharisees benefit from Roman rule, not simply in making use of Roman coins but also by Roman roads and aqueducts, the public peace enforced by Roman police power, and so on. It is hypocritical to receive these benefits and not acknowledge that one should in justice pay a fair share in supporting them.

They are also hypocritical in what they say about God. They are arguing on the premise, which they do not believe, that if someone "shows no human respect" then he will not show respect to Caesar and therefore will try to evade taxes. But in reality, to say that someone "shows no human respect" means that he cares about God's good opinion rather than men's when the two conflict. Jesus has elsewhere convicted the Pharisees of doing the opposite, of preferring a good reputation among men over doing God's will. As if to confirm the point, here they bring along partisans of Herod for assistance in suppressing Jesus.

---

5 The Roman government, like most governments, charged a fee, called "seignorage," for minting coins out of silver and gold. Therefore, any money due to Caesar for the service of minting coins was already paid.

There's a trenchant play on words here. The questioners begin by praising Jesus for the fact that "you show no human respect," which literally in Greek is expressed "you do not look to the face of any man." But then he, by looking to the face on the coin, not only unmasks their plot but also defeats their argument.

23 That same day there came to him Sadducees, who claim
there is no resurrection. They posed a question to him 24
and said,

> **"Teacher, Moses said, 'If a man should die not having**
> **children, his brother shall marry his wife and raise up**
> **seed for his brother.' 25 But among us there were seven**
> **brothers. The first married and died. As he had no**
> **seed, he left his wife to his brother. 26 Likewise also the**
> **second and the third, down to the seventh. 27 Last of**
> **all the woman died. 28 In the resurrection, therefore,**
> **of which of the seven brothers will she be the wife?—**
> **since all of them had her."**

The question is creepy for all kinds of reasons:

- They persist in using the old language of "seed" rather than the then accepted Greek language of "children"
- Their phrasing seems deliberately callous ("last of all she died")
- They refer coarsely to sexual union ("all of them had her")
- They depersonalize Moses's provision and do not care about its rationale
- They are dishonest because they present the case as if it were real ("among us there were.")

It is red meat for the crowds. But Jesus deals with them patiently:

> **29 Jesus said to them in reply,**
> **"You have wandered from the truth, since you do not**
> **know the scriptures nor the power of God. 30 In the**
> **resurrection, they will neither marry nor be given in**
> **marriage; rather, they are like angels in heaven. 31 But**
> **as regards the resurrection of the dead, have you not**
> **read what was spoken to us by God when he said, 32 'I**
> **am the God of Abraham, and the God of Jacob, and the**
> **God of Isaac'? He is not God of the dead, but God of**
> **the living."**
> **33 The crowd listening on was astonished by his teaching.**

That there is a resurrection is indicated by many verses in the Jewish scripture. For example, see Job 19:25–27:

> For I know that my Redeemer lives,
> and at last he will stand upon the earth;
> and after my skin has been thus destroyed,
> then from my flesh I shall see God.

See also Psalm 16:10–11 and Daniel 12:2. There is no marriage in the resurrection because marriage is fundamentally for procreation. It is not a mere bond of close fellowship.

In Greek, the words for "I am" in verse 32 are *ego eimi*. This is the name of God: *I am that I am* (Exodus 3:14). The verse that Jesus quotes in effect says, To exist is my nature, and therefore whatever is mine shares in my existence, and Abraham, Isaac, and Jacob are mine.

34 The Pharisees, learning that he had silenced the Sadducees, gathered together with the same purpose as before. 35 One of them posed him a question, testing him,

36 "Teacher, which commandment is the greatest commandment in the law?"

37 He said to him,

"You shall love the lord your God with the whole of your heart and with the whole of your soul and with the whole of your understanding. This is the greatest and first commandment. 39 The second resembles it: You shall love your neighbor as yourself. 40 In these two commandments the whole of the law depends; the prophets also."

Deuteronomy 6:5 enjoins to love God with all your heart, all your soul, and all your strength. Matthew omits the precept about strength and adds a precept about the understanding. Mark and Luke in their parallel versions (Mark 12:28–34 and Luke 10:25–28) include the precept about strength while adding the precept about the understanding. Overall, we can say that this precept about the understanding is an innovation of Jesus, designed for a Hellenistic culture. It is as if the Greeks had uncovered this other human power, the mind, and therefore, in a development of doctrine, a precept had to be included to cover it.

41 While the Pharisees were gathered together, Jesus posed them a question, 42 saying,

"What is your view of the Christ? Of whom is he the son?"

They say to him,

"Of David."

43 He says to them,
"How therefore does David—in the Spirit!—call him
'Lord,' when he says, 'The Lord said to my Lord, "Sit at
my right, until I put your enemies under your feet"?'. If
therefore David calls him 'Lord,' how is he his son?"
46 No one had the wherewithal to say anything to him in
reply. And from that day no one dared any longer to set
him questions.

He poses a clever question that can only be answered by appealing to the twofold nature of the Christ as the God-man.

What comes next—the denunciation of the scribes and Pharisees, an entire chapter in the traditional division of Matthew's Gospel—has no parallel in another Gospel. (The nearest is Luke 11:39–44.) Let us assume that Jesus spoke these words in the temple, as a single discourse during his final week in Jerusalem ("Holy Week"), before he was arrested and put to death. The discourse could not have been memorized on the spot and passed down in that way, especially as it preceded a time of great disturbance. A disciple had to have written it down after conducting interviews and confirming the language, either with disciples or with Jesus himself. Presumably, this disciple was Matthew. Therefore, there are two questions: First, why would Jesus have delivered such a biting denunciation on the near approach of his death? Second, why would Matthew alone have seen fit to include it in his account of the gospel?

The answer to both questions is that the scribes and Pharisees are the clearest cases of bad bankers. We have seen that the three sins that Jesus particularly hates in them are hardness of heart, self-righteousness, and hypocrisy. Each makes someone a miserable and dishonest banker. The first closes someone off from value in the divine economy. The second requires fraudulent internal accounting—a self-righteous person maintains a false representation of himself to himself; he represents his own poverty as wealth. The third requires a fraudulent representation to others, like counterfeit coins. The scribes and Pharisees are impoverished in true wealth and even become set upon destroying that wealth in others. If Matthew wants his readers to grasp and be grateful for the Payment, which is the Passion, then as a prelude to the Passion he understandably includes a condemnation of how we delude ourselves and shut ourselves out from doing so. Thus, the economic interpretation of Matthew's Gospel gives clear answers to these two questions.

23:1 It was at that time that Jesus spoke to the crowds and
his disciples, saying:
2 "The scribes and the Pharisees have taken their seat on
the chair of Moses. 3 Therefore, everything that they
might say to you—do it, and keep it. But as to what they
do, do not do it. 4 They bundle up heavy burdens and
place them on the shoulders of men, but they themselves
are not willing even to lift a finger to move them. 5 They
do all that they do to be seen by men. They widen their
phylacteries. They exaggerate the tassels on their
garments. 6 They love the highest place at banquets and
the first seats in synagogues and getting greeted in
markets and being called 'Teacher' by men.
8 "But you—you shall not be called 'teacher,' because One
there is who is your Teacher, and all of you are brothers. 9
And you are not to call anyone 'Father' on earth, because
One there is who is your Father, who is in heaven.

But Mary, and therefore Jesus, too, called Joseph his "father" (compare this with "your father and I have been looking for you" in Luke

2:48). The difference, then, is between whether being called "Father" is regarded by you as compensation, or as a kind of payment. If you wish to be called "Father" because you want to be father-like "to be seen by men," then you regard getting called "Father" as compensation, which you place on the income side of the ledger. If in being called "Father," rather, you understand that you have received your fatherhood from your heavenly Father, then you regard someone's calling you "Father" as like an invoicing, which you must pay to discharge the debt that you owe to your heavenly Father. You therefore place your acts as such a "father" on the expenditure side of the ledger. To accept the appellation "Father" in the second sense is to accept the Cross. Here again the worth of the economic interpretation of Matthew's Gospel is proved.

10 "You are not even to be called 'Leaders,' because One there is who is your Leader, the Christ. 11 If someone among you is greater, he will be your server. 12 Whoever will exalt himself will be humbled, and whoever will humble himself will be exalted.

Likewise, to accept the appellation "Leader" is to understand someone's application of the word to you as like an invoicing, which requires payment through service.

13 "But woe to you, scribes and Pharisees, hypocrites!—Because you shut up the Kingdom of Heaven in front of men. For you yourselves are not heading into it, but neither do you allow those who are heading into it, to enter in.[6]

---

6 I agree with those editors and translators who believe that a traditional verse 14 should be omitted. See Mark 12:40 and Luke 20:47.

15 "Woe to you, scribes and Pharisees, hypocrites!—
Because you travel across the sea and across the dry land to make a single proselyte, and if that should happen, you make him twice as much a Son of Gehenna as yourselves.

The phrase "travel across the sea and across the dry land" evokes business activity. Only traders at the time would undertake such journeys. But these men do so to destroy value, not to gain value for themselves or others.

16 "Woe to you, blind guides!—you who say, 'If someone swears by the inner temple, it is nothing, but if someone should swear by the gold of that inner temple, he becomes
bound.' 17 Fools and blind men! For what is greater, the gold, or the inner temple, which renders the gold holy?
18 And this: 'If someone swears by the altar, it is nothing. But if he should swear by the gift placed on it, he is
bound.' 19 You blind men! For what is greater, the gift or
the altar that renders the gift holy? 20 The man who
swears by the altar, therefore, swears by it and by
everything placed on it. 21 And the man who swears by the inner temple, swears by it and by the One who dwells
in it. 22 And the man who swears by heaven swears by the throne of God and by the One who sits upon it.
23 "Woe to you, scribes and Pharisees, hypocrites!—
Because you pay tithes of mint and dill and cumin, and you have neglected the weightier things of the law: good judgment and mercy and faith. You were bound to do these things, while not neglecting those others. 24 Blind
guides!—men who after they strain out a gnat, swallow a camel.

In these verses, with their talk of gold, Matthew sees clearly that Jesus is talking about the proper assessment of value. Again, there is no parallel to these verses in another Gospel. Matthew fastens on them because they distinguish good versus bad trades.

> **25 "Woe to you, scribes and Pharisees, hypocrites!—**
> **Because you clean the outside of the cup and of the dish,**
> **but inside they are teeming with greed and**
> **self-indulgence. 26 Blind Pharisee! Wash first of all the**
> **inside of the cup, so that its outside too might become**
> **clean.**
> **27 "Woe to you, scribes and Pharisees, hypocrites!—**
> **Because you have made yourselves as if whitewashed**
> **tombs, which appear beautiful on the outside, while**
> **inside they teem with dead men's bones and every kind of**
> **uncleanness. 28 So too on the outside you appear**
> **righteous to men, while inside you are chock full of**
> **hypocrisy and lawlessness.**

That is, the hypocrisy of the Pharisees is a consequence of their poor assessment of value. Because they do what they do "to be seen by men," they are concerned with appearances and have neglected to cultivate their true wealth, which involves how they appear to the Father who "sees in secret" (Matthew 6:4). In their accounting of themselves, they account themselves as wealthy, and yet they are impoverished.

> **29 "Woe to you, scribes and Pharisees, hypocrites!—**
> **Because you build the tombs of the prophets and decorate**
> **the monuments to righteous men, 31 and you say, 'If we**
> **had been alive in the days of our fathers, we would not**

have cooperated in shedding the blood of the prophets.'
32 And thus you testify about yourselves, that you are
sons of the men who murdered the prophets. 32 Go fill up
then, you too, the measure of your fathers! 33 Snakes!
Offspring of vipers! How will you escape from the
sentence of Gehenna?

Prophets must be eliminated, because prophets are like whistle-blowers who show up their fraud. But God must send them, because only in this way can the truth be declared, and can they have an occasion to repent.

The next language makes it clear that Jesus is deprecating the scribes and Pharisees because they stand for all corrupt and moralizing elites who will be present throughout history to come, who will persecute his followers:

34 This is why, you see, I am sending prophets to you, and
wise men and scribes. From among these, you will kill.
You will crucify. From among these, you will scourge in
your meeting houses and hunt down, city to city." 35 That
is how all the righteous blood poured out upon the earth
will come upon you, from the blood of Abel, the
righteous, up to the blood of Zachariah, son of Berechiah,
whom you murdered between the temple and the altar. 36
Amen, I say to you, all these things will be owned by this
wicked generation.

He is describing a kind of mechanism of the divine economy whereby sufferings like his own Passion will be repeated in history to come. Moralizing elites will continue to persecute and put to death those like himself, whom he will nevertheless continue to send. The communists of the twentieth century are excellent examples of these types of murderous, self-righteous moralizers. They murdered countless martyrs.

Note that Jesus's clear teaching about this mechanism of persecution ought to have precluded among early Christians the idea that the world would end soon.

> **37 "Jerusalem, Jerusalem, she who kills the prophets and**
> **stones those sent to her—how many times I have wanted**
> **to gather your children to me, in the way that a hen**
> **gathers her chicks under her wings, and you did not want**
> **it. 38 Look, your house is left to you, desolate. 39 I tell**
> **you: you will not see me from now until you should say,**
> **'Blessed is he who comes in the name of the Lord.'"**

Your house is left to you, desolate—This seems to be a prophecy of the destruction of Jerusalem by the Romans in 70 AD, which apparently is meant to serve as a warning against the nihilism of a life of false religiosity.

Sensing that Jesus was saying that the city would be destroyed, the disciples, in reply, say something foolish, the way children do, wanting him to affirm it:

> **24:1 Jesus left the temple and was walking away when his**
> **disciples came up to him to draw attention to the various**
> **structures of the temple. 2 Responding, he said to them,**
> **"Do you not see all these things? Amen, I say to you, no stone will be left here upon another stone—no stone that will not be pulled down."**

The Payment: Our Plight in the Future

The next section, about the end times, occupies the rest of a chapter (chapter 24) in the traditional organization of Matthew. It is found almost verbatim in Mark 13 and Luke 21. In no other passage do the three synoptic Gospels coincide so exactly. But this is precisely as we should expect. Regarding other teachings and parables, Jesus repeated them on many occasions in different contexts, presumably with variations. Many listeners witnessed these, just as many witnessed the healings. But this discourse on the end times was given just once, in response to the disciples' childlike awe of the temple. There were no witnesses except Peter, James, John, and Andrew (as Mark tells us, 13:3). None of the evangelists was a witness. Therefore, there had to have been some definite account in the custody of the Apostles that the evangelists worked from. How might this account have come to be? We assume that Matthew was the scribe among the Apostles. Perhaps, then, after Jesus gave the discourse, the four who heard it shared what was said with the others. As they shared it, Matthew wrote it down on wax tablets. Afterward, perhaps Peter reviewed what was written and confirmed it as accurate. Therefore, the account would have been regarded as authoritative for all. Matthew had a copy in his possession and used it when he composed his Gospel.

3 When he had sat down on the Mount of Olives, his disciples went to him in private.

in private—Therefore, the prediction he had just made in verse 2 was stated in the presence of others, and perhaps that language was used against him in his trial.

"Tell us," they said, "when will these things be? What will be the sign of your coming and of the end of this age?"

Clearly, he had already taught them that the present age is finite and that he would return. That is why they took his comment about the temple to refer to the end of the world. Now they want to know when it will happen and how one can tell it is coming. They are prompted both by his comment about the temple and by their sense of an impending crisis. And yet they are perplexed because Jesus has just foretold how types like the scribes and Pharisees will continue to persecute his followers and put them to death into the future.

4 Replying, Jesus said to them,
"Watch out that no one leads you astray. 5 Many men
will come in my name, claiming, 'I am—the Christ.'

They use the name of God, too, "I am," in claiming to be the Christ. It follows that Jesus too regards the name Christ as including implicitly the name of God.

"They will lead many astray. 6 When you begin to hear
about wars and you hear rumors of wars, do not be
disturbed. It is necessary that this take place, but the end
is not yet. 7 Because nation will rise up against nation,
and kingdom against kingdom. There will be famines and
earthquakes all over. 8 All these are the beginning of the
birth pangs.
9 "Next they will denounce you, to see you oppressed, and
they will kill you. You will be hated by every nation
because of my name.

10 "Next, many will take offense. They will denounce one
another and hate one another. 11 Many false prophets will
arise, and they will deceive many. 12 Because of rampant
lawlessness, the love of many will grow cold.
13 "The man who remains to the end—he is the one who
will be saved. This very gospel of the Kingdom will be
proclaimed throughout the whole world, for a witness to
all the nations. And then the end will come.

It seems impossible that Matthew (as we supposed) could have composed a transcription of this discourse, which contained the self-referential phrase, "This very gospel of the Kingdom," and not have realized that this discourse would need to be embedded in a fuller account. That phrase, right there, may very well be the germ of Matthew's Gospel. It is like a gentle command to write a fuller account.

15 "When you see the Abomination of Desolation that
was spoken of through Daniel the prophet set up in a holy
place (you who are reading this, understand!), 15 that is
when the inhabitants of Judea should flee to the
mountains. 17 A man on his housetop should not come
down to take anything from his house. 18 A man in the
fields should not turn back to take his garment.
19 "It will mean trouble, much trouble, for pregnant
women or mothers nursing infants in those days! 20 Pray
that your flight does not take place in wintertime, or on a
sabbath. 21 Because at that time there will be a great
tribulation, such as has not occurred from the beginning
of the world until now, nor ever shall be. 22 If those days
had not been cut short, no fleshly thing would have

survived. But because of the chosen ones, those days shall be cut short.
23 "Then, if someone should say to you, 'Look, here is the Christ!' or 'Look, he is there!' do not believe it! 24 Because false Christs will arise and false prophets. They will offer great signs and wonders to deceive even the chosen ones, if that were possible. 25. Pay careful attention: I have told you in advance.

Many Christians have come up with theories of the end times and tried to map current events to what Jesus says here. But his main purpose seems to be to convey what is expressed in this last verse—he does not want his followers to be surprised or flustered; he wants to help them persevere to the end.

26 "Therefore, if they should say to you, 'Look!—he is in the wilderness!'—do not go out. 'Look!—in the inner rooms!' Do not believe it. 27 Because just as lightning comes from the east and is seen as far as the west, so it will be with the coming of the Son of Man.
28 "Wherever a carcass happens to be, there the vultures will gather.

The circling of vultures in the sky is a sure sign that there is a carcass below in the center of their circles. A dying world too is beset by vultures. Since birds for the biblical mind represent spirits, these vultures also represent powers of evil. Their circling represents the cyclical and ever more urgent nature of the signs.

29 "Immediately after the tribulation of those days, 'The sun will be darkened. The moon will not give its light. The

stars will be falling from the heavens. The powers that are
in the heavens will be shaken. [Isaiah 13:10].
30 "Then it is that the sign of the Son of Man will appear
in heaven. Then all the tribes of the earth will mourn.
They will see the Son of Man coming on the clouds of
heaven, with power and great glory. 31 He will send forth
his angels with a great trumpet blast. He will gather up his
chosen ones from the four winds, from the highest point
of heaven to its farthest extent.
32 "Learn this parable, taken from a fig tree: when its
branch becomes tender and it puts forth leaves, you know
that summer is near. 33 So too you also, when you see
these things taking place, should know that he is at the
door. 34 Amen, I say to you, that this generation will not
have passed away before all these things have taken place.
35 Heaven and earth will pass away, but my words will not
pass away.

When Matthew heard "my words" in the recounting, he would have taken the Lord's very statement to imply an obligation that he was best suited to satisfy, and he could not have written down *these* words without having understood himself thereby to become bound to write down a fuller account.

36 "But as to the day or hour, no one knows, not even the
angels in heaven, nor the Son, but only the Father.

It is an old chestnut—how could the Son not know, if he is God? The old resolution is that he did know it *qua* God but did not know it *qua* man and as being one like us. Moreover, he is saying, he is not going to reveal it to us on the grounds, simply, that he had taken on human nature. It is better for us that the time be hidden, so that for all we know it could be any time. We will live better in this way—we will strive more earnestly to accrue genuine wealth.

> **37 "Just as the days of Noah—that is how it will be with**
> **the coming of the Son of Man. 38 Just as people in those**
> **days, the days prior to the flood, were eating and**
> **drinking, marrying and giving in marriage, right up to**
> **the day that Noah entered into the ark, 39 and they had no**
> **idea of the flood until it came and carried everything**
> **away, so too will be the coming of the Son of Man. 40**
> **When it happens, two men will be in the field; one will be**
> **taken away, and one will be left. 41 Two women will be**
> **grinding at the mill: one will be taken away, and one will**
> **be left.**
> **42 "So then, stay awake!—because you do not know the**
> **time when the Lord is coming. 43 This you do know: that**
> **if the master of the house had known at what hour of the**
> **night the thief was coming, he would have stayed awake**
> **and would not have let his house be burgled. 44 That is**
> **why you too should be ready, because at an hour that you**
> **are not expecting, the Son of Man is coming.**

The hour is deliberately withheld and cannot be discerned except in a general way. Therefore, his followers should always be expecting him. (A curious upshot is that Christians who believe that we are in the end times are closer to the truth than those who do not.)

> **45 "Who therefore is the reliable servant, and prudent**
> **too, whom his master has placed over his household to**
> **give to them food at the right time? 45 Happy is that**

servant whom the Lord, when he comes, will find doing
so. 47 Amen I tell you, he will place him over all his
possessions.
48 "But if a bad servant says in his heart, 'My Lord delays,'
49 and he begins to beat his fellow servants, and if he eats
and drinks with drunkards, 50 the Lord of that servant
will come on a day he is not expecting and at an hour he
does not know, 51 and he will cut him in half and assign
his part with the hypocrites, where there will be the
weeping and gnashing of teeth."

cut him in half—This is the strict meaning of the Greek verb. Many translations have "cut him to pieces," (although Douay-Rheims and the NASB are exceptions). After he is cut in half, apparently only half of him is sent to Gehenna. Whatever can this mean? Here is a suggestion. Perhaps the person had been placed over the household in some office that situates him, in some sense, forever there. And this assignment is so strong in its significance to the Lord that if such a man is sent to hell, it is as if he needs to be cut off from himself—the man, as having become bad, is damned *over and against* whatever good he had as holding that office. Consider, for example, Peter and Judas, both of them Apostles. Both were to feel the threat of being thus "cut in two," the one because he denied the Lord, the other because he betrayed him. Each after his sin was bad, as a sinner, but good, as an Apostle. In Peter, the good servant, as it were, rejected the bad servant that he had become, whereas in Judas, seemingly the bad servant in him obliterated the good that still remained.

The Settling of Accounts: The Closing of the Books

Now that he has foretold that the world will always provide many occasions for suffering for his sake, he describes the judgment that will come at the end of the world. He conceives of this judgment as a "settling of accounts." Matthew's Gospel alone describes the end of the world in this way (verse 19).

All three vignettes in the traditional chapter 25 of Matthew's Gospel—the foolish and wise virgins, the talents, and the sheep and goats—are peculiar to Matthew. Luke also has a parable about how servants make use of money and are rewarded or punished accordingly (Luke 19:11–27). But it is so different from Matthew's that it should not be counted as a parallel version of the same parable. If these vignettes are about closing the books, then, only Matthew has an extended explanation of that.

The vignettes fall into a sequence that models practical reason. The first considers the harsh judgment that we will receive if we did not pursue our true interest when we had the opportunity. The second assumes that we will be pursuing our genuine interest diligently, but it discusses different returns corresponding to different degrees of initial investment and assumed risk in trading. The third assumes basic prudential self-interest and an energy in making good trades to advance that interest, but it finds fault in the restriction in the scope of one's trading in the divine economy.

25:1 "At that time, the Kingdom of Heaven will be comparable to ten virgins who took their lamps and went out to meet the bridegroom. 2 Five of them were foolish, and five were prudent. 3 The foolish ones, when they took their lamps, did not take oil with them. 4 But the prudent ones took oil in jars along with their lamps.

They bring lamps that are already burning. Those who do not bring extra oil are not prepared in case there is any delay.

5 "When the bridegroom was delayed, they all nodded to sleep and slept soundly.

Against their will they nodded off, just as dying is against our will.

6 "In the middle of the night, there was a cry: 'Look! the
bridegroom! Go out to meet him.' 7 Then all those virgins
got up. They trimmed their lamps.
8 "The foolish ones said to the prudent ones: 'Give us
some of your oil, because our lamps are going out.' 9 But
the prudent ones said in reply, 'We can't risk there not being enough for us and for you. Go instead to the vendors and buy oil for yourselves.'

Saint John Chrysostom says that the vendors are the poor for whom we can distribute alms. Because they cannot repay, we store up treasure in heaven—the oil. And yet after we die, we can no longer benefit the poor. That is why, he says, the foolish virgins were apparently unsuccessful in purchasing any oil.

10 "When they were traveling away to buy it, the bridegroom came. The ones who were ready accompanied
him into the wedding feast. The door was shut. 12 It was
only later that they came—the other virgins—who then
said, 'Lord. Lord! Open the door for us.' 12 But replying,
he said, 'Amen, I say to you, I do not know you.'

The warning that comes next at first seems out of place, as if it does not belong with this parable. One would have thought that the parable was exhorting us to achieve a superabundance of merit in the short time we have available:

> **13 "Therefore, stay awake, because you do not know the day or the hour.**

Also, note how the wise virgins are hardly an example of staying awake, since they as well as the foolish ones fell asleep. And if sleep in the parable stands for death, it seems pointless to be exhorted not to die.

But the message seems rather to be this: Someone is as if already asleep—already dead—if all that he does is to allow his oil to burn. To be awake is to be expecting the arrival of the bridegroom and to be acquiring oil and conserving it, so as to bring a lighted lamp to his presence. That is, Jesus is assuming that to be fully alive is to be engaged in doing good works—not randomly or fecklessly—but precisely in order to please the Lord when he returns. The prudent virgins are good bankers.

> **14 "Just as a man, about to leave for another country, called his own servants and entrusted them with his possessions. 15 To one he gave five silver talents. To another, two. To yet another, one. He gave to each according to the distinctive ability of each.**

The Greek word here for "ability" (*dunamis*), when used in an economic sense, means the capacity to yield produce, such as the fecundity of the land; the skill of a craftsman, which will tend to make him successful; or the potential yield of an investment.

"Then he left for that other country. Without delay, 16 the one who got five silver talents traded with them and realized a gain of five other talents. 17 Likewise, the one who got two silver talents realized a gain of another two.

He gave no instructions about what to do, and yet they immediately put his money to work. Presumably, he was putting his own money to work before he left, and they simply imitated what they saw him do already. Similarly, Jesus gave an example of good trading in his Payment, his Passion and Redemption, and his followers must make similar trades on that example.

18 "But the man who got one went off, dug a hole in the ground, and hid there the silver piece that belonged to his lord.

It was not this servant's property, and therefore he needed to assess whether it matched his lord's intentions that the silver piece be buried in the ground.

19 "After much time had passed, the lord of those servants comes and settles accounts with them.

settles accounts—This is the same phrase used in 18:23 and, as mentioned, it is unique to Matthew.

20 "The one who had gotten five silver talents came up and brought another five talents and said, 'Lord, you had entrusted me with five silver talents. Look, another five talents that I gained.' 21 His lord said to him, 'Well done, good servant, and faithful too. You were faithful with a

> **few goods. I will place you over many. Enter into the joy of your lord.'**

He was faithful in the sense that he showed himself reliable in using the money to the advantage of its owner. He was a good and trustworthy banker.

> **22 "Then came up as well the one with the two silver talents. 'Lord, you had entrusted me with two talents. Look, another two talents that I have gained.' 23 His lord**
> **said to him, 'Well done, good servant, and faithful too. With a few goods you were faithful: I will place you over many. Enter into the joy of your lord.'**

In the tradition, commentators wonder what the progression, five, two, one in the talents might stand for mystically. Some say that the meaning is in the double of these, namely, ten and four, as these taken together stand for complete righteousness (the Decalogue, and the foursquare ethical uprightness of the cardinal virtues). The man with one talent, then, was supposed to yield one other talent.

> **24 "Then came up also the one who had received the one talent and said, 'Lord, as I knew that you are a hard man because you reap where you have not sown, and you**
> **gather from places where you have not scattered, 25 and**
> **as I was afraid; I went and hid your silver talent in the**
> **ground. Look, you have what is yours.' 26 But his lord in**
> **reply said to him, 'Wicked servant, and cowering also. You knew, did you, that I reap where I had not sown and I**
> **gather from places where I had not scattered? 27 Then you**
> **ought to have deposited my money with the bankers, and**

when I came I would have repossessed what was mine with interest.'

This one was risk-averse; he wanted to do what seemed safe to him. The lord draws the servant's attention to opportunity cost, which is what we give up by not taking another alternative. That is to say, this servant did not even return the value of what the lord had given him, because one must subtract, from the value of the talent rendered, the amount that could have been earned in interest over the intervening time.

We see here an implicit endorsement by Jesus of interest insofar as it represents, as we would say, the "time value of money." As this modern conception could not have come from a Hebrew understanding of money and lending, it must have come from Roman culture, with which we are supposing Matthew was well familiar. Note too that if these workers were simply imitating what they saw the master doing, then this man who buried the talent in the ground was imitating, very badly, his master's own practice of depositing some talents in a bank.

28 "Take the talent away from him, then, and give it to the man who has ten talents. 29 For to everyone who has, it shall be given, and he shall superabound, but to the one who has not, even what he has will be taken away from him.
30 Cast the useless servant out into the outer darkness, where there will be weeping and the gnashing of teeth.
31 "But when the Son of Man comes in his glory, and all the angels with him—then he will sit upon his throne of glory. 32 All the nations will be gathered together before him. He will distinguish them from one another, just as a shepherd distinguishes his sheep from the goats.

The Greek term for "distinguish" means to set boundaries and even to articulate different natures. It is as if in the last judgment there will be not simply a discovery of where someone belongs but also a definitive placement of him there by the Lord.

> **33 "He will place the sheep on his right, and the goats on**
> **his left. 34 Then the king will say to those on his right:**
> **'Come, you esteemed ones of my Father, receive as an**
> **inheritance the kingdom prepared for you from the**
> **establishment of the world. 35 Because I was hungry, and**
> **you gave me to eat. I was thirsty, and you gave me to**
> **drink. I was a stranger, and you welcomed me. 36 Naked I**
> **was, and you clothed me. Sick, and you took care of me. In**
> **prison I was, and you came to me.' 37 Then the righteous**
> **will say to him in reply, 'Lord, when was it that we saw you**
> **hungry and we fed you, or thirsty and we gave you to**
> **drink? 38 When was it that we saw you sick or in prison,**
> **and we came to you?' 40 And the king will say to them in**
> **reply, 'Amen I tell you, insofar as you did so to one of the**
> **least of these my brothers, you did so to me.'**

This passage about the final judgment in Matthew is typically interpreted to support a humanism whereby the Lord is identified with every human being, such that any good deed done for any human being counts as being done for the Lord. And yet, strictly, that is not what is said here. Our Lord says that anything done for even the lowest among these who are his brethren—those on his right—is done for him. Likewise in verse 45 below, "the least ones" must mean the least of "these on my right." He seems, rather, to be expressing the doctrine that the saved taken together are identified with himself—he is affirming what is called the "mystical body of Christ." If he wanted to express humanism, he would have said something like, "insofar as you did not do so *to one another*."

> **41 "Then he will furthermore say to those on his left: 'Go away from me, you accursed ones, into the everlasting fire that has been prepared for the devil and his angels. 42 For**
> **I was hungry, and you did not give me to eat. I was thirsty, and you did not give me to drink. 43 A stranger I was, and you did not welcome me. Naked I was, and you did not clothe me. Sick and in prison, and you did not take care of me.' 44 Then these too will say to him in reply, 'Lord, when did we see you hungry or thirsty or a stranger or naked or sick or in prison, and we did not minister to you?' 45 Then**
> **he will say to them in reply, 'Amen I tell you, insofar as you did not do so to one of these least ones, neither did you do so to me.'**
> **46 And these shall proceed into everlasting punishment, but the righteous into everlasting life."**

Note the symmetry between the two fates. If the blessed life enjoyed by the one group is eternal, without end, and entirely secure, then so must be the punishment suffered by the other. Saint Augustine takes this verse to be a definitive refutation of those who deny the eternity of the punishments of the damned in hell: "Some deceive themselves, saying, that the fire indeed is called everlasting, but not the punishment. This the Lord foreseeing, sums up His sentence in these words."[7]

7 St. Augustine, *On Faith and Works*, 15, quoted in St. Thomas Aquinas, *Catena Aurea*, vol. 1, part 2 (Oxford: James Parker and Co., 1874), 868.

The Payment Proper: His Passion and Death

Matthew uses striking language to signal that now his account of the Payment for Redemption begins, understood as the Crucifixion:

> **26:1 What happened, when Jesus had ended saying all of these things, was that he said to his disciples:**
> **2 "You know that after two days the Passover arrives,**
> **and the Son of Man gets handed over to be crucified."**
> **3 It was at that time that the chief priests and elders of the**
> **people were assembled in the courtyard of the high priest**
> **named Caiaphas. 4 They were debating how to arrest Jesus**
> **by some trick and put him to death. 5 Yet they were**
> **saying, "Not during the festival. Otherwise, the people**
> **might riot."**
> **6 When Jesus was in Bethany, in the house of Simon the**
> **leper, 7 there came to him a woman, bringing an alabaster**
> **jar of exclusive fragrant oil,**

In his narration of this anointing, Mark describes the fragrant oil (myrrh) simply as "very expensive" (*polutelos*). Matthew, in contrast, uses a term that means "tending to a high price in the market"—literally, "weightily valued" (*barytimos*)—which shows a sensitivity on his part to the law of supply and demand. For him, the oil is not merely expensive; it is expensive *because it is highly demanded yet scarce*. He also realizes that this myrrh is a commodity that by its nature only a very few in the market can acquire. Thus, he adds that it is "exclusive." In sum, Mark's description of the oil is conventional, while Matthew's shows a keen understanding of the market.

and she poured it out freely over his head as he was reclining at table.

Jesus had just discoursed on the use of goods for almsgiving to the poor, to store up treasure in heaven. The disciples naturally interpret her actions as misguided. She seems to show him the sort self-indulgence that he had just castigated. Hers is not an act of almsgiving, they think. She is like the man who buried money in the ground. The woman needs to be corrected and taught to serve the poor instead:

8 As they saw this, the disciples became indignant and said,
"What justifies this waste? 9 It would have been possible to sell it for a great price and give to the poor."

Mark, in his narrative, quotes the words of the disciples, which name a price: "it could have been sold for 300 denarii to be given to the poor" (Mark 14:4). But Matthew omits the price. Why? Perhaps because he saw that even at the time that they spoke they quoted a fictitious price —just as we often pick a rounded, high number when we don't really know. But also, as mentioned, he had not described the myrrh as *highly priced* but rather as *highly demanded*, and therefore he would have thought of the price of the myrrh as what it would get in the market at the time he was writing (just as he had "marked to market" the price of the sparrows, in Matthew 10:29).

10 Knowing this, Jesus said to them,
"Why do you add to this woman's troubles? She has done a good work, for me. 11 The poor at all times you have among you. You do not always have me.

First, he suggests they are being like the Pharisees (see Matthew 24:3), who bundle up burdens and place them on the shoulders of others without doing anything to lift them. His own language is meant to stir up compassion in them and pity. Second, he draws their attention to the crucial part of his teaching on alms: "insofar as you did it to the least of these my brothers you did it *for me*." Third, he points out that there is no opportunity cost here; "the poor" are anyone for whom a spiritual or corporal act of mercy can be done, and these are all around, always. Typically, too, these acts can be done without any material expenditure—time and affection are usually enough. Fourth, he says that her deed in any case does indeed count as a work of mercy. We would say it falls under the category of "burying the dead":

> **12 "For she poured this fragrant oil onto my body to**
> **prepare me for burial. 13 Amen, I say to you, wherever**
> **this gospel is proclaimed in the entire world, what she has**
> **done will be also be told, in memory of her."**

Referring back to his teaching on almsgiving, Jesus says that she, like the others among the elect, will be one of the heralded and estimable ones (Matthew 25:34). And yet he takes pains to say precisely that "what she has done" will be proclaimed, rather than that her name will be proclaimed—thus he preserves the "hiddenness" of her act and therefore its great merit before God (Matthew 6:3–4).

> **14 Next, one of the Twelve, the one called Judas "Iscariot,"**
> **went to the chief priests, 15 and said,**
> **"What are you willing to give me? I will deliver him to you."**
> **They countered with thirty pieces of silver.**

Here Mark says only that they promised him that sum (Mark 14:11), and Luke says that they agreed on that sum (Luke 22:5). Only Matthew conveys the bargaining. Judas is selling something, and he is asking for their bid.

countered with—Matthew uses a word (Greek, *estēsan*) that here means strictly *placed in the balance so as to equal*. Matthew is thinking of the transaction as an equilibration. He reveals his astonishment that the life of Christ for these men weighed the same as a few pieces of a commodity. Matthew in his narrative is ever concerned with whether valuation is correct or faulty. They are disastrously poor bankers; they lack sound ideas of value.

16 From that time he began to look for the opportunity to betray him.

The chief priests had resolved not to attempt to arrest him during the festival, but Judas's initiative changes their mind. In God's providence the sacrifice of Jesus and the sacrifice of the Passover lamb take place at the same time, yet it was by Judas's treachery that they came to coincide. It is an example of how God brings good out of evil.

17 On the first day of the Festival of Unleavened Bread the disciples came and said to Jesus,
"Where do you want us to get everything ready for you to eat the Passover meal?"
18 He said,
"Go into the city to so-and-so, and tell him, 'The teacher says, "My time is near. I will keep the Passover at your place with my disciples."'"

Matthew keeps the man's identity secret ("so-and-so") so that his house would remain secret. His language therefore indicates that these lines were written before the destruction of Jerusalem in 70 AD.

19 His disciples did as he had instructed them. They got everything ready for the Passover meal.
20 When evening came, he was reclining at table with the Twelve, 21 and, as they were eating, he said,
"Amen I tell you, one among you will betray me."
22 They were deeply distressed and began to say to him, one-by-one,
"Surely it is not I, Lord."

No one except Judas had any inclination to betray him, and yet each was uncertain, because they regarded Jesus as a better authority on their own interior life than they were themselves. But only God has such authority

23 He said in reply,
"A man who has dipped his hand with me in the dish—he will betray me. 24 The Son of Man goes just as it is written about him. But woe to that man through whom the Son of Man is betrayed. It would be a good thing for that man if he had not been born."

Not "better for him" but rather "a good thing"—the Greek word is *kalon*, which means "good to look at." And how could that man have had any good at all, if he had never existed? But that is not what the Lord says. He means *if, once conceived, he had not seen the light of day*, and therefore, this is yet another assertion by Jesus that we exist in the womb.

25 Judas, who was in the act of betraying him, said in response,
"Surely it is not I, Rabbi."

Judas has stopped calling him "Lord."

He says to him,
"You have said so yourself."

The Fathers rightly take these statements of Jesus to be attempts by him to persuade Judas, in the mystery of his freedom, not to betray him after all. First, Jesus quotes a psalm (41:9). Then he says that the necessity of his Passion does not imply that any particular person is necessitated. Next, he warns of the penalty of hell. Finally, he even tells Judas that there is no reason why his outward profession ("Surely it is not I") could not become an affirmation, an act of the will, a resolution not to betray him. "You have said so yourself" means *You have implied that it is not you, and therefore you can make it so happen; this is in your power.*

Matthew's language earlier, "they countered with thirty pieces of silver," now shines light on the decision that Jesus has placed before Judas: Will he reject that equilibration when the Lord now appeals to him, or will he reaffirm it? "Am I really worth only thirty pieces of silver in your eyes?"—is the question Jesus is posing to him.

26 And as they were eating, Jesus, taking bread and blessing it, broke the bread and, after giving it to his disciples, said,
"Take. Eat. This is my body."
27 Taking a cup and giving thanks, he gave it to his disciples and said,

> **"Drink from it, all of you. 28 Because this is my blood of the covenant, which is poured out for many for the forgiveness of sins. 29 I tell you, I will not drink of this product of the vine from now on, until that day when I drink it with you, new, in the Kingdom of my Father."**

What is fresh or new (*kainon*) is the wine, not the drinking of it. Earlier the Lord had used this same word for fresh wineskins (Matthew 9:17). It is new wine because it is his blood.

product of the vine—This is what he says, literally; the word does not mean "fruit." Both bread and wine are human products, although they are derived from wheat and grapes. What Jesus blesses and calls his body and blood has human labor mixed with it. Thus, most strictly, it is a product of the vine, not merely "fruit of the vine."

30 And after they had sung a hymn, they went out to the Mount of Olives.

31 Next, Jesus tells them,

> **"All of you, this very night, will take offense in me. For it is written, 'I will strike the shepherd, and the sheep of the flock will be scattered.' But after I have been raised, I will go before you to Galilee."**

32 Peter, replying, says,

> **"If everyone should take offense at you, I myself will never do so."**

34 Jesus said to him,

> **"Amen I tell you this very night before the cock crows you will deny me three times."**

35 Peter says to him,

> **"Even if I must die with you, I will definitely not deny you."**

All the disciples spoke in the same way.
36 Next, Jesus goes with them to an area called
Gethsemani. He tells his disciples,
"Have a seat here while I go over there and pray."
37 Taking Peter along with him, and the two sons of
Zebedee, he began to feel great sorrow and distress. 38
Next, he tells them,
"My soul is overwhelmed with sorrow to the point of death. Stay here and stay awake with me."

stay awake—This meant also to keep watch, as if a guard. When a guard falls asleep, he fails in his duty to keep watch.

39 He went a short way farther and fell with his face to the ground as he prayed and said,
"My Father, if it is possible, let this cup pass from me: except, not as I will, but as you will."

This is all that they overhear, before they drift off. His return to them seems sudden:

40 He comes to his disciples and finds them sleeping. He says to Peter,
"You were not able to stay awake and keep watch with me for even one hour? Stay awake, keep watch, and pray, that you do not enter into temptation. The spirit indeed is willing, but the flesh is weak."

He is gentle, as he might have said in reproach, *Far from dying with me under threat, you cannot even stay awake for an hour when I ask.* He tells them that good intentions are not enough and that they need divine assistance (what is called "grace") to carry out what they wish.

42 Again for a second time he went off and prayed, saying,
"My Father, if it is not possible that this pass away
unless I drink it, may your will be done."
43 And he came and again found them sleeping—because
their eyes were heavy.

This is a detail that Jesus must have shared with them later. They were asleep and could not have perceived it. If he was not raised from the dead, they could not have learned it.

44 He left them and again went off and prayed, using the same language for a third time.

Matthew's narrative now attempts to convey artfully what they began to sense as they were being roused:

45 Then he comes to his disciples and says to them,
"Sleep and get rest later. . . . Look, the hour is upon us.
The Son of Man is betrayed into the hands of
sinners. . . . 46 Wake up. Let's go. . . . Look, the one who
is betraying me is at hand."
47 He was still speaking when—look!—Judas came, one of
the Twelve, and with him, from the chief priests and
elders of the people, a large crowd with swords and clubs.
48 His betrayer had given them a sign, saying, *The man*
***whom I kiss is he; arrest him.* 49 Going up right away to**
Jesus, he said,
"Greetings, Rabbi!"

He gave him a kiss. 50 Jesus said to him,
"Friend, what brings you here?"

By calling him "friend," Jesus is presenting Judas with the option of changing his mind even after the deed is done.

Then they came up and grabbed Jesus with their hands
and arrested him.
51 And right then one of the men with Jesus stretched out
his hand, drew his sword, and, striking the servant of the
high priest with it, cut off his ear. 52 Jesus then says to
him,
"Return your sword to its place. All who draw the
sword will die by the sword. 53 Or do you suppose I
cannot ask my Father for help, and he will not provide
for me, at this very moment, twelve legions of angels or
more? 54 But how, then, would the scriptures be
fulfilled, that it was necessary that it take place in
this way?"

The literal obligation created by scripture implies a duty to fulfill the scripture.

Jesus's use of words for possibility and necessity bring us back to his prayer just earlier, "if it is possible that this cup pass." The disciples had heard only that prayer and then fell asleep. But suppose they had stayed awake and prayed with him—would they have received the reinforcing insight, perhaps, that it was necessary that it happen in this way? And why not? Suppose that, in that prayer, the Father had intimated to the Son, "Of course, you need only to ask, and I will send legions of angels to protect you," and the Son, in his human will, which initially recoiled in horror at torture and death, freely declined such a proposition? Indeed, verses 52–54 have the feel of something already considered and rejected.

That is to say, verses 53–54 represent Jesus's recognition, presumably already realized in his prayer, of what is gained by his paying the price, and how what is recorded antecedently in scripture has created a debt that must be paid. Matthew's Gospel is the only one that conveys these words, which are highly pertinent to the economic interpretation of his Gospel. There is no parallel in any other Gospel.

55 When that was happening, Jesus said to the crowds,
"As though on the trail of a robber, have you come out with swords and clubs to capture me? Day after day I sat teaching in the temple, and you did not arrest me."
56 But all of this happened so that the writings of the prophets might be fulfilled.
Then it was that all of his disciples deserted him and fled.
57 The men who arrested Jesus led him to Caiaphas the high priest, where the scribes and elders had assembled.
58 Peter followed him from a distance, up to the courtyard of the high priest. Entering in, he sat down with the servants, to see how it would end.
59 The chief priest and the entire Sanhedrin began to look for false testimony against Jesus, enough that they could put him to death.
60 They did not find it, even though many false witnesses had come forward. But later, two came forward
61 and said,
"This one said, 'I have the power to tear down the temple of God, and after three days will build it up.'"
62 Rising to his feet, the chief priest said to him,
"You have nothing in reply to what these men are charging you with?"

63 But Jesus was silent. The chief priest said to him,
"I adjure you, by the living God, that if you are the Christ, the Son of God, you tell us so."
64 Jesus says to him,
"You have said so yourself."

The chief priest would not have asked this question if he had no grounds for believing it, just as you will not ask it of me, and I not of you. Jesus, therefore, in effect challenges him: if you are convinced that I am not, then simply deny that I am and move on. But the chief priest cannot and does not accept this challenge.

We must imagine here a pause, before Jesus breaking the silence goes on to say:

"For all that, I tell you: from now on you will see 'the Son of Man seated at the right hand of power' and 'coming in the clouds of heaven.'"

"From now on" does not mean beginning from this moment you will see him thus, but rather that when you see him, from now on this is how you will see him. "Now" is the hour of his Passion and death, not the instant he says this word. He puts it in this way because he and they are all aware that they intend to destroy him presently.

He is simply citing scripture (Daniel 7:13), and yet:

65 Then the chief priest rent his garments and said,
"He has blasphemed. Do we continue to need witnesses? Look, you have just now heard the
blasphemy. 66 What is your view?"
They said in reply,
"He deserves the sentence of death."

67 Then they spat on his face and slapped him. Some hit
him with sticks 68 and said,
"Prophesy for us, O Christ, and tell us who struck you."
69 Peter was sitting outside in the courtyard. A servant
girl came up to him and said,
"You too were with Jesus of Galilee."
70 He denied it in front of all of them and said,
"I do not know what you are talking about."
71 Another servant girl saw him as he was leaving for the
gate and says to those there,
"This one was with Jesus of Nazareth."
72 Again, he denied it with an oath,
"I do not know the man."
73 A little while later some men standing there went up to
Peter:
"It's true, you too are one of them. It's your accent that gives you away."
74 Then he began to curse and swear,
"I do not know the man!"
And without delay, a cock crowed. 75 Peter remembered
what Jesus had said, that *before the cock crows you will deny me three times.* He went outside and wept bitterly.

He wept bitterly, yet he took pains to do so outside, so that he would not be seen and discovered as a disciple. His was a very imperfect contrition right then.

The following account of the death of Judas and the fate of the thirty pieces of silver (verses 1–10) has no parallel in any other Gospel. Matthew alone "follows the money" and is concerned with how the transaction winds up.

27:1. When it was morning, all the chief priests and elders of the people took counsel against Jesus, as to how to put him to death. 2 Binding him up, they led him away. They handed him over to Pilate, the governor.
3 That was when Judas, the one who betrayed him, seeing that Jesus had been condemned, changing his mind, returned the thirty pieces of silver to the chief priests and elders, 4 saying,
> **"I sinned in betraying innocent blood."**

They said,
> **"What is that to us? It falls to you."**

5 After throwing the pieces of silver into the inner sanctuary, he withdrew from them. Going away, he strangled himself.

Luke in Acts gives the gruesome details that "falling headlong"—presumably because the rope broke—"he burst open in the middle and all his bowels gushed out" (Acts 1:18). The body must have fallen with violence on a sharp rock or tree stump.

6 The chief priests, taking the silver, said,
> **"It is not permissible to put the coins into the Corban, since it is the price of blood."**

7 After taking counsel, they used some of the coins to purchase the Potter's Field as a burial place for foreigners.
8 That is why that field has been referred to as The Field of Blood to this day.

the Corban—The fund for support of the temple and its priests (see Mark 7:11). They pride themselves on their uprightness in not applying the money to their own support.

Luke in Acts says that the field was called the Field of Blood because that was where Judas's body burst with blood pouring all over. The two explanations are not inconsistent. Blood could have become associated with that ground, in the popular mind, from two different pathways.

to this day—Another indication that Matthew wrote before the destruction of Jerusalem in 70 AD.

> **9 It was at that time that it was fulfilled, what was said through Jeremiah, saying, "And they took the thirty pieces of silver, the price of the man valued at a price, on whom a price had been set by the sons of Israel, 10 and they gave them for the potter's field, as the Lord directed me."**

However, Matthew does not give a quotation from Jeremiah so much as a paraphrasic interpretation of Jeremiah 32 combined with Zechariah 11. (The reader might wish to look at those chapters for background.)

Luke in Acts says in contrast that it was Judas who purchased the field. He "obtained a field out of the payment (*misthos*) for his injustice" (Acts 1:18). However, Luke does not say that Judas himself bought the field. His words may simply have been intended to convey a grim irony. If Judas returned the coins to the chief priests, yet they themselves never took possession of them but simply used them to make a purchase, then strictly they were agents for Judas in making this purchase. And if Judas's reward of thirty coins was converted through that transaction to a field, then it remains correct that the field represented Judas's compensation for the betrayal of Jesus. So Luke's description is not incompatible with Matthew's.

Matthew thinks in a similar way about the conversion of value in these transactions. He thinks that Jesus had been "valued" at thirty pieces of silver. Therefore, this price represents the value of the Lord and the Good Shepherd. He thinks that if this value is used by human agents to purchase a field, then it is as if the Lord was the price for the field, and, therefore, one can say that the Lord purchased the field. But if the Lord purchased the field, then the field must stand for something. And that it later gets called Field of Blood supports this idea that it has a mystical meaning. That the field was a burial place for foreigners is suggestive as well, as these foreigners would apparently represent those others who will be gathered into the kingdom—invited to the banquet, in place of the original people who refused the invitation.

This is the way to understand Matthew's reference to Jeremiah the prophet here. Jeremiah in chapter 32 explains how the Lord instructed him to purchase a field in Jerusalem on the eve of the city's destruction by the Babylonians, because of the people's faithlessness and crimes—especially their sacrifice of children to Baal in the Valley of Hinnon. The Valley of Hinnon is precisely where the Field of Blood was located. The purchase of this field, Jeremiah says (in chapter 32), represents the promise of eternal salvation and an eternal covenant, despite these sins.

Matthew clearly believes that Zechariah as a prophet "sees" and describes the very same transaction (in chapter 11), in a passage where he tells of how a "shepherd of the flock doomed to be slain for those who trafficked in the sheep" was rejected by the sheep and compensated with thirty shekels of silver.

The matter is complicated, but we can summarize it as follows: Matthew freely takes language from both accounts, in Jeremiah and Zechariah, because he interprets both as foreseeing the same transaction, whereby the Lord was sold out for thirty pieces of silver. He attributes these accounts to Jeremiah and not Zechariah because Jeremiah is the major prophet and it is in Jeremiah solely that one can see the mystical meaning of the transaction and the promises associated with it.

It is important here to emphasize that Matthew is not using the purchase of the Field of Blood with the money from the selling out of Christ—which he witnessed—as some kind of proof that the prophets were correct. Rather, he is telling us in a concise way to study the prophet Jeremiah for the meaning of the transaction.

11 Jesus stood before the governor. The governor asked him,
"Are you the king of the Jews?"
Jesus said,
"You yourself say it."

Here again, why would Pilate ask it, unless there were some possible grounds for it to be true? He asks a question, which contains implicitly some sort of affirmation. Jesus proposes that he attend to that affirmation and commit to it or not.

12 He said nothing in reply all the while that the chief
priests and elders were accusing him. 13 Pilate, then, says
to him,
"Is it that you fail to hear the many charges they affirm against you?"
14 He did not reply to him, not even to a single charge,
which caused the governor great astonishment.
15 Each festival, it was the governor's custom to release
for the crowd one prisoner of their choosing. 16 They were
holding at the time a high-profile prisoner named
Barabbas. 17 Therefore, when a crowd had gathered,
Pilate said to them,

"Which prisoner do you want me to release for you,
Barabbas, or Jesus who is called 'Christ'?"
18—For he knew that it was out of envy that they had
handed him over.
(19 While he was seated on the Bema, his wife sent word
to him, "Have nothing to do with that righteous man.
Today in a dream I underwent tremendous sufferings
because of him.")
20 But the chief priests and elders persuaded the crowds
to ask for Barrabas and do away with Jesus.

The Bema was a stone speaker's platform with a judgment seat (see Acts 18:12–16).

We can guess that in reply to Pilate's question in verse 17, they were mainly saying "not Jesus." Pilate thinks that they do not grasp that he has not offered them an open-ended choice of a prisoner, but solely a choice between Barabbas and Jesus. Accordingly, he makes it perfectly clear for them. He finds it hard to believe that their envy, a negative emotion of rejection, can so strong as to support the positive choice of a notorious criminal:

21 The governor said in response,
"From these two, which do you want me to release for you?"
They said,
"Release Barabbas."

As an officer of the law, he does not want to release Barabbas. Therefore, he asks something that he thinks will elicit some degree of consideration for Jesus:

22 Pilate says to them,
"What then shall I do with Jesus, the man called Christ?"
They say all together:
"Let him be crucified!"

Their reply creates a new problem for Pilate. Logically, if he releases Barabbas, then Jesus merely takes the place of Barabbas in prison, as Barabbas was not slated to be crucified.

Pilate's steps in these verses (verses 21–22) are reported only in Matthew and reflect Matthew's fascination with trades and transactions.

23 He said,
"On what basis? What bad thing has he done?"
But they all the more shouted out,
"Let him be crucified!"
24 When Pilate saw that it was to no avail but rather a riot was breaking out, taking water, he washed his hands in the sight of the crowd and said,
"I am innocent of the blood of this man. It falls to you."

Pilate's words here almost exactly reenact what Judas said to the chief priests and elders and what they said in reply (Matthew 27:4). Only Matthew records this detail, just as only Matthew records their words to Judas.

We can see why Matthew would be fascinated with the question of whether someone who had the authority to decide, like Pilate, can rightly declare that he has *not* decided, as that declaration raises the issue of opportunity cost—in choosing not to choose, Pilate seems to be accepting the cost of what he might have chosen but has foregone.

There is also what economists call a principal-agent problem: Can a principal turn himself into an agent? Can Pilate, who is the principal, become a mere agent of the crowd, so that it plays the role of a principal?

25 The whole people said in reply,
"Let his blood be upon us and upon our children."
26 That was when he released Barabbas for them, while
Jesus, after having him scourged, handed him over to be
crucified.
27 Then the governor's soldiers took Jesus into the
Praetorium and confronted him with the whole company
of soldiers. 28 They removed his clothing and put a scarlet
robe on him. 29 They wove together a crown from thorny
branches and placed it on his head and a cane pole in his
right hand. Kneeling before him, they mocked him and
said, "Hail, king of the Jews!" 30 They spat on him and
took the cane pole and hit him over the head with it.
31 When they were done with mocking him, they
removed the robe from him. They placed his own clothing
on him. They led him out to crucify him. 32 As they were
going out, they found a Cyrenian man named Simon. This
is the man they compelled to carry his cross.

Matthew's narrative, as we have said, is typically written in the style of an accounting entry. Here he writes as if it is known already that someone meets the description "the man compelled to carry Jesus's cross," and he assigns that description to a certain named man. (Mark, 15:21, and Luke, 22:26, use very different language.)

33 When they came to the place called Golgotha, which is
to say the "Skull" place, 34 they gave him wine mixed with
gall. Taking a taste of it, he declined to drink it.
35 Affixing him to the cross, they divided his clothing,
casting lots. 36 Taking seats, they remained there
guarding him. 37 They placed over his head a written
statement of the cause, "This is Jesus, the King of the
Jews." 38 Then they put two robbers on crosses with him,
one on his right, and one on his left.
39 People passing by reviled him irreverently, shaking
their heads 40 and saying:

"Hey, temple-destroyer, who builds temples in three days—save yourself!

"Come down from the cross, Son of God, if that's what you are!"

41 Likewise the chief priests too, with the scribes and
elders, were saying:

42 "He saved others—he has no power to save himself?"

"The King of Israel! Yup, that's who he is!"

"Let him come down from the cross right now—and we will believe in him."

"He trusted in God. Let God rescue him now, if he favors him. 'I am God's son'—or so he said."

44 In the same way, even the robbers who were being
crucified with him were abusing him.
45 Starting at the sixth hour darkness covered all the land,
until the ninth hour. 46 At around the ninth hour, Jesus
cried out in a loud voice and said,

"Eli, Eli, lema sabachthani,"

which is, "My God, my God, why have you forsaken me?"
47 Some of those standing there when they heard it began
to say,
"Even he calls upon Elijah."

They were delighted because they thought he had stopped believing he was the Son of God, since now he apparently needed Elijah's assistance.

48 Immediately, one of them ran and got a sponge, soaked
it with vinegar, and, placing it on a cane pole, gave it to
him as a drink. 49 The others began to say,
"Hold back. Let's see if Elijah comes to save him."
50 But Jesus again cried out in a loud voice and gave up
his spirit.
51 And—amazingly—the veil of the inner sanctuary was
rent in two from top to bottom. The earth shook. The
rocks were split.

The phrase "the rocks" is odd, as if the reader should understand which rocks were split. Why not just "rocks" or "some rocks", but rather "the rocks"? Early Christian tradition takes them to be the rocks specifically of Golgotha. Indeed, in the Church of the Holy Sepulchre in Jerusalem today, one can see the fissure in the rock, which starts at the base of where the Cross of Golgotha was reputed to be and extends all the way down to "Adam's Chapel" below Golgotha.

The following description, verses 52–53, is in Matthew's Gospel alone.

52 The tombs were opened up. Many bodies of saints who
had fallen asleep were raised. 53 Coming out of the tombs

> **after his resurrection, they went into the holy city and appeared to many.**

Matthew perhaps included this detail to show that the Payment of the price of Redemption was immediately effective. In any case, his narrative continues:

> **54 The centurion and those with him who were guarding**
> **Jesus, when they saw the earthquake and all that had**
> **happened, became extremely afraid and said,**
> **"Truly this man was a son of God."**
> **55 Many women were there who were looking on from a**
> **distance, women who had followed Jesus beginning in**
> **Galilee, to care for his needs. 56 Among them was Mary**
> **Magdalene, Mary the mother of James and Joseph, and**
> **the mother of the sons of Zebedee.**

It needs to be explained how the body of someone crucified as a common criminal, instead of being buried in a common grave, ended up being returned to the followers of Jesus and placed in a fitting tomb. Because the coming torture and death of Jesus had never really been believed by his disciples, no provisions would have been made in advance. Moreover, they were poor and lacked money or connections, and they were scattered and hunted as criminals; therefore, they had no power to do anything after the fact. It seemed extraordinary and miraculous, then, that a wealthy, well-connected man turned up just then who could take such exquisite care of this:

> **57 When it was evening, a wealthy man from Arimathea**
> **came, whose name was Joseph, who himself had become a**
> **disciple of Jesus. 58 This is the man who went to Pilate**

and requested the body of Jesus. It was then that Pilate
ordered that it be surrendered. 59 Joseph took the body,
wrapped it in a clean linen cloth, and placed it in his own
unused tomb, which he had had cut into the rock. After
rolling a large stone up to the entrance of the tomb, he
went away. 61 Mary Magdalene was there, and the other
Mary, both of them sitting across from the tomb.

this is the man who went to Pilate and requested the body—More accounting language, assigning a description to a name, just as "it was then that" is accounting language assigning an event to a time.

But Pilate and the others had second thoughts about surrendering the body to the followers of Jesus. The following verses, verses 62–66, which have no parallel in another Gospel, reflect Matthew's distinctive interest in matters of confirmation, assurance, and chain of custody:

62 On the next day, which is after the Preparation, the
chief priests and the Pharisees were together in a meeting
with Pilate 63 and said,
"Lord, it occurs to us that that deceiver had said while
he was still living, 'After three days I arise.' 64
Command, then, that the tomb be secured until three
days have passed, so that his disciples do not come, steal
the body, and say to the people, 'He is risen from the
dead.' The last deception will be worse than the first."
65 Pilate told them,
"An armed guard is yours. Go and secure the tomb as
you see fit."
66 They went and secured the tomb by sealing it,
accompanied by the armed guard.

So ends Matthew's accounting of payments out of the household of the Kingdom of God. The sealing of the tomb, overseen by the highest legal authorities of that jurisdiction, is as if a presentation of a hard copy receipt of the Payment. The tomb is sealed; the debt is paid in full.

But this is not quite the end of Part Two, which, recall, had been introduced with these words: "It was from that time that Jesus began to show his disciples that it was necessary for him to depart for Jerusalem and to suffer many things from the elders and chief priests and scribes and to be put to death and on the third day to be raised" (Matthew 16:21). The Resurrection must therefore be included in Part Two. Why? Because the Payment that purchases freedom from sin is also an initiation into a new form of life. That is why baptism, the sacrament of Christian initiation, is a kind of reenactment of the Passion and Resurrection. Baptism was originally by immersion; the lowering of the baptismal candidate into the water represents death and entombment, while the rising of the candidate out of the water represents resurrection into new life. Through baptism, it is held, a new Christian enjoys not simply forgiveness of sin but also a new life of grace, a divine life of being a son or daughter of God. The Payment purchased both of these things. To understand any payment, one needs to give a full accounting of what it purchased. Thus, to under stand the Payment, we need to see how it not only covered outstanding debt but also recapitalized the original entity.

The Recapitalization of the Household of God (Matthew 28:1–19)

28:1 On the evening of the sabbath, at the break of dawn of the first day of the week, Mary Magdalene went, and the other Mary, to see the tomb.

Matthew tells us that they went simply *to see*, to visit the tomb, to contemplate it, just as they had stood at a distance and contemplated the crucifixion. The Greek verb is the same and has the same root as *theôria*. They did not go there to see the resurrection.

2 And amazingly there was a great earthquake because an angel of the Lord had come down from heaven; it went up to the tomb, rolled away the stone, and sat on top of it. 3 Its countenance was as if lightning and its garments as if snow.

The image of snow is presumably drawn from Mount Hermon, about 60 miles north of Capernaum, which retains snow all year round. Visible from Galilee, its summit ridge appears blazingly white after a storm. Snow would not have been a natural image for an author from Jerusalem, but the detail is consistent with Matthew's authorship.

4 Out of fear of the angel, the men guarding the tomb were themselves shaken and had fallen to the ground as if dead men. 5 The angel in response said to the women,

"You—you be not afraid. Because it is Jesus the Crucified, I know you are looking for. 6 He is not here, because he is risen, just as he said. Come, see the place where he was lying. . . . 7 Go quickly and tell his disciples that he is risen from the dead, and—attend carefully—he goes before you to Galilee. There you will see him. Look, I have told you."

Here we see again Jesus's bias in favor of intermediaries. Even though he was going to tell the women himself, he preferred to have a messenger tell them as well, and first. We are in a position by this point to see why he likes intermediaries so much. To enlist an intermediary is fundamentally to share an action with another; if doing an action is a good, and if generally to do is a greater good than to have done to you, then enlisting an intermediary is a high form of beneficence. In the divine economy, the use of an intermediary increases the value of one's activity, while also giving space for the intermediary to acquire value. Any good banker, then, will make ample use of intermediaries.

8 And going away from the tomb quickly with fear and also great joy, the women ran to give the message to the disciples. 9 And right then Jesus encountered them and said,

"Greetings to you!"

They went to him, held him by his feet, and adored him.
10 Then Jesus says to them,

"Do not be afraid. Go and tell my brothers that they should go to Galilee, and there they will see me."

The following account, which refers to the necessary amount of money for an effective bribe, is found only in Matthew. This sort of arrangement would have been familiar territory for Matthew because tax collectors were notorious for taking bribes:

> **11 As they went on their way, it happened that some men**
> **from the armed guard went to the city to give a report to**
> **the chief priests of everything that had taken place. 13**
> **These men, after meeting with the elders and taking**
> **counsel, gave the necessary sum of money to the soldiers,**
> **13 saying,**
> **"Say that his disciples came during the night and stole**
> **him while you were sleeping. 14 And if this report**
> **should reach the governor's court, we will ourselves**
> **assure him and see that you are held blameless."**
> **15 They took the money and did as they were instructed.**
> **And this story has been repeated among the Jews even to**
> **this present day.**
> **16 The eleven disciples went to Galilee, to the mountain**
> **that Jesus had designated for them. 17 Upon seeing him,**
> **they adored him, although some doubted.**

The meaning in Greek might just be "but they also (all of them) doubted." In any case, both belief and doubt were among them. Perhaps the suggestion is that the doubts were temporary and left them after they spent more time with him:

> **18 Jesus came up and spoke to them, saying,**
> **"All authority in heaven and on earth has been given to**
> **me. 19 Go therefore and make disciples of all the**
> **nations, baptizing them in the name of the Father, and**

> **of the Son, and of the Holy Spirit, 20 teaching them to keep everything that I have commanded you. And—look!—I am with you every single day until the final conclusion of the age."**

has been given to me—Matthew's approach leads us to ask whether all authority in heaven and earth was "given" to him in the manner of a gratuitous gift, or rather in the manner of wages due to him, for undergoing the Passion. We perhaps suppose the former. But what if it is the latter? After all, the same verb for "given" is used throughout Part Two of Matthew's Gospel to mean something due:

- In Matthew 20:4 it means the payment of wages to workers in the vineyard.
- In Matthew 22:17 it means tribute paid to Caesar.
- In Matthew 26:15 it means the payment to Judas for his treachery.

But if that is the meaning of what Jesus says, then we are meant to understand his death as also purchasing that authority. On the economic interpretation of Matthew's Gospel, then, we should put the whole matter this way:

- By divesting himself of the characteristics of divine life, the Son purchases the Incarnation.
- In purchasing the Incarnation, he deposits divine nature into human nature.
- In suffering the Passion, at the cost of his human life, he purchases the freedom of the fallen human race from slavery to sin.

- In suffering the Passion, he becomes owed (with respect to his human nature) the characteristics of divine life.
- In the Resurrection, he receives in the manner of something due (with respect to his human nature) the characteristics of divine life.

Conclusion

In this book I have looked for the person behind the person in the Gospel of Matthew, just as I have discovered Peter to be the preacher behind the Gospel of Mark and Mary to be the subtle, feminine influence behind the Gospel of John. Is Matthew, the tax collector, the person behind the Gospel of that Matthew who was an Apostle and Evangelist?

To find the tax collector behind Matthew's Gospel, I needed, as it were, to match that presumed ambitious tax collector to the Christian message. Hence in the introduction I argued that it was highly illuminating to formulate the Christian message using economic analogies. I argued, too, that that ambitious tax collector—if he was familiar with Roman best practices of accounting, banking, and contracts—would be well placed to see the power of these economic analogies. I took as my warrant for so matching the one to the other the teaching of Jesus, passed down in the tradition of "Be good bankers."

Has this approach been valuable simply as an interpretation of the text? Yes it has, in three ways. First, it has illuminated the structure of the Gospel of Matthew, which we see is constructed on the pattern of a ledger, dealing first with deposits credited to an account and then with payments out of that account. Second, it has shown that an economic way of thinking is implicit in the parables and teachings of Jesus. Third, it has led us to discover many small details in the language of Matthew's Gospel that, taken together, present a compelling portrait of the evangelist.

Given that Matthew's Gospel counts as the most popular book in all of history—because it is the most popular book within the Bible, which is the most popular published book ever—these results are not insignificant.

But what are the wider-ranging consequences? What is the cash value of this economic interpretation? That notion of the cash value of a truth was introduced by the American pragmatist philosopher William James. "The great assumption of the intellectualists," James wrote, "is that truth means essentially an inert static relation." In contrast, pragmatism tell us to ask, "What concrete difference will its being true make in any one's actual life? How will the truth be realized? . . . What, in short, is the truth's cash-value in experiential terms?"[1]

The conclusions of this book have a cash value for Christians and for business professionals. For Christians, the economic interpretation of Matthew's Gospel teaches them to look at their Christian life with the same realism and savvy with which they watch over their assets and carry out business. The interpretation is an antidote to anyone who conceives of Christian faith as a matter of good feelings and good intentions. It emphasizes that, as John Henry Newman said in his celebrated sermon "The Ventures of Faith," the measure of a Christian's faith is what he would lose if Christianity proves to be

1 William James, *Pragmatism: A New Name for Some Old Ways of Thinking. Popular Lectures on Philosophy by William James* (New York: Longmans, Green, and Company, 1931), 200.

false.[2] What has he wagered on its truth? What has he invested? What risks has he taken?

For entrepreneurs, or professionals in finance, accounting, or banking—or anyone engaged in business—my conclusions point to a higher economy than the merely material. How should we think rationally and effectively about these higher goods? The economic interpretation of Matthew's Gospel tells us how. Here we find spelled out exactly what people mean today when they speak of being a "cultural Christian." Recently, Elon Musk, the CEO of Tesla and SpaceX, commented, "While I'm not a particularly religious person, I do believe that the teachings of Jesus are good and wise. . . . I would say I'm probably a cultural Christian. . . . I'm actually a big believer in the principles of Christianity. I think they're very good."[3] But what are these "principles of Christianity"? How might we sum them up?

Looking at the economic interpretation of Matthew's Gospel, we can say confidently that they are summed up in that maxim that Jesus was fond of and used to say: "Be good bankers."

---

2 John Henry Newman, "The Ventures of Faith," *Parochial and Plain Sermons*, vol. 4 (London: Longman's, Green, and Company, 1909), 295–306.

3 Elon Musk, "Elon Musk: I'm a Cultural Christian," interview by Jordan Peterson, UnHerd, July 23, 2024, https://unherd.com/newsroom/elon-musk-im-a-cultural-christian/.

Postscript: Matthew's Authorship and "Marcan Priority"

The Direct Case for Matthew's Authorship

In this book I adopted the working hypothesis that Matthew the tax collector was the author of what is called traditionally the Gospel according to Saint Matthew. Was that hypothesis supported by the structure and details of the text? Yes it was, amply so! Indeed, given the insights yielded by the economic interpretation, it seems incredible that anyone other than Matthew could have written that Gospel.

But this is an indirect argument for Matthew's authorship. Despite the skepticism of recent scholars,[1] there are many strong direct arguments as well:

- First, the early Church was unanimous in the attribution of this text to the Apostle Matthew. There were no alternative suggestions and no other claimants—not even a conjecture as regards some other claimant!

1 That Matthew was the author of Matthew was hardly doubted by scholars before the middle of the nineteenth century.

- Second, the early Church was unanimous in the attribution, precisely when it was also presupposed that a composition should be within the canon of sacred scripture only if it had an apostolic origin. If a composition did not have an apostolic origin, there was a strong motive for that fact to be uncovered.
- Third, in the manuscript tradition (which includes some very early manuscripts), only Matthew is ever identified as the author.
- Fourth, Matthew is identified as the author precisely in a Hellenistic culture in which generally people cared greatly about authorship. Books were not regarded as anonymous chunks of information sent out into some public space, but rather as definite expressions of the excellence of a particular person. To get the author wrong would be like getting the sculptor of a magnificent statue wrong.

These are the strongest and most obvious arguments. But there are other plausible arguments, although more subtle. I shall give three.[2]

One argument is that, in the early Church, the Gospel of Matthew was identified as the first Gospel to have been written down and no other Gospel is identified in this way. But this suggests that the early

---

2 Here I am indebted to a book by Edgar Johnson Goodspeed, a papyrologist in the last century at the University of Chicago, titled *Matthew, Apostle and Evangelist: A Study on the Authorship of the First Gospel* (Philadelphia: John C. Winston, 1959). In researching for this book on ancient tax and bookkeeping practices, I have benefited from consulting Goodspeed's monograph *Greek Papyri from the Cairo Museum, Together with Papyri of Roman Egypt from American Collections* (Chicago: University of Chicago Press, 1902). Goodspeed there describes papyri that record, for instance, "A Certified List of Taxpayers" (p. 14) and a statement of "Accounts" (pp. 31–73), which goes into great detail over the course of forty pages.

Church regarded the author of Matthew's Gospel as a writer or recorder of some sort—and a tax collector was a writer or recorder. The early Christians as a rule were not literate. Their culture was predominantly an oral one. Writing was even regarded as inferior to speaking. Some kind of special reason, then, was needed to write something down, rather than say it person-to-person. Saint Paul had such a reason, for example, since he could not communicate with distant churches except through writing. But what would be the reason for writing down a Gospel? Stories of healings, parables, and teachings can be handed down well enough through an oral culture. There is no evidence that the Gospels were written down to authorize or preserve particular versions of the life of Christ or to immunize them from change. There was a body of written Scripture already, later called the Old Testament, that apparently was sufficient for Jesus. However, if Matthew was a tax collector, then there would be a reason why he might write things down—because writing was his professional work. Tax collectors did nothing without making a record of it. Documentation (as we call it today) was part and parcel of the work of a tax collector.[3]

3 Note that this subtle argument does not depend on the truth of the belief of the early Church, that Matthew really was the first to write a Gospel. In fact, the argument is even stronger if, as Goodspeed himself believed, Mark was first rather than Matthew—as this would show that the connection between authorship of the Gospel according to Matthew and Matthew's being a dedicated writer and recorder was so firmly established in the early Church, that it led people to believe that Matthew's Gospel had to be the first, even if it wasn't. Goodspeed, *Matthew, Apostle and Evangelist*, 35.

A second argument of involves the extensive use of Isaiah in the Gospel ascribed to Matthew, as this chart shows:

Verse in Matthew Quoting	Verse in Isaiah Quoted
1:23	7:14
3:3	40:3
4:15–16	9:1f
8:17	53:4
11:5	61:1
11:23	14:13–15
12:18–21	42:1–4; 41:8, 9
13:14, 15	6:9, 10
15:8, 9	29:13
21:5	62:11
21:13	56:7
21:33	5:1f
24:7	19:2
24:29	13:10; 34:4
24:31	27:13

The author of the Gospel ascribed to Matthew was clearly a keen student of Isaiah. And yet Isaiah took care to see that his prophecies were written down by his followers (Isaiah 8:16–18)—a fact that the author of Matthew would have well appreciated. Indeed, that Isaiah's prophecies were written down is the reason that the author could even quote from them. Thus, the author of the Gospel of Matthew can be described as someone who recognized that the followers of Jesus were similarly bound to make a written record of his teachings. But who else among the followers of Jesus could this have been, except Matthew? At least, Matthew is the most plausible candidate, since, again, Matthew's specific professional expertise included being a recorder.

Note how these last two arguments complement the first four. The first four point out that no one except Matthew, presumed to be the Apostle, is identified as the author of his Gospel; these last two point out how Matthew the Apostle is indeed the sort of person who could easily have authored a book about Jesus and would have had a motive for doing so. Moreover, he would have regarded himself as in effect bound to write such a book, so that if the Gospel traditionally ascribed to Matthew is not that book, we really ought to be able to find some other book that is "the Gospel according to Matthew."

Then there is the curious detail about the numbers in the genealogy in the Gospel ascribed to Matthew, where the author divides the ancestors of Jesus going back to Abraham into three groups of fourteen. We can debate the meaning of the numbering, but why was there even a number at all? Isn't this a declaration by the author that he is a man conversant with numbers? [4]

Against Marcan Priority

It was widely believed in the early Church that Matthew wrote his Gospel in Hebrew—either Aramaic, the local language in Palestine at the time, or as Charles Tresmontant has argued,[5] the Hebrew still

---

4 As Goodspeed puts it, the three groups of fourteen are "the tax collector's way of saying, not flatly, but much more interestingly, 'Jesus is the leading figure of the seventh seven, the climax of it all.' It is precisely here that the tax collector's 'figure-imagination' speaks so authoritatively; he thinks in numbers. . . . It is in this page that the author declares himself; he is a man of figures, the tax collector, the statistician." Goodspeed, *Matthew, Apostle and Evangelist*, 25.

5 Charles Tresmontant, *The Gospel of Matthew: Translation and Notes*, trans. Kenneth D. Whitehead (Front Royal, VA: Christendom Press, 1996).

used then for religious purposes. If so, the version we now have in Greek would be a translation, perhaps by Matthew too. Also, it was widely held in the early Church that Matthew wrote for a Jewish readership to prove that Jesus was the Messiah. These beliefs are not relevant to my project in this book; therefore, I have not needed to consider them.

However, I do need to engage briefly the common view of modern scholars that Mark was the first to write a Gospel (the view called "Marcan priority" or simply "the Marcan hypothesis"), as this view can seem at odds with my approach.

Consider the following argument, which for clarity's sake I present in the form of a list:

1. The correspondences between the Gospel of Mark and the Gospel of Matthew are so extensive and close that they cannot be explained except by holding either that the author of the Gospel of Mark made use of an already written Gospel of Matthew, or that the author of the Gospel of Matthew made use of an already written Gospel of Mark. Call this first premise the thesis of the "literary dependence" of one of these two Gospels upon the other.
2. Of these two alternatives, it is more plausible to hold the latter, that the author of the Gospel of Matthew made use of an already written Gospel of Mark.
3. But if the author of the Gospel of Matthew were himself an eyewitness to the life of Christ, he wouldn't have needed to make such extensive use of an already written Gospel of Mark, and he would not have done so.
4. Therefore, the author of the Gospel of Matthew was not an eyewitness to the life of Christ.

5. But the tax collector, Matthew, was an eyewitness to the life of Christ.
6. Therefore, the author of the Gospel of Matthew was not the tax collector Matthew.

As many observers have pointed out, this argument carries with it many deeply corrosive, skeptical implications. If the Gospel of Matthew presents itself as the account of an eyewitness but it is not, then why should we take the Gospel of Mark, on which it supposedly depends, to convey the account of an eyewitness? And if the early Church was so dramatically wrong about something so basic as the authorship and standing of the Gospel of Matthew, then why should its views be regarded as trustworthy in anything?

But I do not think we need to accept premises 1–3. To the contrary, it seems to me reasonable to reject them.

In considering premise 1, we should remind ourselves of a general logical principle, that if A and B resemble each other, the resemblance may be explained in either of three ways: that B depends on A, or that A depends on B, or that both depend upon a prior thing—call it C. In the case of the Gospels of Matthew and Mark, C would be an oral tradition that preceded the writing of the Gospels.

Scholars rule out C based on subjective assessments of likelihood. They look at the correspondences, which indeed are often very close and extensive, and they do not find it credible that such could be the result of memorization within an oral tradition. It is true that, within a highly literate culture such as our own, such correspondences could hardly arise except from a written text. But it would be hazardous to draw a similar conclusion for a mainly non-literate, oral culture, in which people's memories tend to be much stronger.

Even within a highly literate culture, many Christians have memorized the entire Bible. Orestes Brownson, for instance, in his autobiography attests that he memorized "a great part" of the Bible before he was fourteen years old.[6] Most of us have no motive to do so. But suppose you were a disciple of Jesus himself, and suppose he instructed you and your friends to memorize the equivalent of a few pages. Surely if you worked together at it, you could do so.[7]

In nonliterate cultures, the power of memory is much greater, because memory is being exercised constantly. People would even develop techniques for memorization, such as the "Memory Palace," which derives from classical times. The locations along the Sea of Galilee, which one can see at a glance from any point on the shore, would be ideal for the use of such a technique.[8] Members of nonliterate cultures also memorize complex data by, as it were, encoding it and then generating it again, rather than by brute direct memorization, as shown by fieldwork done on the pattern of Albert Lord[9] and Milman Parry. One researcher found that a genealogy that included over one hundred relatives could be recited in exactly the same form

---

6 Orestes Augustus Brownson, *The Convert: Or, Leaves from My Experience* (New York: D.& J. Sadlier, 1889), 26. Thousands of Muslims have memorized the Koran to become, as they are called, *Hafizim*. A popular guidebook for the practice states, "If someone is facing difficulty in memorizing . . . he should not listen to sports commentary, not watch TV, not listen to music, should go to bed and wake up early." Muhammed Aslam Sheikhupuri, translated by Muhammad Faisal, *Guide Book for Huffaz* (ScribeDigital.com, 2014), n.p.

7 If printed double-spaced on standard print paper, the Gospel of Mark would run sixty pages. It is not even necessary to assimilate Jesus to those later rabbinical schools where disciples were expected to memorize lengthy teachings first delivered orally: Birger Gerhardsson, *Memory and Manuscript: Oral Tradition and Written Transmission in Rabbinic Judaism and Early Christianity*, trans. Eric John Sharpe (Uppsala, Sweden: C.W.K. Gleerup, 1961).

8 Frances A. Yates, *The Art of Memory* (London: Routledge & Kegan Paul, 1966). In *De Inventione*, II.53, Cicero makes deliberate memorization a skill that is a part of the virtue of prudence.

9 Albert B. Lord, *The Singer of Tales* (Cambridge, Massachusetts: Harvard University Press, 1960).

and with all the same details by an ordinary Serbian villager on two different occasions, fourteen years apart.[10]

And then the Apostles might have used wax tablets, the notepads of the ancient world, as aids to memory—to set down outlines, schemata, or other mnemonics. In fact, it would be most surprising if Matthew the tax collector was not writing on wax tablets on a daily basis. Very few wax tablets from the ancient world have survived because they are not durable. Also, among Christians, any early wax tablets would presumably have been discarded once the standard four Gospels became available on scrolls or in codices. A common wax tablet would hold typically about four hundred characters, and very often outlines of the "pericopes" (episodes) in the New Testament can be condensed to about four hundred characters. Is such a correspondence a coincidence or evidence of an earlier mode of recording?

Here is another consideration. We know that Jesus sent his disciples out to preach the "good news of the kingdom of God" on multiple occasions: What, then, did they preach? Did they agree on what they would preach? Was there some sequence of striking or edifying or illuminating miracles that Jesus picked out for them (out of the thousands they might have picked randomly, each of them) and reviewed with them, so that they were of one mind in recounting them as they went out to preach? It seems incredible that he would not do something like that. But if an agreement on healings, parables, and teachings was already in place twenty or thirty years before any

10 Barbara Kerewsky Halpern, "Genealogy as Oral Genre in a Serbian Village," in *Oral Traditional Literature: A Festschrift for Albert Bates Lord*, ed. John Miles Foley (Columbus, Ohio: Slavica Publishers, 1981), 317n. "The content of genealogies is not memorized," she writes, "data are rather retrieved and recollected according to abstract rules in the head of the narrator."

of the four Gospels was written, why should we think that this foundation could not have separately informed two or more Gospels?

In sum, for many reasons, the assertion in premise 1 of literary dependence should be treated with skepticism.

But suppose we affirm premise 1 anyway and then must take a position on which was earlier and which is dependent. For most of the history of Christianity, those who studied the Gospels carefully and were in a position to entertain literary dependence believed that Matthew wrote his Gospel first and Mark shortened it. This fact in itself proves nothing, of course—except that it is apparently easy for intelligent persons to conceive of the Gospel of Mark as an abbreviation. If, in contrast, we find it difficult to do so, perhaps the reason is in the different philosophical presuppositions we accept, which are independent of considerations of pure textual scholarship. For example, since the modern discovery of atoms at least, we prefer to explain wholes in terms of parts, rather than parts in terms of wholes. William R. Farmer has argued along these lines that the main reason for the shift toward Marcan primacy was an intent among scholars to undermine ecclesiastical authority in favor of the secular authority of professors underwritten by the state.[11]

After all, correlation is not causation. From the mere existence of parallels between one text with the other, the direction of causation cannot be inferred. Hans-Herbert Stoldt makes this point very clearly in his treatise against Marcan priority. He exhaustively submits all relevant evidence and challenges the reader to say why the evidence

11 William R. Farmer, "State *Interesse* and Marcan Primacy 1870–1914," in *The Four Gospels 1992: Festschrift Frans Neirynck*, ed. F. Van Segbroeck et al. (Leuven, Belgium: Leuven University Press, 1992), 2477–98; and William R. Farmer, *The Synoptic Problem: A Critical Analysis* (Hillsboro, North Carolina: Western North Carolina Press, 1976).

is not at least indeterminate.[12] He argues, strongly, that it is just as easy to say that Matthew is first and to become occupied with explaining away apparent incongruities as it is to do the reverse.[13]

Because correlation cannot imply causation, in the absence of concrete evidence of chronology, all arguments for priority must hinge on assessments of what is more likely or more credible—for example, that it is more likely that one author would wish to expand on what another author wrote than to excerpt from it. Yet arguments of greater plausibility, if examined carefully, appear inconclusive. For instance, it is common for scholars to argue, "If Mark's purpose was to create a shorter gospel than Matthew's, then why is it the case [as it is] that his accounts of particular miracles and parables tend to be longer than Matthew's?"[14]—as if someone who shortens in one respect is irrational unless he shortens in all respects. Perhaps Mark wanted to shorten the Gospel as a whole precisely so that he could give more attention to detail in the accounts that he did retain, say, because his Gospel conveys additional eyewitness details from Peter. Such a purpose, far from lacking likelihood, is perfectly plausible.

Premise 3 assumes Marcan priority and then says in effect that if Matthew was an eyewitness, he would have no reason for drawing so heavily on Mark. Another way of putting the point would be this: Matthew's witness is *completely dependent* on that of Mark (and that

12 Hans-Herbert Stoldt, *History and Criticism of the Marcan Hypothesis*, trans. and ed. Donald L. Niewyk, with an introduction by William R. Farmer (Macon, Georgia: Mercer University Press, 1977).

13 Nothing is more common for scholars in this matter than to describe the evidence in the way that needs to be proved: they inadvertently use language of dependence when all they may licitly help themselves to is language of correlation. A great exemplar is B. H. Streeter, *The Four Gospels* (London: MacMillan & Company, 1930). A similar error is seen in many other areas of scholarship.

14 See for instance Robert H. Stein, *The Synoptic Problem: An Introduction* (Grand Rapids, Michigan: Baker Books, 1987), 49–51.

of others, such as a hypothetical source, "Q"). Some scholars, notably Dom Butler and John Rist,[15] have argued quite strongly that, even granting literary dependence and Marcan priority, Matthew is reasonably regarded as independent. After all, someone can *depend* on something without being *completely dependent* on it. For example, if I were composing my own narrative of events I had lived through and witnessed myself, I might nonetheless make use of a narrative that I found in a book. In that case, I would be dependent on that book, but not completely so. Similarly, Matthew the eyewitness might have depended on Mark's Gospel without being completely dependent on it for what it relayed.

Nearly all scholarship neglects the difference it would make if Mark's Gospel is indebted to Peter[16]—that is, if its apostolic authority is that of Peter—and if Peter truly enjoyed preeminent authority among the Apostles. If so, then (again granting literary dependence and Marcan priority) it becomes easy to understand why Matthew might think he should rely on Mark's Gospel and incorporate as much of it as possible, even though he was himself an eyewitness and did not *need* to rely upon it. He might do so in deference to Peter and his authority. Indeed, suppose that Peter was understood to have special authority among the Apostles, conferred by Christ, and suppose that Mark's Gospel conveys Peter's preaching. In that case, Mark's account of Christ would be as if a Christ-certified account of Christ. Who in composing his own account would not wish to make use of it, even if he did not need to?

---

15 John Rist, *On the Independence of Matthew and Mark*, Society for New Testament Studies Monograph Series (Cambridge: Cambridge University Press, 1978); and B. C. Butler, *The Originality of St. Matthew* (Cambridge: Cambridge University Press, 1951).

16 Michael Pakaluk, introduction to *The Memoirs of St. Peter* (Washington, D.C.: Regnery Gateway, 2019), xiii–xxviii.

Since I *do* believe these things about Mark's Gospel and Peter, far from finding no reason to affirm premise 3, I think it rational to deny this premise firmly. One might even flip around the usual way of reasoning and say that the fact that Matthew, although an eyewitness himself, incorporates into his account nearly all of Mark's, is additional evidence for belief in Petrine primacy from the very earliest days of the Church.[17]

I conclude this necessary postscript by saying that this common argument from within the historico-critical school is unsound. My working hypothesis was reasonable, and the direct and indirect evidence supports it: Matthew was the author of Matthew.

17 For an account of the other evidence, see John Henry Newman, "Instances in Illustration," chap. 4 in *An Essay on the Development of Christian Doctrine* (London: Longmans, Green, and Company, 1909), section 3, "The Papal Supremacy," 148–65.

Acknowledgments

I wish to thank Dr. Catherine R. Pakaluk for originally impressing upon me how pervasive is the economic way of thinking and that the real economy in which we are embedded is open-ended and far-reaching, extending to goods higher than material goods. Eric Mader, my best reader, offered excellent comments based on his close reading of the entire penultimate draft. My excellent editor at Skyhorse, Kathryn Riggs, gave me highly perceptive editorial directions—exactly what every author needs. Finally, I wish to thank Saint Matthew, Saint Alphonsus Liguori, and Saint John Chrysostom, in the communion of the saints, for, as I believe, their unfailing encouragement and assistance.

Select Bibliography

What follows is a list of the books I consulted for this work, by topic, for readers who wish to go into an area more deeply.

Agrapha

Cassianus, Johannes. *Opera Omnia. Tomus Secundus*. Edited by Alard Gazet. Douai, France: Balthazar Bellerus, 1616.

Cassian, John, and Michael Petschenig. *Iohannis Cassiani Conlationes XXIIII*. Vindobonae, Austria: apvd C. Geroldi filivm, 1886.

DeSales, Francis. *Introduction à la vie dévote. Texte intégral, publié d'apres l'édition de 1619 [par] Fernand Boulenger*. Paris: Ch. Poussielgue, 1909.

Hutt, Curtis. "'Be You Approved Money Changers!': Reexaming the Social Contexts of the Saying and Its Interpretation." *Journal of Biblical Literature* 131, no. 3 (2012): 589–609.

Jeremias, Joachim. *Unknown Sayings of Jesus*. Translated by Reginald H. Fuller. New York: Macmillan, 1957.

Resch, Alfred. *Agrapha: Aussercanonishe Schriftfragmente*. Leipzig, Germany: J. C. Hinrich'sche Buchhandlung, 1906.

Ropes, James Hardy. "The So-Called Agrapha." *American Journal of Theology* 1, no. 3 (July, 1897): 758–76.

Roman Banking

Andreau, Jean. *Banking and Business in the Roman World.* Cambridge: Cambridge University Press, 1999.

Calhoun, George M. *The Business Life of Ancient Athens.* Chicago: University of Chicago Press, 1926.

Hamilton, Neill Q. "Temple Cleansing and Temple Bank." *Journal of Biblical Literature* 83 (1964): 365–72.

Peck, Harry Thurston. "Trapezitae." In *Harpers Dictionary of Classical Antiquities.* New York: Harper and Brothers, 1898.

Sieber, Johann Gottfried. *Dissertatio Inauguralis de Argentariis Eorumque Imprimis Officiis.* Leipzig, Germany: Augustus Samuel Crucigerus, 1739.

Westermann, William Linn. "Warehousing and Trapezite Banking in Antiquity." *Journal of Economic and Business History* 3 (November 1930): 30–54.

Ancient Accounting

Andreau, Jean. "Structure et Fonction du Livre de Comptes de Kellis." *Comptes rendus des séances de l'Académie des Inscriptions et Belles-Lettres* 148, no. 1, (2004): 431–43.

Bagnall, Roger S. *The Kellis Agricultural Account Book (P. Kell. IV Gr. 96).* Oxford: Oxbow Books, 1997.

Bandi, Lydia. "I conti privati nei papyri dell'Egitto greco-romano." *Aegyptus* 17, no. 4 (October–December, 1937): 349–451.

Goodspeed, Edgar J. *Greek Papyri from the Cairo Museum, Together with Papyri of Roman Egypt from American Collections.* Chicago: University of Chicago Press, 1902.

Grier, Elizabeth. *Accounting in the Zenon Papyri*. New York: Columbia University Press, 1934.

LaGroue, Lance Elliot. "Accounting and Auditing in Roman Society." Diss., University of North Carolina, Chapel Hill, 2014.

Mickwitz, Gunnar, "Economic Rationalism in Graeco-Roman Agriculture." *English Historical Review* 52 (October 1937): 577–89.

Ogereau, J. M. "The Earliest Piece of Evidence of Christian Accounting: The Significance of the Phrase *eis logon doseos kai lempseos (Phil 4 :15)*." *Comptabilités* 6 (2014): 1–16.

Oldroyd, David. "The Role of Accounting in Public Expenditure and Monetary Policy in the First Century AD Roman Empire." *Accounting Historians Journal* 22, no. 2, (December 1995): 117–29.

Ste. Croix, G. E. M "Greek and Roman Accounting." In *Studies in the History of Accounting*, edited by A. C. Littlejohn and B. S. Yamey, 14–74. London: Eastern Press, 1956.

Codex Accepti et Expensi

Cicero, M. Tullius. *Orationes*. Vol. 1, edited by Albert Curtis Clark, and Vol. 2, edited by William Peterson. Oxford: Clarendon Press, 1961.

Cicero, M. Tullius. *The Orations of Marcus Tullius Cicero*. Translated by C. D. Yonge. London: George Bell & Sons, 1903.

Cicero, M. Tullius. *Rhetorica*. Vol. 1, edited by A. S. Wilkins. Oxford: Clarendon Press, 1957.

Jouanique, P. "Le codex accepti et expensi chez Ciceron." *Revue historique de droit français et étranger* 46 (1968): 5–31.

Minaud, Gerard. *La Comptabilité à Rome: Essai d'histoire économique sur la pensée comptable commerciale et privée dans le monde antique romain*. Laussane, Switzerland: Presses Polytechniques et Universitaires Romandes, 2006.

Pliny the Elder. *The Natural History*. Translated by John Bostock, and H.T. Riley. London: Taylor and Francis, 1855.

Rees, B. R. "*N.H.* ii.22." *The Classical Review* 8, no. 3/4 (December 1958): 213–15.

Smith, William, William Wayte, and G. E. Marindin. *A Dictionary of Greek and Roman Antiquities*. London: John Murray, 1890.

Thilo, Ralf Michael. *Der Codex accepti et expensi im Römischen Recht: Ein Beitrag zure Lehre von den Literalobligation*. Gottingen, Germany: Muster-Schmidt, 1980.

Obligatio Litteris

Appert, G. "Essai sur L'Evolution de Contrat Litteral et sur la place qu'il a Tenue chez les Romains", *Revue historique de droit français et étranger* (1922–) Quatrième série 11, no. 4 (1932): 619–59.

Birks, Peter. *The Roman Law of Obligations*. Edited by Eric Descheemaeker. Oxford: Oxford University Press, 2014.

Buckland, W. W. *A Text-Book of Roman Law from Augustus to Justinian*. Cambridge: Cambridge University Press, 1921.

Monro, Charles Henry, trans. and ed. *The Digest of Justinian*. Vol. 1. Cambridge: Cambridge University Press, 1904.

Poste, Edward, trans. and commentator. *Gai Institutiones: Or, Institutes of Roman Law by Gaius*, 4th ed. Oxford: Clarendon Press, 1904.

Watson, Alan. *The Law of Obligations in the Later Roman Republic*. Oxford: Oxford University Press, 1965.

Taxes and Tax Collectors

Brunt, P. "The Revenues of Rome." *Journal of Roman Studies* 71 (1981): 161–72.

King, Darwin L., Carl J. Case, and Jared L. Roosa., "The Comprehensive Taxation System Existing During the Roman Empire." *Journal of Business and Accounting* 13, no. 1 (Fall 2019): 64–78.

Kloppenborg, John S., "Jesus, Fishermen and Tax Collectors: Papyrology and the Construction of the Ancient Economy of Roman Palestine." *Ephemerides Theologicae Lovanienses* 94, no. 4 (2018): 571–99.

Pulliam, R. "Taxation in the Roman State," *Classical Journal* 19, no. 9, (1924): 545–53.

Richardson, John. "The Administration of the Empire." In *The Cambridge Ancient History*. Vol. 9, *The Last Age of the Roman Republic, 146–4 B.D.*, 564–98. Cambridge: Cambridge University Press.

Capernaum and the Galilean Economy

Edwards, Douglas R. "Identity and Social Location in Roman Galilean Villages." In *Religion, Ethnicity, and Identity in Ancient Galilee: A Region in Transition*, edited by Jürgen Zangenberg, Harold W. Attridge, and Dale B. Martin, 357–74. Tübingen, Germany: Mohr Siebeck, 2007.

Harland, Philip A. "The Economy of First-Century Palestine: State of the Scholarly Discussion." In *Handbook of Early Christianity: Social Science Approaches*, edited by Anthony J. Blasi, Jean Duhaime, and Paul André Turcotte, 511–27. Oxford: AltaMira, 2002.

Loffreda, Stanislao. *Recovering Capharnaum*. Jerusalem: Edizioni Custodia Terra Santa, 1985.

Mattila, Sharon Lea, "Revisiting Jesus' Capernaum: A Village of Only Subsistence-Level Fishers and Farmers?"*The Galilean Economy in the Time of Jesus*, edited by David A. Fiensy and Ralph K. Hawkins, 75–138. Atlanta: Society for Biblical Literature, 2013. https://doi.org/10.2307/j.ctt1b7x6b4.8.

New Testament and Matthew

Aland, Kurt, Barbara Aland, Johannes Karavidopoulos, Carlo M. Martin, and Bruce M. Metzger, eds. *The Greek New Testament*. 3rd corrected ed. Stuttgart, Germany: Biblia-Durck GmbH, 1983.

Albright, C. S., and W. F. Mann., *The Anchor Bible: Matthew*. New York: Doubleday, 1971.

Aquinas, Thomas. *Catena Aurea*. Vol. 1, Part 1. Oxford: James Parker and Co., 1874.

———. *Catena Aurea*. Vol. 1, Part 2. Oxford: James Parker and Co., 1874.

Bengel, Johann Albrecht. *Gnomon of the New Testament*. Translated by James Bandinel. Edinburgh: T. & T. Clark, 1863.

Carr, A. *The Gospel According to St. Matthew*. Cambridge: Cambridge University Press, 1893.

Chrysostom, John. *Homilies on the Gospel of Saint Matthew*. Translated by George Prevost. New York: Charles Scribner, 1888.

Eubank, Nathan. *Wages of Cross-Bearing and Debt of Sin: The Economy of Heaven in Matthew's Gospel*. Berlin: De Gruyter, 2013. https://doi.org/10.1515/9783110304077.

Jacquier, Jacque Eugène. "Gospel of St. Matthew." *The Catholic Encyclopedia*. Vol. 10. New York: Robert Appleton Company, 1911. July 29, 2023. http://www.newadvent.org/cathen/10057a.htm.

Meyer, Heinrich August Wilhelm. *Commentary on the New Testament*. Edited by Frederick Crombie. Translated by Peter Christie. Edinburgh: T. & T. Clark, 1880.

Pakaluk, Michael. *The Memoirs of St. Peter*. Washington, D.C.: Regnery Gateway, 2019.

Tresmontant, Charles. *The Gospel of Matthew: Translation and Notes*. Translated by Kenneth D. Whitehead. Front Royal, VA: Christendom Press, 1996.

Synoptic Problem

Butler, B. C. *The Originality of St. Matthew*. Cambridge: Cambridge University Press, 1951.

Farmer, William R. "State *Interesse* and Marcan Primacy 1870–1914." In *The Four Gospels 1992: Festschrift Frans Neirynck*, edited by F. Van Segbroeck, C. M. Tuckett, G. Van Belle, and J. Verheyden, 2477–98. Leuven, Belgium: Leuven University Press, 1992.

———. *The Synoptic Problem: A Critical Analysis*. Hillsboro, North Carolina: Western North Carolina Press, 1976.

Gerhardsson, Birger. *Memory and Manuscript: Oral Tradition and Written Transmission in Rabbinic Judaism and Early Christianity*. Translated by Eric John Sharpe. Uppsala, Sweden: C. W. K. Gleerup, 1961.

Huck, Albert. *Synopse der Drei Ersten Evangelien*. 9th ed. Tübingen, Germany: Verlag Von J.C.B. Mohr (Paul Siebeck), 1936.

Mattila, Sharon Lea. "A Question Too Often Neglected." *New Testament Studies* 41 (1995): 199–217.

Rist, John. *On the Independence of Matthew and Mark*. Society for New Testament Studies Monograph Series. Cambridge: Cambridge University Press, 1978.

Stein, Robert H. *The Synoptic Problem: An Introduction*. Grand Rapids, Michigan: Baker Books, 1987.

Stoldt, Hans-Herbert. *History and Criticism of the Marcan Hypothesis*. Translated and edited by Donald L. Niewyk, with an introduction by William R. Farmer. Macon, Georgia: Mercer University Press, 1980.

Streeter, B. H. *The Four Gospels.* London: MacMillan & Company, 1930.

Theology of Merit and Atonement

Anselm of Canterbury. *St. Anselm: Proslogium; Monologium; An Appendix in Behalf of the Fool by Gaunilon; and Cur Deus Homo,* Translated by Sidney Norton Deane. Chicago: Open Court, 1926.

Aquinas, Thomas. *Summa Theologiae,* I–II, q. 114, "Of Merit." Translated by Fathers of the English Dominican Province. New York: Benzinger Brothers, 1920.

Bonhoeffer, Dietrich. *The Cost of Discipleship.* Rev. ed. New York: Macmillan, 1959.

Council of Trent, Sess. VI, cap. xvi, in *The Canons and Decrees of the Council of Trent.* Translated by H. J. Schroeder. Gastonia, North Carolina: TAN Books. 2005.

Pohle, Joseph. "Merit." *The Catholic Encyclopedia.* Vol. 10. New York: Robert Appleton Company, 1911. http://www.newadvent.org/cathen/10202b.htm.

Scheck, Thomas P. "Bishop John Fisher's Response to Martin Luther." *Franciscan Studies* 71 (2013): 463–509.

Other Spiritual and Religious

Aquinas, Thomas. *Commentary on Saint Paul's Letter to the Philippians.* Translated by F. R. Larcher. Albany, New York: Magi Books, 1969.

Bowden, John William, John Henry Newman, Richard Hurrel Froude, John Keble, Robert Isaac Wilberforce, and Isaac Williams *Lyra Apostolica.* London: Longmans, Green, and Company, 1901.

Cano, Melchior. *De Locis Theologicis*. Salamanca, Spain: Mathias Gastius,: 1563.

Catechism of the Catholic Church. New York: Doubleday, 1995.

Catherine of Siena. *Dialogue*. Translated by Suzanne Noffke. New York: Paulist Press, 1980.

Delany, Joseph. "Corporal and Spiritual Works of Mercy." *The Catholic Encyclopedia*. Vol. 10. New York: Robert Appleton Company, 1911. http://www.newadvent.org/cathen/10198d.htm.

de Sales, St. Francis. *Introduction to the Devout Life*. Translated by John K. Ryan. Garden City, New York: Doubleday Image Books, 1955.

Escriva, St. Josemaria. *Friends of God*. Manila: Sinag-Tala, 1989.

Lewis, C. S. *God in the Dock*. Grand Rapids, Michigan: William B. Eerdmans Publishing, 1970.

Liguori, St. Alfonso Maria de' *The Passion and Death of Jesus Christ*. Translated by Eugene Grimm. New York: Benzinger Brothers, 1887.

Newman, John Henry. *Apologia Pro Vitâ Suâ*. London: Longmans, Green, and Company, 1908.

Newman, John Henry. *An Essay on the Development of Christian Doctrine*. London: Longmans, Green, and Company, 1909.

———. "The Dream of Gerontius." In *Verses on Various Occasions*. London: Longmans, Green, and Company, 1903.

———. *Parochial and Plain Sermons*. Vol. 4. London: Longmans, Green, and Company, 1909.

Pakaluk, Michael. "The Gospels Begin with Sex." The Catholic Thing, January 5, 2022. https://www.thecatholicthing.org/2022/01/05/the-gospels-begin-with-sex/.

———. "The Lord of Substance." The Catholic Thing. June 7, 2023. https://www.thecatholicthing.org/2023/06/07/the-lord-of-substance/.

———. "Philosophy as a Path of Salvation in the Ancient World." In *Proceedings of the XIX Session of the Pontifical Academy of St. Thomas*, edited by Serge-Thomas Bonino and Guido Mazzotta, 11–27.

———. "Redeeming the Time the Christian Way." The Catholic Thing, June 8, 2022. https://www.thecatholicthing.org/2022/06/08/redeeming-the-time-the-christian-way/.

Roberts, Alexander, James Donaldson, and A. Cleveland Coxe, eds. *Ante Nicene Fathers*. Vol. 8. Buffalo, New York: Christian Literature Publishing, 1886.

Scruton, Roger. *The Face of God: The Gifford Lectures*. London: Bloomsbury Continuum, 2014.

———. "Forgiveness and Irony." *City Journal*. December 2009: 56–63.

Sheikhupuri, Muhammed Aslam. *Guide Book for Huffaz*. Translated by Muhammad Faisal. ScribeDigital.com, 2014.

Tertullian, *De resurrectione carnis*. In *Patrologia Latina*, edited by Jacques Paul Migne. Vol. 2. Turnhout, Belgium: Brepols, 1844.

General

Adams, Henry. *The Education of Henry Adams*. New York: Barnes & Noble, 2009. First published 1918 by Houghton Mifflin (Boston).

Aeschylus. *Aeschylus*. Translated and edited by Herbert Weir Smyth. 2 vols. Cambridge, Massachusetts: Harvard University Press, 1926.

Brownson, Orestes Augustus. *The Convert: Or, Leaves from My Experience*. New York: D.& J. Sadlier, 1889.

Cicero, Marcus Tullius. *De Inventione. De Optimo Genere Oratorum. Topica*. Translated by H. M. Hubell. Cambridge, Massachusetts: William Heinemann, 1968.

Dickens, Charles. *A Christmas Carol [by] Charles Dickens*. New York: Hodder & Stoughton, 1913.

Friedman, Milton, and Rose D Friedman. *Free to Choose : A Personal Statement*. New York: Harcourt Brace Jovanovich, 1980.

Halpern, Barbara Kerewsky, "Genealogy as Oral Genre in a Serbian Village." In *Oral Traditional Literature: A Festschrift for Albert Bates Lord*, edited by John Miles Foley, 301–21. Columbus, Ohio: Slavica Publishers, 1981.

James, William. *Pragmatism: A New Name for Some Old Ways of Thinking. Popular Lectures on Philosophy by William James*. New York: Longmans, Green, and Company, 1931.

La Rochefoucauld, François. *et Réflexions Morales*. London: A. Dulau et Co., 1799.

Lord, Albert B. *The Singer of Tales*. Cambridge, Massachusetts: Harvard University Press, 1960.

Pakaluk, Catherine Ruth. *Hannah's Children: Stories of Women Quietly Defying the Birth Dearth*. Washington, D.C.: Regnery Gateway, 2024.

Pakaluk, Michael. *Aristotle's Nicomachean Ethics. An Introduction*. Cambridge: Cambridge University Press, 2005.

Read, Leonard E. "I, Pencil: My Family Tree as Told to Leonard E. Read." *The Freeman* 8 (December 1958): 32–37.

Scheler, Max. *Ressentiment*. Translated by William W. Holdheim. New York: Schocken, 1972.

Scruton, Roger. *The Aesthetics of Architecture*. Princeton, New Jersey: Princeton University Press, 2013.

Smith, Adam. *An Inquiry Into the Nature and Causes of the Wealth of Nations*. Cannan ed. Vol. 1. London: Methuen, 1776.

Yates, Frances A. *The Art of Memory*. London: Routledge & Kegan Paul, 1966.